Scottish Fiddle Music
in the 18th Century

This book is affectionately dedicated to
Mary Anne Alburger

Scottish Fiddle Music in the 18th Century

A music collection and historical study

DAVID JOHNSON

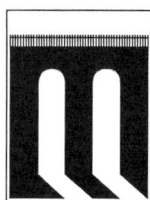

MERCAT
PRESS

First published in 1984 by John Donald Publishers Ltd
This second edition published in 1997 by
Mercat Press, 53 South Bridge, Edinburgh EH1 1YS

ISBN: 1873644 663

*The illustration on the title page shows an Edinburgh
drawing room with fiddler and harpsichordist, c.1728
(from Stewart's* Musick for Allan Ramsay's Collection
of Scots Songs, *National Library of Scotland;* see page 36)

Music typesetting by Barry Peter Ould
Small music examples drawn by the author
Typesetting of text by HM Repros, Glasgow, and Mercat Press
Printed in Great Britain by the Cromwell Press, Melksham

Contents

	page
PREFACE TO THE SECOND EDITION	ix
Acknowledgements	xvi
INTRODUCTION	1
The making of a manuscript	7
The making of a printed collection	9
I. SONG AND DANCE-TUNES TO 1720	14
Tunes based on five notes	16
Tunes based on two chords	18
Tunes based on Italian chord progressions	19
1. Highland laddie	22
2. I wish I were where Helen lies	22
3. Allan Water	23
4. Gowd on your gartens, Marion	23
5. Macpherson's testament	23
6. Killiecrankie	24
7. Saw na ye my Peggie	24
8. Sour plums of Galashiels	25
9. I love my love in secret	26
10. Bride next	26
11. Lasses gar your tails toddle	27
12. The collier's daughter	27
13. The horseman's port	28
14. Drunken wives of Carlisle	29
15. When she cam ben, she bobbit (set by John McLachlan)	30
EDITORIAL METHOD	31
SUGGESTIONS FOR PERFORMANCE	31
NOTES ON THE MUSIC	32
II. THE 'SCOTS DRAWING ROOM' STYLE	34
With or without accompaniment?	39
16. Johnnie Faa (set by Francesco Barsanti)	41
17. Leith Wynd (set by William McGibbon)	42
18. There's three good fellows ayont yon glen (set by William McGibbon)	44
19. Through the wood, laddie (set by William McGibbon)	46
20. When she cam ben, she bobbit (set by William McGibbon)	48
21. Pentland Hills (James Oswald)	51
22. Rory Dall's port (James Oswald)	53
23. Will you go to Flanders? (? set by Robert Bremner)	56
24. Robaidh dona gòrach (set by Nathaniel Gow)	61
NOTES ON THE MUSIC	63

III. LONG VARIATION SETS   65
Decorative variations   69
Replacement variations   69
Chordal variations   71
European influences on variation sets   72
    25. *A wife of my ain*   76
    26. *My Nanny-O* (set by William Forbes of Disblair)   77
    27. *Up tails a'* (set by William Forbes of Disblair) 78
    28. *Cailleach odhar* (set by David Young)   79
    29. *Allan Water* (set by David Young)   81
    30. *The reel of Tulloch* (after David Young)   82
    31. *Old Sir Symon the king* (after Henry Purcell)   84
    32. *Black Jock* (after Charles McLean)   86
    33. *The maltman comes on Monday*   89
    34. *The East Neuk of Fife*   92
    35. *Duncan Gray*   94
    36. *Lumps of puddings* (set by James Oswald)   95
    37. *The lea rig*   96
    38. *Johnnie Cope*   97
    39. *The Highlander's farewell*   98
    40. *Sweden's march*   98
    41. *Mount your baggage*   99
    42. *The hare among the corn*   100
NOTES ON THE MUSIC   102

IV. SCORDATURA   106
Scordatura after 1800   109
    43. *Practice piece I*   111
    44. *Practice piece II*   111
    45. *Black sloven*   111
    46. *Willie Wink's testament*   112
    47. *The fox lamentation*   112
    48. *Donald McIntosh*   113
    49. *Wat ye wha I met yestreen*   114
    50. *The miller's wedding*   114
    51. *Duke of Argyle's strathspey* (set by Nathaniel Gow)   115
NOTES ON THE MUSIC   117

V. BAGPIPE PIECES   119
Pibroch   122
Battle pieces   124
    52. *Pibroch*   128
    53. *Piobaireachd Dhomhnaill*   130
    54. *Cumha Easbuig Earraghàidheal*   131
    55. *Cumha Iarla Wigton*   132

56. Mackintosh's lament	134
57. The battle of Harlaw	135
58. A Highland battle (James Oswald)	138
NOTES ON THE MUSIC	141

VI. MINUETS	143
Minuets by Scottish composers	144
Minuets made from traditional tunes	146
Instrumentation	146
Flat keys	147
Dedications	149
59. Minuet in A, with variations (William McGibbon)	152
60. Miss Carmichael's minuet	153
61. Miss Faw's minuet/She's sweetest when she's naked	153
62. Lady Jean Lindsay's minuet (Daniel Dow)	154
63. Mrs Grant of Arndilly's/General Burgoine's minuet (Earl of Kelly)	154
64. Miss Kinloch's minuet (J.G.C. Schetky)	158
NOTES ON THE MUSIC	159

VII. VARIATION SONATAS	161
Formal structures	161
Alterations during transmission	166
65. Sonata on 'Bonny Jean of Aberdeen' (Alexander Munro)	170
66. Sonata on 'Twas within a furlong of Edinburgh town' (Charles McLean, after Henry Purcell)	180
67. Sonata on 'The lea rig'	183
68. Sonata on 'Pinkie House' (Robert Mackintosh and Charles McLean)	186
NOTES ON THE MUSIC	190

VIII. SONATAS	192
William McGibbon	192
Charles McLean	195
James Oswald	197
John Reid	198
David Foulis	199
The Earl of Kelly	200
Robert Mackintosh	202
69. Sonata in G (John Reid)	204
NOTES ON THE MUSIC	211

IX. REELS, HORNPIPES, STRATHSPEYS AND JIGS FROM 1760	212
Dance tunes as local celebrations	214
Dance tunes as tools for professional advancement	215
Blueprint for a ducal orchestra at Blair Atholl	216

What the Duke of Atholl did instead   217

The Gow collections   219

    70. *Green grows the rashes*   223

    71. *The flowers of the forest*   223

    72. *The Duke of Perth's reel*   223

    73. *St. Bernard's Well*   224

    74. *The Earl of Dalhousie's reel* (Nathaniel Gow)   224

    75. *The De'il's among the tailors*   225

    76. *Dusty Miller*   225

    77. *Welcome home, my dearie*   226

    78. *O'er the muir among the heather*   226

    79. *Rose Street strathspey* (Robert Ferguson)   226

    80. *Miss Admiral Gordon's strathspey* (William Marshall)   227

    81. *Mrs Fordyce of Ayton's strathspey* (Robert Mackintosh)   227

    82. *Sir Archibald Grant of Monymusk's strathspey* (Daniel Dow)   228

    83. *I'll lay no more with my mother*   228

    84. *Greensleeves*   228

    85. *Dunkeld House* (Niel Gow)   229

    86. *The South Bridge of Edinburgh/The Haddington Assembly*   229

    87. *Colonel Hamilton's delight* (Joseph Reinagle)   230

NOTES ON THE MUSIC   231

X.   SPECIAL EFFECTS   234

    88. *The hen's march* (? Robert Bremner)   236

    89. *Marriage and money*   238

    90. *The sow's tail, with variations* (set by William Nisbet of Dirleton)   239

NOTES ON THE MUSIC   243

CONCLUSION: FIDDLE MUSIC AFTER 1800   244

REFERENCES   248

INDEX   254

Preface to the Second Edition

SCOTS fiddling has undergone considerable changes since this book was first published thirteen years ago. It has become better accepted into educational institutions, more played by classically-trained violinists, more commercially marketed; research into its history has also moved on. All this demands a new preface.

ADDITIONS AND CORRECTIONS

page 7

James Oswald's biography is much clearer than it was in 1984 thanks to the research work of Heather Melvill (still awaiting publication). Melvill establishes that Oswald was born in Crail in the East Neuk of Fife in 1710 (baptised on 21 March), and that his father was Crail's town drummer.

page 9

The *McLean* collection was engraved by James Johnson, but actually published by Neil Stewart. Its date is a little approximate.

page 16

Tunes with sophisticated pentatonic constructions were probably mainly the work of professional harpists. A notable example, of a type not previously discussed, is the air *My Lord Aboyne's welcome home from London*, which has an accompaniment which is itself strictly pentatonic. This suggests a re-tuning of the harp to exclude 4th and 7th degrees of the scale from its whole compass. (The source – NLS MS.9450, dating from *c.* 1650 – is a setting for harpsichord, but is probably derived from contemporary harp playing.)

page 19

Another chord progression of the *passamezzo antico/moderno* type is the bass line to *Hit her on the bum*, given in Bremner's *Curious Collection* of 1759:

I have, however, discovered no name for this chord sequence, nor traced it anywhere else than this one source. Perhaps Bremner invented it, despite its ring of authority and tradition. See also page 234.

page 35

The 'refinement' which Ramsay recommended for pibroch may well refer to pibrochs being transcribed for violin. Cf. the other evidence for this in Chapter V.

page 38

I assumed that William McGibbon knew Adam Craig since his childhood on the basis of Tytler's statement that McGibbon was born in Edinburgh, the son of the oboist Malcolm McGibbon. Recent research indicates, however, that he was born in Glasgow (baptised 12 April 1696), the son of the violinist Duncan McGibbon. This being the case, McGibbon would not have met Craig until the 1720s.

Further to Charles McLean's disappearance from the records after 1740: the chances are high that he went to London. Dr H. Diack Johnstone has turned up information (from 18th-century rate-books in the Westminster Public Library) about a flat in Angel Court, Piccadilly, rented by 'Chas. Macklain' from 1743 onwards, the flat having been previously occupied by the composer Michael Christian Festing. Given the tendency of musicians to pass accommodation on to each other, this is probably the same person. What did McLean do in London? We don't know.

page 40

I would still maintain that, generally, 18th-century long variation sets are better without accompaniment; but there are exceptional cases. In October 1996 I was at last able to organise a performance of Robert Riddell's variations on *The hare among the corn* (a variant of no.42: see p.74), and discovered that the accompaniment was not only first class, but essential to the set's concept.

page 63

Note **16**: there is a further 17th-century text of this tune in Robert Edwards' commonplace book of *c.* 1650 (NLS MS. 9450), under the title *Sueit smylling Katie loves me*.

Note **19**: it should be added that Max Bruch used this tune in 1880 in his *Schottische Fantasie* for violin and orchestra; also that, strangely, Bruch's source for the tune seems to have been McGibbon's setting, exactly as given here.

Note **21**: there is another source for this piece in Francis Peacock's *Fifty favourite Scotch airs* (London, *c.* 1762), p.2 (as 'Pentland Hill, a new Scotch Air').

page 69

Walter Scott's comments on Oswald were probably derived from his friend the antiquary David Laing. In 1822 the library of Oswald's half-sister Susanna Oswald or Weatherley (1740-1821) came up for sale, including copies of Oswald's music with family annotations. Laing took an interest in this library and may well have purchased items from it. (See his preface to *The Scots Musical Museum*, p.li.) He would also have told Scott about it. But Scott probably garbled Laing's information; he wrote his novels at high speed, and rarely revised his script or re-checked his facts.

page 104

Note **34**: once one knows that Oswald was born in Crail, it becomes obvious it was he who retitled this tune *The East Neuk of Fife* – in honour of his birthplace; since Crail is *the* town at the corner of Fife, only a mile from the lighthouse at the point. Oswald may well have composed the tune too. See Mary Anne Alburger's *Scottish fiddlers and their music* (London, 1983), p.47.

Note **36**: it should be added that Burns wrote one of his finest lyrics to this tune, the self-portrait 'Contented wi' little and cantie wi' mair'.

page 109

Scordatura has, sadly, not caught on in the last decade as widely as hoped. Many players fear damage to their instruments by re-tuning, or are simply not willing to experiment with it. But see the march *Kenmore*, written in 1988, below.

page 123

One further fiddle pibroch is now available in a modern edition: this is *Failte MhicGilleain*, from the McFarlane MS. of 1740. See the author's collection *Scots on the Fiddle*, Edinburgh, 1991.

page 164

I have been unfair to Oswald's *Sonata of Scots Tunes*, which I did not hear until the Scottish Baroque Ensemble performed it in 1985. The piece has unexpected subtleties; its movements are balanced as to tonality, speed and weight in a totally original way. It needs a viola part added. I am convinced that Oswald wrote one but then suppressed it, feeling that a trio sonata was more marketable than a string quartet.

pages 192-5

Some more Scottish violin sonatas have recently come to light, notably one by John Clerk of Penicuik (*c.* 1702), which is short and oddly proportioned but grateful to play and enjoyable to listen to. I have made an edition of this (Edinburgh, 1990).

Lorenzo Bocchi's *Musicall Entertainment for a Chamber* (composed in Edinburgh in the early 1720s; published in Dublin in 1726) also contains violin sonatas. The best of these is no.4 in D, which is unusually and imaginatively set in the scordatura A D A D. The McGibbon Ensemble broadcast this in 1989.

My views on McGibbon's sonatas have changed considerably. His 1740 set are by no means solid quality throughout; the good ones are nos. 2, 5 and 6, the others less successful. On the other hand, the shortcomings of his early works worry me less than they used to; many of the 1729 and 1734 trio sonatas are only intended to be light Italianate pieces anyway. The Trio Sonata in G, no.5 of the 1734 set, is a more serious piece. In December 1996 it had a carefully prepared performance at Napier University which revealed surprising beauty in details that had previously seemed clumsy and awkward; for instance, in this passage in the first movement:

Adagio

Violin 1

Violin 2

Harpsichord,
Cello

6   [7 9] 3

Here the bracketed notes in the violin 2 part seem, at first sight, either incompetent or a misprint. (They are 'corrected' in the editions of Elliott, 1963, and Holman, 1991.) But with sensitive playing – including getting the speed right – the passage is striking and original, its harmony as satisfying as J. S. Bach's at the same period.

I have regrettably had no opportunity to publish an edition of McGibbon's 'La folia' sonata. This survives only as a violin part, but its bass is easily reconstructed. It is one of McGibbon's finest pieces, and deserves to be widely known.

page 198

The relationship between Oswald and General Reid becomes stranger the more one looks into it. Around 1750 Oswald founded a fictitious music club in London, the 'Temple of Apollo', whose 'members' were gentlemen amateurs eager to write theatre music for only a small handling fee (the fees payable to Oswald). 'Some of the members had much original genius…' Oswald said to the theatre-manager Garrick, who 'listened attentively'. In actuality Oswald wrote all the music himself, with assistance from Charles Burney; there were no members. (See Klima, Bowers, and Grant, *Memoirs of Dr Charles Burney 1726-1769*, University of Nebraska, 1988, p.88.) Evidently Oswald's composition had become so fluent by then that he could afford to discount his rates. The function of the club was to disguise the fact that he was giving discounts to some, but not all, of his customers.

Yet in 1762 the title-page of Reid's second set of sonatas describes its composer as 'I. R. Esq.ʳ A Member of the Temple of Apollo'.

Jeremy Barlow has found evidence that, around 1760, the Temple of Apollo was giving genuine concerts at an address in Queen Square, probably at the home of Oswald's patrons John and Leonora Robinson-Lytton, which had a well-equipped music room.

One explanation to hold these facts together would be that, at some point in the 1750s, the club's reputation became so great that real gentlemen amateurs insisted on joining it, including Reid. Oswald would have been forced to alter its scope completely. That would in turn explain why Oswald's heirs, after his death, were confused as to whether 'I. R.' was a real person or a pseudonym, resulting in Reid's sonatas being accidentally reprinted under Oswald's name.

page 200

Much new chamber music by the Earl of Kelly has come to light with the discovery of the Kilravock Manuscript in 1989. This MS. (copied for Kilravock Castle *c.* 1770; now NLS MS. Acc.10303) contains 9 trio sonatas, 6 quartets, and a duo sonata for two violins of Kelly's, all previously unknown. Not all these pieces are excellent – some are student experiments which Kelly rightly decided not to publish – but there are masterpieces among them, particularly the trio sonata in F and the quartet in A. The F major trio sonata has been published in the author's edition (Edinburgh, 1991). The duo sonata for two violins is also an exciting piece, with considerable technical difficulties in some places, sumptuous lyricism in others – such as this 'nightingale at midnight' passage in the slow movement:

page 243

Note **90**: a present-day version of this tune – *The sow's lament for sma' tatties*, notated from the fiddler Sophie Hay in 1990 – is published in the author's collection *Scots on the Fiddle.*

page 244

Long variation sets were also reprinted at the end of the 19th century in Köhler's *Violin Repository*, edited by W. B. Laybourn (Edinburgh, 1885). Laybourn seems to have taken them from an old copy of Bremner's *Curious Collection*; it is not known whether his Victorian purchasers appreciated them.

COMMERCIAL RECORDINGS FROM THE BOOK

There have been two: *Music of Classical Edinburgh* (SCH 001, published 1987), and *Fiddle Pibroch and Other Fancies* (SCH 002, published 1989). Both are recorded by the McGibbon Ensemble (Edna Arthur, violin, Bryce Gould, harpsichord, and the author, cello). Owing to the demise of the record company which produced them (the Scotland's Cultural Heritage Unit at Edinburgh University), these are at the moment only available from the author in cassette form, but this situation will hopefully change.

Music of Classical Edinburgh includes nos. **23**, **30**, **73**, **79** and **86** from the book, along with McGibbon's Sonata in C minor (discussed on p.148), the Earl of Kelly's Trio Sonata in C (p.200), *The New Bridge of Edinburgh* (p.215), and *Hit her on the bum* (p.234).

Fiddle Pibroch and Other Fancies contains nos. **25**, **37**, **42-46**, **49**, **54**, **56**, **66**, **69**, **87**, and McGibbon's La folia Sonata (p.195).

NEW FIDDLE COLLECTIONS

The advent of desk-top publishing has made it possible for fiddlers all over Scotland – and fiddlers of Scottish descent in America and Canada – to get their own collections into print with an ease that the 18th century would have envied. Some collections have appeared that might have been better left as private manuscripts (see page 8!) but there have also been some extremely worthwhile ones.

Christine Martin's *Ceol na Fidhle* (4 books, Breacais Ard, Skye, 1986-91) is one of the good ones, clearly and beautifully produced, full of interesting new material, a genuine expansion of the repertory. Also admirable is the collection of tunes by the north-east fiddler Joe Murray (1907-91), published by the composer's grandson in Ballater in 1993. Mr Murray's work was previously unknown outside his circle of friends. The best of his tunes deserve places in future national collections (I especially like the jig *Miss Grant of Dalvey* and the slow air *The braes of Moine-na-Vey*), and they shed a new light on what I had thought to be a bleak period for Scots-fiddle composition, the 1930s and 40s (see p.246).

Kate Dunlay and David Greenberg's *Traditional Celtic Violin Music of Cape Breton* (Toronto, 1996) is a larger work. This is a collection of 139 current Cape Breton tunes, expertly transcribed with careful analytical and historical notes. Its analysis of modes – making the point that, to do the job thoroughly, the underlying harmony must be taken into account as well as the melody – is the best I have yet seen. Most interesting is that this is about a specifically *Highland* tradition: Cape Breton fiddling was evidently exported to Canada from the Highlands between about 1760 and 1880, and owes little to Lowland practices. The book therefore gives a quite different picture of fiddling from any collection previously published.

DEVELOPMENTS IN PLAYING

Hi-tech machinery has opened up possibilities for studying fiddling technique in enormous detail, both in its current forms and in recordings back to about 1950. Grace notes, out-of-tune pitchings, rhythmic bendings, accidental collisions of the bow with adjacent strings and other kinds of scrapy sounds can all now be minutely analysed. Also, these techniques can now be painstakingly taught to students at specialist summer schools.

As a result, there seems to be emerging a new type of Scots fiddler who has determinedly, self-consciously learnt up these techniques and treats them as an alternative to classical violin playing. One of the finest players of this new kind, in my opinion, is the American fiddler Bonnie Rideout, who appeared with panache at the Edinburgh Festival in 1996 and is fast making a powerful reputation for herself.

Compared with what went on in the past, however, this approach to technique seems ridiculously educated and artificial. Certainly it is respectful of tradition, and is perhaps necessary for fiddling's survival in the modern world. But its aims would have been incomprehensible to players 250 years ago. In the 18th century all Scots fiddlers wanted to play like William McGibbon. They regarded the scrapy noises they made as a limitation, a form of failure rather than success.

DEVELOPMENTS IN COMPOSITION

A new era was launched in the 1980s with the discovery, by educationalists, that secondary-school pupils were capable of writing reels and strathspeys for exams. This movement – unprecedented in fiddling's history – seems to have been kicked off by changes in the Higher Music syllabus in 1984.

Composition exam portfolios are not open to public inspection, so one can only guess how many fiddle tunes may have been written in schools in the last ten or twelve years. Between 1,000 and 2,000 might be a reasonable estimate. It has occurred to me that a collection drawn from this body of work (perhaps entitled *The Best of Scottish Exam Fiddling, 1985-95*) would find a sympathetic public, be a national status symbol, and probably sell well. The legal and administrative problems involved in setting it up, however, would be a nightmare.

I would like to conclude the preface with one sample of this work, a march composed by Eli Cradock, a pupil at the Rudolf Steiner School in Edinburgh in 1988. The composer writesabout it as follows: 'This tune was written on Orkney – Kenmore is the name of the house – where they play a lot of Scandinavian music. It would be repeated as often as necessary. The guitar chords are optional. The G and D strings of the fiddle should be re-tuned to A and E, and although they are not played they resound to give the effect of the Norwegian "Hardanger fiel".'

This is a successful piece, and distinctive even if one did not know it had been written by a schoolgirl. Its structure, consisting of one-bar phrases repeated endlessly in varied order, belongs to a central Scottish tradition. At the same time it reaches out into

Scandinavian music (as explained) and also, through its country-and-western style syncopations, into American music. If new tunes like this keep being written, there may yet be hope for the world.

D. J.
Department of Music
Napier University
14 February 1997

Kenmore

Acknowledgements

AMONG the many friends who took part in speculative discussions and, at a later stage, commented upon draft bits of this book, I must especially thank Mary Anne Alburger, Freddie Freeman, Francis Cowan, Alastair Hardie and Neil Mackay. I should also like to thank the helpful performers who were willing to learn obscure pieces and inflict them on unsuspecting audiences, and without whom I would have had a much poorer idea of the music of this period: Helen McArthur, Sandra Brown, Leonard Friedman, David Edwards, George Gwilt, Kenneth Elliott, Michael Tilmouth, and Jeremy Barlow. My greatest debt here, however, is to Edna Arthur and Bryce Gould, who have been sensitive and persuasive advocates for my musical discoveries for over a decade.

Financial acknowledgements are also due: to the Carnegie Trust for the Universities of Scotland and to Lothian Regional Council, for grants towards music type-setting; and to the Scottish Arts Council for a generous Writer's Bursary, the University of Edinburgh for the award of the Helen Doig Bursary, and the Family Income Supplements board for personal sustenance.

Much of the music in this book has been printed from 18th-century manuscripts for the first time. I should like to thank the owners of the manuscripts for kindly agreeing to this: Francis Collinson, for pieces nos. **1-3, 9** and **15**; the Trustees of the National Library of Scotland, for nos. **4-8, 11-14, 27, 35-37, 43-48, 53, 60-62, 70-71, 73, 76, 79, 83-84** and **86**; the National Museum of Antiquities of Scotland, for nos. **25-26, 28-29, 52, 54, 59, 66** and **89**; Anne Macaulay for no. **40**; and Edinburgh City Library for nos. **41-42** and **49.**

Finally, I must thank Alan Bruford for help with the Gaelic, and for reading the book through in final typescript and making many valuable last-minute suggestions.

Edinburgh, St Valentine's Day, 1983   D.J.

FURTHER acknowledgements are due in respect of the second edition: to Mr and Mrs D. T. C. Caldow; to Dr Gerald Gifford of the Royal College of Music, for his enthusiastic interest and practical help; to Roderick Long, Philip Sawyer, and various Napier University students, for their fine performances of newly-discovered pieces; and to Tom Johnstone of the Mercat Press, for his clarity of purpose and unfailing courtesy.

D.J.

Introduction

THIS book is both an anthology and a study of the fiddle music current in Scotland between 1700 and 1800. I hope that it will be played from, and enjoyed, by a large number of Scots fiddlers. Some of the pieces given here will be familiar, or at any rate recognisable, to such players; but only some, for the fiddle repertory changed considerably during the period 1780–1830, and much of the music popular in the 18th century did not survive beyond its own time.

However, this book is also intended to interest lovers of 18th-century European art music, to whom the pieces presented here will come as a surprise in a different way. For Scots fiddle music in the 18th century was poised interestingly — and at times perilously — between the European and the native Scottish musical traditions. Lovers of European music will have no difficulty in spotting its Scottish characteristics, but Scots fiddlers may more readily notice its European characteristics. As will become clear, however, this music needs to be studied from both angles for it to be fully appreciated.

The ninety pieces of music which I have selected, out of the reams which survive from 200 years ago, are necessarily a personal choice; and I have arranged and laid them out rather differently from the arrangements and layouts of such pieces in actual 18th-century fiddle books. Nevertheless, I believe that an 18th-century fiddler would have approved of this selection and found it representative.

The commentaries are designed to be read in order; but they will also, hopefully, make sense if dipped into at random by readers whose main interest is playing the music.

In writing the commentaries it was necessary for me to choose between two possible approaches. I could have put all my comments on each tune together, and produced a book which consisted, in effect, of a series of ninety programme notes. This is the classic method of William Stenhouse's *Illustrations of the Lyric Poetry and Music of Scotland* (1839), and it is undeniably a useful one for concert performers who need material with which to chat to audiences. But anyone who has tried to read Stenhouse from cover to cover knows how hopeless this method is for coming to grips with the larger historical issues, how quickly the general outlines of the subject disappear into a fog of repetitive detail and irrelevant anecdote.

So I have opted instead — partly because it was more fun to write the book this way — for an approach which highlights the general issues, and uses the tunes to illustrate the historical trends rather than the other way round. The disadvantage of this scheme is that comments on individual tunes are not concentrated in one place, but tend to get scattered. Readers who wish to find everything I have to say about the tune *Sweden's march* (no. **40**), for example, will have to turn to page 20 for the tune's relationship to the Italian *passamezzo moderno* chord sequence, page 65 for the variations being modern ones in the 18th century, page 72 for the variations being mostly 'chordal' in type, and page 105 for the tune's use of Baroque trumpet idioms, its full title, and a selection of fiddle-books where it appears. The Index is there to help readers who want to use the book like this.

Scots fiddling is nowadays regarded as a type of traditional music. We must pause, however, before attaching the label 'traditional' too firmly to the fiddling of 200 years ago. *Traditional,* in its basic Latin sense, means 'handed down'; as in handed-down clothes, it means something which one acquires from another person, which has already been used, and which may perhaps be a little worn out. A traditional culture is one that has stayed the same for many generations. A traditional tune is one so old that everybody has forgotten who composed it. In this sense, *traditional* is the opposite of *progressive.*

Scots fiddling in the 18th century, however, was progressive. In the first half of the century composers put great energy into making new arrangements of tunes: bagpipe pieces were reset for fiddle, new principles of harmonisation were evolved, and huge sets of variations blossomed as from nowhere. After 1760 the emphasis turned more to original composition, and large quantities of new dance-tunes were written in a very short space of time.

Other 20th-century ideas about traditional music — that it appeals to all classes of society, and that it is peculiar to its locality — do not entirely fit here either. 18th-century Scots fiddle music was certainly a local culture, and carried a strong sense of Scottish identity; but its 'Scottish' qualities developed and changed as the century progressed, mainly due to the influence of European art music. Most of its repertory was certainly within the reach of ordinary people; nevertheless, its finest pieces made great demands on players' technique and audiences' powers of attention, and can hardly be described as popular music at all.

Above all, much of this music is not anonymous. A great deal is on record about the individuals who wrote it, and we shall meet many of them: John McLachlan, an Edinburgh fiddler whose personal settings of Scots tunes were renowned in the years around 1700; Adam Craig, Edinburgh's leading concert violinist in the early 18th century, who published the first native collection of Scots airs in about 1727; William Forbes of Disblair, an Aberdeen bailie who, in his old age, made influential experiments in combining Scots and Italian musical styles; Alexander Munro, who invented the variation-sonata form in 1732; Francesco Barsanti, an Italian composer and lover of Scots music who, during his eight years' stay in Edinburgh, raised many people's sights as to what was possible; William McGibbon, who was simultaneously the best concert violinist and the finest Scots fiddler of his generation; David Young, who divided his time between Aberdeen and Edinburgh, composed many sets of variations, and compiled the great McFarlane manuscript of 1740; Charles McLean, who wrote twelve Baroque sonatas and six lengthy fiddle sets of Scots tunes; the energetic James Oswald who, though he left Scotland at the age of 30, continued to be a mainstay of Scots-fiddle publishing from London; Robert Bremner, who followed Oswald to London at the age of 50 and, like Oswald, included many of his own compositions and arrangements in the fiddle-books that he published; John Reid, an army general who wrote Baroque sonatas with a Scots accent; and the Earl of Kelly, a Fife landowner who studied music in Germany, and introduced Scots fiddlers to the 'difficult' keys of B flat major and E flat major.

After 1770 we begin to meet composers whose names are still known in Scotland at the present day: Niel Gow, who founded the modern era of Scots fiddling; his son Nathaniel Gow, a precocious composer, arranger and entrepreneur who at 21 masterminded his father's first printed collection; Daniel Dow from Perthshire, composer of reels, strathspeys and minuets; Robert Mackintosh, also from Perthshire, a heroic figure with up-to-date ideas about spiccato bowing and other Italian tricks; John Riddell, a blind fiddler in Ayr; Alexander McGlashan, leader of Edinburgh's finest dance-band in the 1780s; and William Marshall, the Duke of Gordon's protégé, whom Burns called 'the first composer of strathspeys of the age'.

Our first task, however, must be to investigate the fiddle itself.

The present-day Scots fiddle is, of course, the same instrument as the orchestral violin. (This fact needs stating; not long ago a well-known television company offered a friend of mine a doubling fee for playing 'both' instruments in the same programme.) The violin was originally an Italian instrument, used in the 16th century mainly to play dance music. Its tone and expressive range gradually improved, until it reached perfection in the hands of the 17th-century makers Amati, Guaneri, and Stradivari. Simultaneously it spread round Europe, becoming by 1680 *the* instrument for up-to-date music: concerts, opera, church festivals, dances and domestic music-making were soon unthinkable without violins, if one's taste were not to be considered hopelessly old-fashioned. All the compositions of the internationally famed Arcangelo Corelli (1653–1713) were for violin; after Corelli all composers, whether or not they played the instrument, had to be able to write for it. The modern orchestra assembled itself round the violin: ever since 1680 the orchestra's most responsible, highly paid member has been the principal violinist.

Exactly when the violin reached Scotland is anyone's guess; 1670 seems a likely date, but it may have been rather earlier. Violins had become fashionable in England soon after the Restoration of 1660, for Charles II had spent his years of exile at the French court and had been so impressed by Louis XIV's personal violin-band, the '24 violons du roi', that on his return he set up a similar band of royal fiddlers in London. The spread of this fashion from England to Scotland would have been slowed down, however, by the Church of Scotland's attitude to dancing at the time. In England the violin was quickly taken to country areas by dancing-masters; but in Scotland the Church ruthlessly suppressed dancing, making the profession of dancing-master a difficult one until 1700 or later. Nevertheless, the violin caught on in Scotland's main musical centre, Edinburgh; and the earliest Scottish manuscript to specify the instrument, 'Lessones for yᵉ Violin', comes from Newbattle Abbey, nine miles south-east of Edinburgh, and dates from about 1680.

The native musical traditions which the violin found on its arrival in Scotland included fiddling. This was carried out on two bowed-string instruments played, like the violin, on the arm: the medieval fiddle and the rebec. The violin, however, was so superior to either of these — being more resonant, expressive, and grateful to play — that within a generation every fiddler who could afford to buy one, or knew how to make one, had transferred to it. The violin thus acquired the ready-made status of a 'traditional' Scottish instrument.

It is tantalisingly difficult to get a clear picture of fiddling in Scotland before the violin's arrival. 'Fiddles' are mentioned in many Scottish documents from 1450 onwards, the most famous reference being to a fiddle serenade which the loyal citizens of Edinburgh inflicted on Mary, Queen of Scots for several nights running in August 1561. A thorough search of town-council records, kirk-session minutes, and private letters would probably turn up much new information on the subject. The major difficulty in assessing what fiddling was like on the old instruments, however, is that the music was — apparently — never written down. A number of Scots tunes were notated in the 17th century for mandora, cittern, viol and lute, but it seems to have taken the dual-purpose violin, with its uses in both European and native Scottish music, to persuade fiddlers that notation was worthwhile; for no fiddle texts of Scots tunes survive from earlier than 1680.

It is possible, of course, to estimate what 17th-century Scots fiddle music was like simply by taking the 18th-century repertory and deducting all its contemporary features. Short dance pieces — jigs and reels — seem to be the answer, along with a few slow airs. (It is significant that reels and jigs are commonly played with only a few inches of bow; the style was probably designed for the much shorter bow of the rebec.) Some of these pieces were probably extended by short sets of variations; but there are no firm indications that 17th-century fiddling ran to a *ceòl mór* or 'big music' — a repertory of long pieces designed for sustained listening and virtuoso performance. Such sophisticated matters seem to have been left to the bagpipes and harp.

What is clear, however, is that the arrival of the Italian violin altered the balance of power between 'fiddles' and other Scottish instruments. The violin brought new types of dance, new ways of making variations, with it from England and the Continent, and added them to the existing fiddle repertory; it also began to purloin the idioms of other instruments. By 1740, Scots fiddling had become a kind of cultural melting-pot. This can be seen from the McFarlane manuscript, written that year — 'A Collection of Scotch Airs With the latest Variations, Written for the use of Walter Mcfarlane of that ilk By David Young W[riting] M[aster] in Ed[i]n[bu]r[gh] 1740' — which includes, alongside indigenous Scottish pieces, English country dances, hornpipes, and transcriptions of harpsichord pieces; pieces with arpeggios derived from the German flute; pieces in Italian sonata style, with special reference to Corelli's *gigas*, which tie up interestingly with the native Scots jig; Baroque-trumpet imitations; and looking north once more, fiddle settings of *pìobaireachd* and Highland pipe marches. These are even a few pieces in a pseudo 'Italian bagpipe' style, filtered into Scotland through such art-music works as Corelli's *Christmas Concerto*. Out of this came an 18th-century *ceòl mór* for the fiddle, or rather three 'big musics', for the tradition put forth three exotic blooms simultaneously: the Long Variation Set, the Variation Sonata, and the Fiddle Pibroch.

By 1760 the violin had swept its competitors off the board and achieved a central position in Scottish music, just as it had earlier done in European music. It had become *the* instrument of Scottish traditional music.

The violin's dominance caused the whole concept of 'Scottish music' to shift position. Scottish composers, acting on ideas suggested by current English and Italian music, began to give their fiddle pieces a modern elegance and mellifluousness. They shaped a new Scottish style suited to the 18th century, incorporating various European elements, but without losing the music's national identity. Overall, they were highly successful. Bad work was produced, too: music which mixed Scottish and European styles, only to lose the point of both. But the 18th century, being a creative era, carried such mistakes along with it and learned useful lessons from them.

The fiddle's three 'big musics' varied in the amounts they owed to foreign influence. The variation sonata was the most European of the three, its format taken neat from Corelli's *da camera* sonatas, only the tunes on which it was based being Scottish. The fiddle pibroch was the least European, since it derived directly from an indigenous 17th-century bagpipe form; if outside influence had a foothold here, it was only in the transcription process from pipes to fiddle. The long variation set came somewhere between the other two.

The result was that, by the mid-18th century, Scots fiddle music formed a complete spectrum of styles. European violin sonatas at one end of the spectrum were connected to reel tunes at the other end by these new 'big music' genres. It is an impressive achievement when one considers that, in 1690, Scottish reels, English country dances, and Corelli's sonatas had been disjunct types of music, with hardly any common elements at all except the fact that they could all be played on the same instrument. The new compositions had the effect of making the repertory into an integrated whole.

This is not to say that every fiddler, or violinist, in Scotland played every kind of music that was available. There were certainly players who saw their *forte* as performing sonatas in concert halls and would not have been seen dead playing reels in pubs: and vice versa. There would have been dance-band players who never touched long variation sets because there was no money to be made from them; experts at fiddle pibroch who were unable to master strathspeys; fiddlers who adored jigs and despised minuets, and so on. Printed fiddle collections often appear to be catering for such specialist players. The *McLean* collection of 1772, for example, consists almost entirely of variation sonatas, while Bremner's *Curious Collection of Scots Tunes* (1759) is made up largely of long variation sets. Bremner published reels and minuets in other books. Fiddle pibrochs were mainly printed in antiquarian collections like Dow's *Ancient Scots Music* (1776) and Macdonald's *Highland Vocal Airs* (1784). Many fiddlers, however, did have a go at everything the repertory had to offer, and this can be seen from manuscript books, where one is liable to find all types of pieces written out alongside each other, in no particular order.

Nowadays we tend to have a soft spot for illiterate fiddlers with limited, old-fashioned repertories. The 18th century, in contrast, rewarded players who, due to their literacy, had formed up-to-date tastes, and whose compositions put forward an image of Scotland as a part of Europe. Many of the great fiddlers of the 18th century were actually the leading players and teachers of European art music as well. William McGibbon, whose Scots-tune collections sold well for over half a century, was also Edinburgh's finest concert violinist. Daniel Dow, Robert Mackintosh, Alexander McGlashan and Nathaniel Gow all played in the orchestra of the Edinburgh Musical Society: this was Scotland's premier musical organisation, and gave professional concerts at St. Cecilia's Hall every Friday evening. On other nights of the week, McGlashan and Gow played alongside each other in Edinburgh's highest-paid dance-band.

Even Niel Gow, who lived at Dunkeld in the middle of Perthshire, seems to have played Corelli's sonatas at home for fun. (The evidence for this is Nathaniel Gow's *Select Collection of Original Dances*, where Nathaniel reprints part of Corelli's violin sonata op.V no.9 and says that 'of all Italian Compositions this was my Father's Favourite'.)

It follows that mainstream Scots-fiddle playing and mainstream European-violin playing cannot have differed from each other in the 18th century nearly as much as 'folk fiddle' and 'classical violin' playing do today. Dow, McGlashan, and co. could have coped with different musical idioms on successive nights, but not with two fundamentally different techniques. What has happened in the meantime is that art-music violin playing has developed, while Scots-fiddle playing has stayed largely the same.

This point is supported by recent musicological research. Since 1960, scholars have laboriously reconstructed the violin's defunct 18th-century art-music technique, and have decided that its elements included: holding the bow some inches up the stick, not at the nut; playing without chin-rest or shoulder-rest; using open strings and first-position fingerings as much as possible; reserving vibrato for special effects; generally aiming at a light rhythmical sound which bounces off the walls, rather than at a huge actual tone. All these elements are still very much alive in present-day Scots-fiddle playing, where they have been handed down unchanged for the last 200 years.

The question of notation deserves to be looked into further.

I have already suggested that Scots fiddlers seem to have managed very well without notation up to 1680; all repertory was simply passed on by ear. With the coming of the violin, however, fiddle lessons began to include instruction in staff notation, for the pupil might well wish also to play fashionable English country dances, for which fluency in notation would be useful, or to play European concert music, for which it would be essential. Conversely, lessons which aimed primarily at equipping the pupil to play European art music were liable to include Scots tunes as practice pieces. Scots-fiddle pieces continued to be performed from memory, as had always been the custom; increasingly, however, players liked to own written copies, for occasional reference and to help them learn new tunes.

The growing literacy of fiddlers is first noticeable in manuscripts. Considerable numbers of fiddle manuscripts survive from the period 1700–20, compared with the dearth of them the century before. It was not long before enterprising composers realised that there was a market for printed fiddle collections. Two books of Scots-fiddle tunes had already been published in London, Henry Playford's in 1700, and John Young's *c*. 1720. Very well: the same thing could be done locally. Adam Craig published Scotland's first native collection in about 1727 (actually of harpsichord settings, but very clearly based on his own fiddle-playing), and other collections followed from Alexander Stuart (*c*. 1728), Alexander Munro (1732), James Oswald (*c*. 1739), Francesco Barsanti (1742), and William McGibbon (1742). These books were all the work of composers in Edinburgh, issuing their own arrangements as a private speculation. They were expensive books, intended to appeal to the kind of upper-class fiddler who also played, and purchased, European music. As literacy spread, however, collections appealing to a wider public also became viable propositions. James Oswald, after moving to London, brought out an extended series of small volumes, each individually cheap, under the title *The Caledonian Pocket Companion.* These sold very well in Scotland. Soon after that, the first commercial music publishers in Edinburgh went into business: Robert Bremner in 1754, and Neil Stewart around 1760. Bremner and Stewart both put a lot of effort into fiddle books aimed at a mass market.

Printed collections were enormously influential in moulding the 18th-century fiddling tradition. This was so despite the fact that many books were printed in quite small runs, and priced well above the average man's pocket. For hard-up literate fiddlers could — and did — make handwritten copies of printed pieces they liked, once a colleague in the district had bought a volume. Illiterate fiddlers could learn pieces by ear as soon as they heard another fiddler play them. Twenty years after McGibbon's death there can have been few fiddlers in Scotland who did not know his settings, even if they did not realise who had composed them.

This must not be taken as a picture — all too familiar to the 20th century — of a centralised commercial product overriding and undermining local initiative. In the 18th century local initiative was likely to retaliate by reaching for the Edinburgh presses itself. This can be seen from the collections of John Riddell (*c.* 1770), William Marshall (1781), Isaac Cooper (*c.* 1783), Charles Duff (*c.* 1792), Alex Leburn (1793) and Robert Riddell (1794) which, though printed in Edinburgh, were actually compiled and/or composed in Ayr, Morayshire, Banff, Dundee, Fife and Dumfriesshire. It should be noted, too, that even the celebrated fiddlers in Edinburgh had mostly not been born and brought up there, but had come to the metropolis from other parts of Scotland, bearing with them local repertories and regional styles of playing. Dow, Mackintosh and Nathaniel Gow all came from Perthshire; Oswald probably came from the Stirling area, and Charles McLean from the north-east. Among the great Scots fiddlers who lived in Edinburgh, only McGibbon and McGlashan seem to have been natives of the town.

The overall effect of printed fiddle collections was beneficial. They enabled the best music from different parts of Scotland to circulate quickly; they provided examples of notation for those who wished to write down their own repertories, and examples of the new up-to-date Scottish style for those who wished to compose. Their negative value as irritants should also not be overlooked. Many fiddlers must have been extremely annoyed by, for example, Oswald's fly-by-night variation sets in *The Caledonian Pocket Companion.* (It is one of the worst, as well as one of the best, 18th-century collections; one can well imagine poor overworked Oswald sitting down at midnight to cobble something, anything, together to meet his printing deadlines.) Such fiddlers often reacted by trying to compose something better themselves.

Printed collections do, nevertheless, show 18th-century fiddling in a somewhat commercialised light. A truer picture of what fiddlers actually liked can be gained from an examination of manuscript books.

The making of a manuscript

When we turn to manuscripts, it becomes clear at once that fiddlers were influenced by printed collections but were by no means bound by their contents. For many pieces appear in manuscripts which have no connection with printed books at all: pieces written by local composers; pieces that have crossed the country in handwritten copies; pieces which have just surfaced from aural tradition.

It is an intriguing question why fiddlers made these manuscripts at all. In order to explain the pieces in them, one has to assume that players were in the habit of writing out music-sheets bearing single tunes and passing them round their friends. Such music-sheets would be useful for learning new repertory, and would probably be discarded once the tunes were memorised, so it is not surprising that none have survived for present-day inspection. The large manuscript books which do survive, on the other hand, are not so obviously practical. They are usually bound in such a way that they will not stay open on music stands; are too bulky to carry around comfortably; and show no signs of use (e.g. pencilled fingerings and bowings, turned-down pages). Most of them seem to have been made purely for private satisfaction, by fiddlers who liked exercising their skill at notation and wanted to see their repertories set down on paper.

(A few manuscripts also survive which were made by masters and pupils during lessons, and which were made by professional copyists for patrons; but these are only a small proportion of the total.)

It is likely that many fiddlers in the second half of the 18th century had pipe-dreams of producing, one day, a printed collection of their own. Those not named Dow, Riddell, McGlashan, etc. knew perfectly well, however, that they lacked the talent to fill a complete book with original compositions, the energy to deal with printers, booksellers and subscribers, and the capital to float the whole venture off. So they settled for making a private manuscript instead. Into this they would put the 'correct' versions of famous tunes (i.e. as they played them themselves — differently from the printed sets); new variations which they had made up or learnt from friends; and other excellent pieces which, scandalously, no one in Edinburgh had yet had the good sense to publish. Any remaining spaces could be filled up with items copied from the Bremner collection belonging to their friend down the road. They would spend months discussing their selection procedures and notation problems, driving their wife to distraction; gradually, their parlour would submerge in small bits of music-paper. Finally the fair copy would be made, and might be bound personally by its maker.

Completed, the manuscript was naturally far too precious to be played from, marked with fingering, or even shown to anyone but old, trusted friends. Its destiny was to become a family heirloom.

Not all manuscripts were created in such a painstaking, de luxe way; nevertheless, this prototype that I have outlined exactly fits the magnificent manuscript made by James Gillespie in Perth in 1768. Gillespie's book is beautifully written, carefully planned to avoid page-turns in the middle of pieces, and sectionalised in an attractive and unique way. Gillespie also numbered the strains of his pieces — an unusual scheme, but one so practical that I have in fact adopted it for the present book. Many of the items that he chose are treasures: a superb set of variations on *Duncan Gray*, much finer than the sets printed by McGibbon and Oswald; three minuets made out of old Scottish pentatonic tunes, a type of minuet that never reached print at all; two minuets by Daniel Dow, five years prior to publication and not yet dedicated to Miss Babie Gray and Lady Jean Lindsay; the only known reel-version of the song *The flowers of the forest*; a few more otherwise unrecorded reels, some with socially unacceptable titles like *Bring her ben and bore her better*; a small clutch of pieces evidently copied from a manuscript of *c.* 1710 vintage, prior to the printing era; and a rare, late text of Forbes of Disblair's *Maggie Lauder* variations, which for most fiddlers had been superseded by McGibbon's set.

One can see, however, why Gillespie's book would not have worked as a printed collection. Gillespie's original material tended to run dry on him at certain points: his 'Airs and March's' section (pages 23–36), in particular, is heavily dependent on Bremner's *Collection of Airs and Marches* of *c.* 1756–61. Its size would have made it prohibitively expensive to print; and its mixed format, however satisfying to Gillespie, was not what a publisher would have considered the public was willing to buy.

The making of a printed collection

Yet the problems of compiling a printed collection were not essentially different from those of compiling a manuscript; the publisher simply had to solve them with an additional regard for printing costs and market trends. Printed collections did not grow on trees. Their material had to be gathered, like that of manuscripts, from four sources: aural tradition; the editor's own compositions; existing manuscripts; and existing printed collections.

The *McLean* collection — *A Collection of Favourite Scots Tunes . . . By the Late M^r Ch^s McLean and other Eminent Masters,* published by James Johnson in Edinburgh in 1772 — makes an interesting comparison with the Gillespie manuscript. Its contents are set out in Table I; a high proportion of the pieces are variation sonatas. The book is nicely laid out in an oblong format, and is planned, like Gillespie's manuscript, in openings — units of one left and one right-hand page — so as to avoid the need to turn over in the middles of pieces. None of the pieces in it had been printed before in anything like the same forms, apart

Table I

CONTENTS OF THE *McLEAN* COLLECTION

Page	Title	Ascription in Glen's copy	Variant texts	Remarks
1	Had away frae me, Donald	Daniel Grant	—	—
2–3	My ain Kind Dearie O	—	Gill, 55	18 strains to Gillespie's 10, otherwise very similar; bass added
4–5	Birks of Invermay	Mr Charles McLean (*at strain 11*: Gigg R. McIntosh)	McF ii, 210	strains 11–12 not in McF; bass added
6–7	Pinkie House	Mr McLean	McF ii, 110	in E flat where McF is in G; strains 7–8 (of 12) and bass added
8–9	Bonny Jean of Aberdeen	—	*Munro,* 20 McF iii, 259	different bass from *Munro; Munro's* Grazioso and Vivace sections run together as 'Minuet'
10–11	Nansy's to the Green wood gane	—	*Munro,* 15	different bass from *Munro; Munro's* Largo and Vivace sections run together as 'Minuet', and Gavotta and Presto as 'Gavot'
12–13	Corn Riggs	Mr R. McIntosh	—	—
14–15	Logan Water	Mr R. McIntosh	—	—

Page	Title	Ascription in Glen's copy	Variant texts	Remarks
16–17	Caber Feigh	—	McF ii, 113	strains 1–2, 4–9, 12, 14–16 near-identical to McF's 1–2, 6–11, 18, 20–22; bass added
18–19	Lasses Likes nae Brandy	—	Mc F ii, 117	lacks McF's strain 12, otherwise near-identical; bass added
—	Suters of Selkirk	—	—	—
20–21	Tail Todle	—	—	—
—	Well may the Keel row	—	—	—
22–23	the Old Woman in the Glen	—	McF iii, 221	strains 1–2 identical to McF, otherwise set very different
—	Johnie Cope	—	Gill, 52	near-identical; bass added
24–25	Willie was a Wanton wag	—	McF ii, 32	lacks McF's strains 15–22; bass added
—	Cailleach Ouer	—	McF ii, 4	near-identical; bass added
26–27	My Nanio	Mr McLean	McF ii, 108	in D minor where McF is in E minor; strains 1–2 not in McF; bass added
—	Jackie Latin	—	*Br-McG*, 110 Gill, 62	19 strains to *Br-McG's* 20 and Gillespie's 23, otherwise very similar
28–29	Ailen a Roon	Mr McLean	—	—
—	up and ware them a Willie	—	—	—
30–31	Old Ireland Rejoice	—	McF ii, 52	strains 1–6 near-identical to McF; bass added
—	Humours of Glen	—	—	—
32–33	the Breas of Balandine	R. McIntosh	—	—
34–35	Gilder Roy	Mr R. McIntosh	—	—
36–37	Jockie was the Blythest Lad	Mr R. McIntosh	—	—

from *Bonny Jean of Aberdeen* and *Nansy's to the Green wood gane*, which are in Munro's 1732 collection, and *Jackie Latin*, which is in Bremner's 1768 McGibbon collection in a transposed flute version.

Several more of the pieces can be found in near-identical forms in manuscripts. There are three overlaps with the Gillespie manuscript: these show that Gillespie and the *Mclean* editor both liked the same up-to-date kind of variations, and that both belonged to some sort of informal fiddling network which was actively circulating copies. There are also ten overlaps with the McFarlane manuscript of 1740. These seem to be more significant; indeed, they prompt one to ask several detailed questions.

Question one: which pieces did McLean write, and who were the other composers represented in the book? As printed, the collection gives no clues. Fortunately, however, John Glen possessed a copy — now in the National Library of Scotland, pressmark Glen 228(1) — to which some ascriptions were added by hand soon after the book was published. Four of these ascriptions are to Charles McLean, six to Robert Mackintosh, and one to Daniel Grant.

This answers part of the question, but not all of it. In 1772, Mackintosh was only about 27, and had recently moved to Edinburgh from Perthshire; Grant was also in his 20s, and lived in Elgin in the north of Scotland. Both were far too young and obscure to be the 'other Eminent Masters' of the title-page. At least two more composers of McLean's generation must have been represented, probably composers who were legendary figures in informed circles but were not well known to the general public, and whose names were therefore not good enough selling-points to be worth putting on the front cover.

Obviously, the editor must have known who had written what, even if he decided to suppress the information. This means that he must have worked from manuscripts with ascriptions. It is rare for manuscripts to give composers' names, but the McFarlane manuscript, as it happens, is one of those that does: the ten McFarlane texts listed in Table I bear three ascriptions to McLean, three to David Young, and two to Forbes of Disblair, so giving us a group of 'Eminent Masters' exactly like that we were expecting.

Question two: why in the world would anyone rewrite Munro's bass line to *Bonny Jean of Aberdeen* when the original is so splendid; or be so careless as to run the two 3/4 sections of the piece, which are intended to go at quite different speeds, together into a single minuet? What is interesting here is that the McFarlane text of *Bonny Jean of Aberdeen* omits the bass line and the section headings, and runs the (unnamed) Grazioso on into the (unnamed) Vivace without beginning a fresh line. Anyone finding the piece in the McFarlane manuscript would not, therefore, necessarily know to refer to Munro's collection for the original text. They might very well simply reconstruct the bass line and headings as best they could.

Question three: is it not a strange coincidence that the two strains missing from the McFarlane text of *Birks of Invermay* are exactly the two which Glen's copy of the *McLean* collection credits Mackintosh with having composed?

Taken together, these points lead irresistibly to two conclusions: (*a*) that the editor had the actual McFarlane manuscript in front of him; and (*b*) that the editor was Robert Mackintosh himself. Neither conclusion can be absolutely proved, but once one has reached them, many other odd details fit smoothly into place. Three of these details may be mentioned briefly: the McFarlane book was a patron's manuscript rather than a jealously-guarded personal one, and is known to have been lent out round Edinburgh occasionally; the 9–8 suspensions in the harmonisation of *Pinkie House* are strongly characteristic of Mackintosh; and the collection is remarkably full of Mackintosh's compositions (6 pieces out of 26) had anyone other than he been editing it.

Table II is drawn up on the basis of these conclusions. It shows the ten pieces common to the McFarlane manscript and the *McLean* collection, and extrapolates the editorial tasks that Mackintosh would have had to do, in order to turn the one set of texts into the other. These tasks have a convincing ring about them; reading down the farthest right-hand column of the table, one gets an extremely believable, coherent picture of an 18th-century fiddler-editor at work.

Table II

OVERLAPS BETWEEN THE *McLEAN* COLLECTION
AND THE McFARLANE MANUSCRIPT

Title in *McL* (McF title in brackets, if significantly different)	Ascription in McF	Ascription in Glen's copy of *McL*	Mackintosh's editorial work to create *McL* texts from McF
			General: alter melodic decorations; revise bowings
Birks of Invermay	MacLean	Mr Charles McLean (*at strain 11:* Gigg R. McIntosh)	compose extra jig section (strains 11–12) at end; add bass
Pinkie House	MacLean	Mr McLean	transpose into trendy key of E flat major; compose 2 extra strains midway; add bass
Bonny Jean of Aberdeen	—	—	add bass and section headings (editor not aware of the definitive text in Munro's collection)
Caber Feigh (Caber-fei)	D[avid] Y[oung]	—	cut three sections midway (strains 3–5, 12–17, 19) and substitute new, briefer links; add bass; improve Gaelic spelling of title
Lasses Likes nae Brandy (Lasses drink at Brandy)	D[avid] Y[oung]	—	shorten set by cutting last strain; add bass; alter title to suit sensibility of upper-class purchasers
the Old Woman in the Glen (Barbara Allan)	McLean	—	cut McLean's variations back to the opening theme (strains 1–2) and write new ones; alter title to suit own preference for other words to the same tune
Willie was a Wanton wag	Disb[lair]	—	shorten set by cutting last 8 strains; add bass
Cailleach Ouer (Cailleach Ouir)	D[avid] Y[oung]	—	add bass; improve Gaelic spelling
My Nanio	Disb[lair]	Mr McLean (*sic*)	transpose down a tone; tack undecorated set of tune on to opening to introduce the variations; add bass
Old Ireland Rejoice	—	—	cut last 8 strains and substitute new, briefer ending; add bass

Mackintosh's editorial methods of 1772, as revealed in Table II, are not ones which would appeal to 20th-century musicologists. By present-day standards, Mackintosh was too confident by half: he blue-pencilled other composers' work before he had fully grasped its subtleties, and altered it to suit the taste of his own generation, assuming without question that the previous generation's taste was inferior. But we must remember that he was promoting a living tradition, not excavating a dead one. And perhaps his confidence was justified at a personal level; for Mackintosh was soon to become a far more famous fiddle-composer himself than McLean had ever been, or any of the other 'Eminent Masters' featured in the collection.

Nevertheless, such editing would hardly be acceptable today; and so the ninety tunes in the present book are edited on principles different from Mackintosh's, even though four of them *(My Nanny-O, Cailleach odhar, Bonny Jean of Aberdeen* and *Pinkie House)* also appear in this book and are, in fact, the same pieces of music that are listed in Table II. I, however, unlike Mackintosh, found a copy of Munro's 1732 collection and used it for *Bonny Jean of Aberdeen* (**65**). I used the McFarlane manuscript, rather than the *McLean* collection, for *My Nanny-O* (**26**) and *Cailleach odhar* (**28**). *Pinkie House* (**68**), however, is based on Mackintosh's text; it seemed fair in the circumstances to ascribe it to McLean and Mackintosh jointly.

Perhaps it is time, now, that we looked more closely at the actual music.

CHAPTER I
Song and Dance-tunes to 1720

THIS chapter presents a selection of song and dance-tunes as they were played on the fiddle in the first twenty years of the 18th century. No instrumental music had yet been printed in Scotland at this time; so the sources are manuscript books (all from the south of Scotland except one, George Skene's, which was made in Aberdeenshire), plus one printed collection, *A Collection of Original Scotch-Tunes . . . for the Violin*, published by Henry Playford in London in 1700. I have accepted the contents of Playford's book as authentic, since it appears to have been printed from genuine Scottish manuscripts. Two pieces in this chapter, *Sour plums of Galashiels* (8) and *The collier's daughter* (12), are taken from a later source, James Gillespie's manuscript; the style of these pieces shows, however, that they belong to the period around 1710.

Nos. **1, 9** and **12** are Scotch measures; **5** is a strathspey; **6** is a slow march, similar in style to the theme of a pibroch; **7** is a hornpipe; **10** and **13** are jigs, and **11** is a reel. The other pieces can only be classified as airs, though **2** has some of the characteristics of a 17th-century French sarabande, and **15** is related, through its alternating 6/4 and 3/2 rhythms, to the 16th-century English coranto.

Many of the titles of these pieces are the first lines of songs. *Allan Water* (3), for example, was a song which began:

> Allan Water's wide and deep,
> And my dear Annie's very bonnie.

The words are given in Martha Brown's music-book of 1714. However, the fiddle version does not fit the words exactly: it has too many notes, and would have to be pruned and simplified before it could be sung.

It seems that most Scottish tunes at this time could be performed in three ways: *(a)* as songs; *(b)* as accompaniment to dancing; *(c)* as instrumental recital pieces. These fiddle versions often seem to fall uncomfortably between categories. They are too complex and wide-ranging to be sung; they are too highly ornamented, and have to be played a little too slowly, for dancing; yet most of them are not musically developed enough to be fully satisfying as recital pieces apart, perhaps, from the excellent sets of *Saw na ye my Peggie* (7) and *When she cam ben, she bobbit* (15). This was probably due to the violin's being a recent importation into Scotland; it was still a new-fangled instrument, in the process of acquiring a repertory of Scots tunes. Its moment of supreme success, when it would emerge as pre-eminent among Scottish instruments, was not to come for another forty years.

A few long fiddle pieces survive from this early period. Four of them I shall introduce later: the fiddle pibrochs *Cumha Easbuig Earraghàidheal* (54), *Cumha Iarla Wigton* (55) and *The battle of Harlaw* (57), which date on stylistic grounds from about 1720, and *Marriage and money* (89), which Robert Riddell notes as having been played in Newton Stewart around 1705. Three other long pieces deserve a brief mention here: an ambitious bagpipe rant called *The gum-ga'd aiver* (Gairdyn MS.); a multi-sectional setting of *John come kiss me now*, of English origin (Cuming MS.); and a vigorous set of variations on *I'll hae her awa in spite o' her minnie*, not recorded until the *Flores Musicae* collection of 1773 but almost certainly dating from the beginning of the century.

This chapter concentrates on the shorter pieces of the period. Even these, however, can be analysed and shown to contain a wealth of variation procedures; all the techniques needed to construct large-scale pieces are, in fact, here if one looks for them.

Scots songs in the 17th century seem mostly to have had only one strain of music, which was repeated over and over again until all the words had been sung. Fiddle settings of the songs, on the other hand, nearly always had two strains. From the late 17th century onwards fiddlers had begun to add second strains to the tunes, generally making the strain 2 by creating a variation on strain 1. A favourite method for doing this was to put strain 1 up an octave and then adjust any notes which ran off the top of the instrument's compass. Usually the melody was forced to come down the octave again at some point, so that strain 2 closed with the same final notes as strain 1. This method has obviously been used to make strain 2 of *Bonny Jean of Aberdeen* (65). It can also be seen in the second strains of *Highland laddie* (1), *Killiecrankie* (6), *The collier's daughter* (12), and *When she cam ben, she bobbit* (15), though in some of these cases it has been combined with other constructional devices.

Once a 2-strain instrumental version of a song-tune had been established, fiddlers could create further variations on it, this time regarding strains 1–2, rather than merely strain 1, as the theme. *When she cam ben, she bobbit* is a good example of this; strains 3–4 and 5–6 are organised as pairs of strains, and both have been arrived at by varying strains 1–2.

There was one major Scots fiddle-composer at this time: John McLachlan. McLachlan's life is obscure, but he is known to have played violin in an orchestral concert in Edinburgh in 1695, and he composed the dance-tune *McLachlan's Scotch measure*, which appears in Playford's 1700 collection. He also made settings of traditional tunes for fiddle. A large number of these survive in the Balcarres lute-book of *c.*1700.

The Balcarres lute-book gives McLachlan's pieces under such titles as: 'Where will our goodman lye, m^r m^claughlans way, by m^r beck. This can be glossed as: *'Where will our Goodman lie,* with the variations composed and played by Mr McLachlan, rearranged for lute by Mr Beck'. Here is a specimen section of this particular piece:

Beck was an Edinburgh lute-teacher. All that he did, when rearranging McLachlan's fiddle settings for his own instrument, was to put the fiddle line down an octave and add a few harmony notes; for the piece also appears in the Bowie fiddle manuscript (Edinburgh, 1705) as follows:

This version must be McLachlan's original, or something very near to it. However, the Bowie manuscript does not bother to mention McLachlan's name, so without the Balcarres lute-book we would have had no idea who made the setting.

When she cam ben, she bobbit **(15)** is another of McLachlan's settings, again given anonymously in the Bowie manuscript and with an ascription in the Balcarres lute-book. McLachlan's work deserves further study.

Scottish fiddle pieces of the 1700–20 period are written in a variety of styles, the most characteristic of which are: *(a)* tunes based on five notes; *(b)* tunes based on two chords; *(c)* tunes based on Italian chord progressions. Each of these merits a brief investigation.

Tunes based on five notes

Nos. **1–9** are all five-note (or pentatonic) tunes. In these, the 4th and 7th degrees of the scale are either omitted or else are used very sparingly, in unaccented places in the melody. Pentatonic tunes in the key of G (for example) are thus virtually limited to the notes G, A, B, D and E.

Pentatonic music is often thought of as naive and primitive. This was not the case, however, with pentatonic music in late-medieval Scotland which, on the contrary, was often put together in a sophisticated, self-conscious, and almost mathematical way. By 1700 this style was old-fashioned and had begun to break down; but enough of it remains in these fiddle pieces for its flavour to be demonstrated.

Sequences

Sequences in pentatonic music were similar to those in European art music, except that intervals of a tone and a minor third had to be treated as equivalent to each other because of the gaps in the scale. The repeated figure thus changed shape as the sequence proceeded. *Sour plums of Galashiels* **(8)** contains several of these sequences, such as the following:

Whole phrases could also be arranged in sequence, as for example in *Killiecrankie* **(6)**, strain 2, where bars 5–8 form a sequence with bars 1–4:

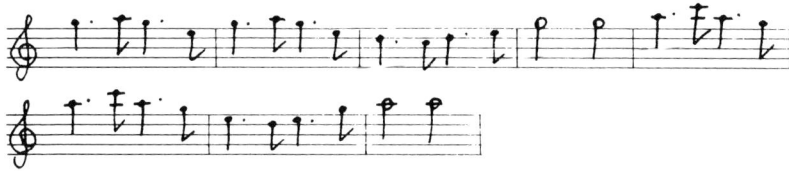

(The Cs in bars 5 and 6 are taken from a recorder text of the piece; the fiddle text given in this chapter alters them to Bs to avoid a shift out of first position.)

Permutations of notes

Melodic figures in pentatonic pieces were often repeated with the notes shuffled into a different order. There are examples of this in *I wish I were where Helen lies* **(2)**, where the phrase:

returns varied as:

and in *Allan Water* **(3)**, where:

returns changed into:

The curiously lop-sided arpeggio in strain 6 of *Saw na ye my Peggie* **(7)**:

is also a result of permutated note-order; the norm here is the regular Alberti-bass type of arpeggio.

Permutations of rhythm

Melodic figures could also be juggled with from a rhythmic angle. *Saw na ye my Peggie* (**7**) contains a splendid set of examples of this. The five-note figure with which the piece starts (bracketed):

reappears first in a bunched-up form:

then in bunched-up form and off the beat:

and finally is restored to its original size in a new rhythm which gives the second note much more weight:

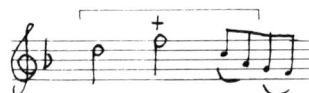

These devices were all melodic ones, and worked without any reference to supporting harmony. Indeed, they were only possible because pentatonic tunes generally had so little sense of harmonic direction.

Tunes based on two chords

Nos. **10** and **12–14** come into this category. Often known as 'double tonic' tunes, they have a sense of being supported by two alternating chords a tone apart, whether or not they are actually played with an accompaniment. The higher (or upper) of the two chords may be either major or minor, but the lower chord is always major. Either the upper or the lower chord can feel like the predominant tonality, depending on how the tune is structured. Thus a tune based on the chords of G and A can either have a sense of being in G major, with some bars shifting to the supertonic; or of being in A major/minor, with some bars shifting to the flattened seventh.

Double-tonic tunes were not unique to Scotland; they were also popular in England in the 16th and 17th centuries. After 1700, however, they dropped out of use in English music and acquired strongly Scottish national associations.

It was possible for double-tonic tunes also to be pentatonic ones, for the notes of the pentatonic scale in key G (G A B D E) could easily be grouped into the chords of G and A

(G B D / A E). The upper chord here, however, contains no third, so leaving it an open question whether it is intended to be major or minor. This would depend on whether the gap in the pentatonic scale were filled in by C natural or C sharp, assuming that it were filled in at all. *Greig's Pipes* is a good example of a double-tonic tune which is also pentatonic. It goes as follows:

In this case the tune eventually comes down in favour of A minor and introduces some C naturals in its fourth strain. (This text is based on the Gillespie MS.; see also a strathspey set of the same tune, *Willie Wink's testament*, given as no. **46.**)

Many early 18th-century tunes show an ambivalence between major and minor upper chords which is probably due to this pentatonic background. The version of *The collier's daughter* **(12)** given here, for instance, is firmly in G minor (with some bars in F major), but texts of it are also known in a G major version.

Double-tonic tunes can be played on bagpipes as well as on fiddle. As the bagpipes have a fixed scale of nine notes (A major with flattened 7th: g' to a''), many of these tunes have become standardised with the passage of time. If *Drunken wives of Carlisle* **(14)**, for example, were transposed up a tone and played on the pipes, its upper chord would have no choice but to be major, and the scale passages would necessarily come out with flattened 7ths in the upper key, sharpened 4ths in the lower key. The violin, however, is chromatically flexible, so fiddle versions rarely turn out as systematic and logical as this. Indeed, fiddle texts of double-tonic tunes usually contain a great range of chromatic inflections, and modes which change without warning from one bar to the next.

Considering how crude the double-tonic scheme is as a musical idea, it is surprising what an abundance or repertory it has brought forth. Perhaps a sixth of all Scots tunes current between 1700 and 1800 are based on it; and one seldom confuses one tune with another which is similarly constructed, even when they are disguised by complex variations. Even as few as two chords can, it seems, be used in a lot of different ways.

Tunes based on Italian chord progressions

There were several stock chord progressions which evolved in Italy in the 16th century, spread to other countries, and were used in popular music all over Europe during the century that followed. Two of these took root in Scotland, the *passamezzo antico* and the *passamezzo moderno*: they are given below (after Reese).

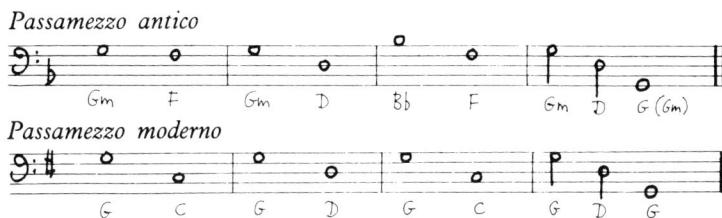

It should be pointed out that most Scots would not have known the origins of these chord progressions, or the Italian names for them. However, tunes based on these chords are so distinctive, because of their strong harmonic sense, that they are easily recognised even if the sequence of chords is slightly changed.

Passamezzo antico tunes were nearly always in the key of G minor. The one most popular in Scotland was the English tune *Greensleeves;* a local jig set of this is given as no. **84**. The natively-composed *When she cam ben, she bobbit* **(15, 20)** ran it a close second. *Johnnie Cope* **(38)** and *Up in the morning early* were also based on the *passamezzo antico* chords, though in both tunes the progression is slightly altered. The accompaniment of *Three good fellows* **(18)** also derives from these chords.

The most famous *passamezzo moderno* tune was *John come kiss me now*, which was widely known in both England and Scotland in the 16th and 17th centuries. *Lasses gar your tails toddle* **(11)** was probably partly copied from it, for it uses the same chords in a slightly haphazard order. In *John come kiss me now*, the subdominant and dominant chords are carefully separated from each other by tonic chords; but in *Lasses gar your tails toddle*, subdominant and dominant chords occur consecutively, so producing a kind of double-tonic effect which sounds more Scottish than Italian.

Another Scottish *passamezzo moderno* tune is *Sweden's March* **(40)**. Here the Italian chords are used faithfully up to strain 3. From strain 4 onwards, however, the subdominant chords are replaced by supertonic ones, giving this piece, too, a local double-tonic flavour. Three more tunes based on these chords are *St. Bernard's Well* **(73)**, *Up and waur them a', Willie*, and *There's nae luck about the house*. All three of these seem to have been newly composed in the 18th century.

Scots fiddle music of the period 1700–20 thus had a number of interesting European connections. Despite these, however, it was an old-fashioned and insular tradition: the tunes were played on a brand-new imported instrument, but mainly reflected fashions and tastes which had been on the go since the 16th century. No one in 1720 can have foreseen the enormous impact which up-to-date European art-music was shortly to make on Scots fiddling.

c

1. Highland laddie

2. I wish I were where Helen lies

3. Allan Water

[Moderato]

4. Gowd on your gartens, Marion

[Slow]

5. Macpherson's testament

[Moderato]

repeat
strain 2

6. Killiecrankie

[Slow, rhythmic]

7. Saw na ye my Peggie

[Brisk]

[D.C. strains 1 and 2]

8. Sour plums of Galashiels

[Moderato con moto]

9. I love my love in secret

10. Bride next

11. Lasses gar your tails toddle

12. The collier's daughter

13. The horseman's port

14. Drunken wives of Carlisle

[Fast, rhythmic]

15. When she cam ben, she bobbit

set by JOHN McLACHLAN (fl. 1700)

[D.C. strain 1]

EDITORIAL METHOD

Each piece is edited from a single source as far as possible. Added accidentals are given in small type; added slurs are ticked. Repeat-signs have been adjusted to fit the prevailing notation of the piece. Appoggiaturas and incompletely-notated rhythms are glossed above the stave. Other editorial additions are shown in brackets or in small note-heads. A few wrong slurs have been deleted, and a few staccato dots added, without notice.

Strain-numbers have been added to all pieces with more than 2 strains. The first full bar of a strain counts as bar 1; 1st and 2nd-time bars are referred to as (e.g.) bars 8a and 8b.

Pieces in score are for violin with harpsichord and cello accompaniment if not specified otherwise. Spelling, capitalisation and punctuation of the titles have been modernised.

SUGGESTIONS FOR PERFORMANCE

Decorations. In pieces before 1725, + and ⋀ are mordents, and ⁄⁄ and ⨯ are trills (equivalent to *tr* after 1725). All these are generally short decorations, consisting of only one or two grace-notes at the beginning of the main note. Trills in 'Scots drawing-room' pieces, however, are often played in European art-music style, i.e. they begin on the upper note, continue throughout the main note's length, and end with a turn.

The decorations ♫♩ and ♫♩ (slurred, usually rising stepwise) are played roughly as ♫♩. ; they are in fact equivalents of each other, though both notations can be found in the same piece. See no. **8** for examples.

For birls (repeated-note ♫♩ , bowed separately) see Chapter V.

Fingering. Two golden rules: use first position as much as possible; use open strings in preference to stopped notes.

Bowing. It is unlikely that any two 18th-century fiddlers bowed a tune in exactly the same way. (The keen student might like to compare bowings of the *Johnnie Cope* variations, no. **38**, in *(a)* the Gillespie MS. *(b)* the Trotter MS. *(c)* the *McLean* collection.) Modern players can thus feel free to experiment.

The Scots-fiddle 'loop' bowing (two repeated notes taken in one bow, the bow being re-pressed, not detached, for the second note) occurs in many 18th-century pieces, shown by a somewhat ambiguous slur. I have glossed these slurs with extra bowing marks; see nos. **9** and **15** for examples.

Scoratura notation. See Chapter IV.

Repeat signs. The double-bar forms ‖ (before 1725) and ⫴ (after 1725) are equivalents, both indicating a point at which the fiddler *may* play a repeat *if* he wishes. Here also the modern player can experiment. (Exceptions are nos. **30, 31** and **32**, which Bremner printed with double bars in ‖ form as late as 1759; Bremner clearly intended these pieces to be played straight through without repeats.)

In pieces where the even-numbered strains are twice as long as the odd-numbered ones (nos. **3, 8, 35** and **41**), a case can be made out for repeating odd-numbered strains only; this repeat scheme must have been used when the tunes were sung, since it always fits the words. Whether it was used for fiddling would depend, however, on how closely the player felt tied to the words.

Da capos. The Gillespie manuscript glosses *da capo* as 'begin again and End with the first Strain'. Many pieces in this book will benefit from having strain 1 (or strains 1–2) played again at the end; I have added directions in some cases, such as nos. **7** and **15**.

NOTES ON THE MUSIC

1 *Highland laddie*
Source: Bowie MS.
The tune was also known in the 18th century as *The lass of Livingston*. Readers interested in looking up words associated with these times are warmly recommended to the following collections: James Johnson's *Scots Musical Museum* (1787–1803); Robert Chambers' *Songs of Scotland prior to Burns* (1862); Thomas Crawford's *Love, labour and liberty* (1976).
Revisions: strain 2 bar 2 note 4 orig *b♭'*.

2 *I wish I were where Helen lies*
Source: Bowie MS.
The words to the tune show that it was a lament, not a love song (it is a grave Helen is lying in, not a bed).
Revisions: strain 2 bar 6 notes 2–3 orig *e"*, *d"* (cf. strain 2 bar 2).

3 *Allan Water*
Source: Bowie MS.
Compare David Young's slower, more decorated set of the same tune, no. **29**.

4 *Gowd on your gartens, Marion*
Source: George Skene MS., f.4r.
The words to the tune begin 'Will ye go to the ewe-buchts, Marion'; this title is the opening line of the third verse.
Revisions: tune orig barred in C
  rhythm of strain 1 bar 4 notes 6–11 editorial.

5 *Macpherson's testament*
Source: Sinkler MS, p.5.
This is the earlist known fiddle tune in strathspey rhythm; it is the tune to the broadside ballad about James Macpherson, the famous fiddler-brigand executed at Banff in 1700.
Revisions: repeat of strain 2 orig written out in full.

6 *Killiecrankie*
Source: James Thomson MS., p.20. Title supplied from a recorder setting in the same manuscript.
This tune celebrates the battle of Killiecrankie in Perthshire in 1689. It was later renamed Tranent Muir, after a different battle (usually known as the Battle of Prestonpans) in East Lothian in 1745. It should not be confused with another *Killiecrankie* tune for which Burns wrote words beginning 'Where hae ye been sae braw, lad'.
Revisions: strain 1 bar 6 is editorial (cf. strain 1 bar 5).

7 *Saw na ye my Peggie*
Source: Sinkler MS., p.21. Title supplied from *Flores Musicae*, p.20.
Later, different variations on this tune are given in the *Caledonian Pocket Companion* and the Gillespie MS.

8 *Sour plums of Galashiels*
Source: Gillespie MS., p.70.
It is perhaps unnecessary to mention that Galashiels is a town in the Borders, on the River Tweed.
Revisions strain 3 bar 2 note 3 orig *e"*.

9 *I love my love in secret*
Source: Bowie MS.
This tune was also played in standard tuning (in C major: texts in Playford's *Original Scotch-Tunes* and the Hume MS).
Revisions: scordatura prefatory-stave editorial
  strain 2 bar 7 note 5 orig *f"*.

10 *Bride next*
Source: Playford's *Original Scotch-Tunes*, p.8.
The tune was also known in the 18th century as *My wife's a wanton wee thing;* it is still widely current in Scotland under this title.
Revisions: strain 1 bar 3 note 4 orig *b'*.

11 *Lasses gar your tails toddle*
Source; George Skene MS., f.12r.
Skene's original title is: 'Lasses gar your Tails Todle, Spread your houghs lat in the Dodle, that will gar your Tails Todle'. The decorations seem excessive: it is likely that Skene was simply enjoying writing out the signs, in which case most of them could be ignored, but strain 1 bars 3–4, for example, could be rendered as:

Revisions: the text is a compound of two notations given in the MS.
  repeat of strain 2 orig written out in full.

12 *The collier's daughter*
Source: Gillespie MS., p.38.
This tune also existed in major versions (texts in the Sinkler and Cuming MSS.). For its words, see Johnson, *Music and Society*, p.138.

13 *The horseman's port*
Source: Sinkler MS., p.6.
Port (properly *peurt*) is Gaelic for 'instrumental piece'.
Other titles for this tune were *The black and the brown* and *John Paterson's mare.*

14 *Drunken wives of Carlisle*
Source: Sinkler MS., p.9.
This was originally a bagpipe piece, as can be seen from its restricted compass. It was also known as *Gie the mawking mair o't.*

15 *When she cam ben, she bobbit*
Source: Bowie MS. Ascription to McLachlan from the Balcarres lute-book, p.90.
Translated into standard English the title is: 'When she came through to the parlour, she curtseyed'. Since about 1810 this tune has been known as *The laird of Cockpen,* after Lady Nairne's words to it. Compare McGibbon's more ornate, Italian-baroque setting, no. **20.**
Revisions: trills and editorial accidentals from Balcarres
  editorial accompaniment based on Balcarres.

CHAPTER II

The 'Scots drawing room' style

THE 'Scots drawing room' style was the invention of a small group of composers in Edinburgh between 1720 and 1745. The style was created, in essence, by harmonising Scots tunes in an up-to-date art-music manner, though most of the composers not only harmonised the tunes they chose but added variations to them which also have marked art-music characteristics. The Variation Sonata genre was also created in Edinburgh at this time: this will be discussed more fully in Chapter VII. The central problem of the drawing-room style, however, was harmonisation, for Scottish melodic clichés and European harmonic clichés had evolved separately up to 1720, and there was no guarantee that they could be fitted together with any satisfactory results at all. I have presented the pieces in this chapter with their original harmonisations, in order to show how the various composers coped with this problem. Nos. **16–21** are examples of the drawing-room style up to 1745, while nos. **22–24** show how it developed later in the century.

The instruments accompanying the fiddle should ideally be harpsichord and cello. However, 18th-century performers might well have used a lute, harp, or small pipe-organ instead, and there is no very strong reason why 20th-century performers should not use a piano.

The Scots drawing-room style had its psychological roots in the Act of Union of 1707 between Scotland and England. Losing its separate parliament damaged Scotland's self-esteem badly; and the Edinburgh upper classes felt the blow particularly keenly, for Edinburgh was transformed at a stroke from a capital city and seat of government to a dirty, provincial town twelve days' journey from London, a town of little consequence to the rest of the world. Edinburgh tried to compensate culturally for its lost political power by starting a new artistic movement which was both aggressively nationalistic and aggressively fashionable. The chief spokesman of the movement was Allan Ramsay, who — in a triple role of poet, playwright, and editor — undertook a full-scale remoulding of Scottish literature with a view to putting Edinburgh back on the international map.

Ramsay's work covered a large area. His *Ever Green* (1724) was an anthology of hitherto unpublished 15th and 16th-century Scottish court poetry, while *The Tea-table Miscellany* (four volumes, 1723 onwards) was a collection of new lyrics to folk-songs, many of them in Scots dialect but modelled closely on London types of fashionable verse. His play *The Gentle Shepherd* (1721–9), on the other hand, was a pastoral which mixed Arcadian literary conventions with realistic pictures of Scottish country life.

There was a curious inside/outside dichotomy in Ramsay's work, for he was attempting to get together a body of literature which would not only be enjoyed in Edinburgh, but also be respected in London. This was a dangerous aim, and it sowed the seeds for Scotland's present-day cultural insecurity; for trying to please local and international audiences simultaneously, and worrying about one's prestige in foreign countries, tend to inhibit an artist from producing sincere, coherent work. As a wiser poet than Ramsay was to observe, a more secure tactic is to concentrate so hard on making the poem, sermon or

34

mouse-trap to one's own satisfaction that one hardly notices the rest of the world arriving on the doorstep to watch.

Ramsay had views about music, too. He set these down in 1721 in a poem addressed to the Edinburgh Musical Society:

> Then you, whose symphony of souls proclaim
> Your kin to heav'n, add to your country's fame,
> And shew that music may have as good fate
> In *Albion's* [Scotland's] glens, as *Umbria's* [Italy's] green retreat;
> And with *Correlli's* soft Italian song
> Mix *Cowden Knows,* and *Winter nights are long.*
> Nor should the martial *Pibrough* be despis'd;
> Own'd and refin'd by you, these shall the more be priz'd.

This passage outlined a development scheme for Scottish music exactly parallel to that which Ramsay already had under way for Scottish literature. It amounted to a set of recommendations: dig up the best Scottish traditional music, most of which had never been printed; put it before the civilised world in a suitably 'refin'd' form; and enhance Scotland's reputation abroad. 'Refinement' would be achieved by mixing the Scots tunes with elements of Italian music, just as Ramsay's *Tea-table Miscellany* was mixing traditional Scots lyrics with elements of London fashionable verse.

Ramsay mentions two Scots songs as suitable material for this treatment. It is likely, in fact, that Scots songs were already being sung at formal concerts in Edinburgh by the time Ramsay wrote his poem, with trained singers and up-to-date kinds of accompaniment. In 1722, at any rate, the Edinburgh singer William Thomson included a Scots song in an extremely high-class concert in London; and in 1725 Thomson published, also from London, a whole book of Scots songs with Italianate accompaniments. The stage was all set for a 'drawing room' kind of fiddle music to make its entry.

The group of Edinburgh composers who created this new fiddle style — Adam Craig, Alexander Stuart, Alexander Munro, James Oswald, Francesco Barsanti, Charles McLean, and William McGibbon — did not have to bridge profound social or cultural chasms in order to achieve what they did. All of them had a good working knowledge of European music; at the same time, all but Barsanti had been brought up in Scotland, and could hardly have avoided knowing Scots tunes any more than they could have avoided speaking with Scots accents. Barsanti, the odd man out of the group, was Italian; but he had a remarkable affinity with Scottish music, and liked it almost from the moment he arrived in Edinburgh in 1735. His Scots-tune settings are probably the most sensitive ones ever made by a foreigner. (Barsanti also, incidentally, married a Scots girl.)

The problems of the drawing-room style were therefore not cultural, but technical. How much Italianate decoration, for example, could a given Scots tune stand? Could one modulate to a new key at such-and-such a point without destroying the tune's shape? How was one to harmonise pentatonic sequences? To bring these difficulties home, the reader might like to turn back to *Sour plums of Galashiels* **(8)** and try composing an Italianate bass part to it: this was exactly the problem that Munro set himself on page 32 of his *Collection of Scots Tunes.*

Not all the composers solved such problems well. Craig's *Scots Tunes* (*c*.1727, second edition 1730) has moments of great elegance, but its harmonies tend to be static and awkward. Stuart's *Musick for Allan Ramsay's . . . Scots Songs* (c. 1728) is clumsy and primitive; its best feature is probably its frontispiece, showing an Edinburgh drawing-room with gentleman fiddler, lady harpsichordist, and fawning spaniel, which at least makes clear the social image that the collection was trying to create.

Munro's *Scots Tunes* (1732) is ambitious but erratic. Munro's flair considerably outstripped his technique, leading him to take terrible risks without realising what disasters lay just round the corner. His best work, however, is excellent, and his masterly variation sonata on *Bonny Jean of Aberdeen* (65) will be introduced later in the book.

James Oswald's *Curious Collection* (c.1739), on the other hand, is cautious, and maintains a high average standard. Oswald was ambitious in a different sense from Munro, and knew that professional careers were not enhanced by rushing into print with half-baked experiments. Between 1736 and 1741 Oswald ran round Edinburgh pursuing a multiple career as dancing-master, fiddler, cellist, publisher, and concert promoter, but as a composer he was carefully grooming himself for the final move to London. It was only when he was established in London that his compositions became fluent and occasionally slapdash. His *Pentland Hills* (21) was probably basically composed in Edinburgh, though it may have been revised later. His *Rory Dall's port* (22) dates from his London period.

Barsanti's *Old Scots Tunes* (1742) is an exciting collection, for though it is limited to short, 2-strain tunes without variations, the settings are virtuosic and extremely personal. *Johnnie Faa* (16) is one of the simplest and finest of them. With the experience that he gained from this collection, Barsanti began a set of string overtures incorporating quotations from Scottish and English dance tunes. These overtures are a spin-off from the Scots drawing-room style but interestingly reverse its conditions, for they are Italian pieces influenced by traditional music rather than the other way round. As an example, here is part of Barsanti's overture in G, op.IV no.9, which introduces the jig *Babbity Bowster* as a fugue subject (the jig is in the violin 1 part):

Charles McLean's contribution to the drawing-room style is hard to assess, since no collection of his Scots-tune settings was published during his lifetime. Several of his settings appeared posthumously in the *McLean* collection (1772) but, as has already been explained in the Introduction, these were heavily edited by Robert Mackintosh and cannot be taken as authentic texts. The McFarlane manuscript (1740), however, contains six McLean settings in texts which are authentic apart from lacking the bass lines. One of these *(Black Jock,* ii, 207) is a long variation set; the others *(Pinkie House,* ii, 110; *Tweedside,* ii, 209; *Birks of Invermay,* ii, 210; *Twas within a furlong of Edinburgh town,* iii, 214; and *Barbara Allan,* iii, 221) are in drawing-room style. Without the bass lines one cannot tell how well McLean handled the harmonisations, but as melodies with delicate Italian decorations they seem extremely fine. I have attempted to reconstruct the missing accompaniment to *Twas within a furlong of Edinburgh town,* and this piece will be presented later as no. **66.**

The settings of William Forbes of Disblair also deserve a mention here, though they are only partly drawing-room in style. Disblair lived on an estate in Aberdeenshire, 140 miles from Edinburgh, and had little contact with the other composers in this chapter; he seems to have taken up composing in his old age, when he was left almost penniless through paying extravagent sums of aliment to his ex-wife (see Johnson, 'Forbes family'). Twenty-one of his Scots-tune settings survive (in the McFarlane MS. and in NLS Adv. MS.5.2.25). They are quirky, but full of original methods of mixing Italian and Scottish ideas in the same piece. Two of them, *My Nanny-O* **(26)** and *Up tails a'* **(27),** are included in the next chapter.

It was William McGibbon's *Scots Tunes* of 1742, however, that were the crowning achievement of the period. With the publication of McGibbon's collection one can sense cultured Edinburgh heaving a sigh of relief: at last, the drawing-room style had been done perfectly. McGibbon had produced a set of centre-of-the-road, classic solutions which would serve as models for all later settings, just as Corelli's sonatas were models for all later European works of their kind. McGibbon, who was highly aware of Corelli, no doubt saw his 1742 collection in this light himself.

It was a turning-point in his own career, too. Up to 1742 McGibbon had been a second-rate composer of Italian music who happened to live in Scotland; suddenly he emerged as a first-rate — indeed, the finest living — composer of Scottish music.

The ironical thing about McGibbon's achievement, and the respect which Edinburgh and Scotland paid to it, was that McGibbon's Scots-tune settings were based to a considerable extent on the work of his immediate predecessors and rivals. Of the four McGibbon pieces in this chapter (nos. **17–20**), three were closely derived from recent settings by other composers. *Leith Wynd* **(17)** is heavily indebted to Craig's version of the same tune; *Three good fellows* **(18)** is almost identical to Disblair's version; and *When she cam ben* **(20)** is very similar to Oswald's. The creative effort which McGibbon put into his settings must actually have been quite slight, compared with that needed to write his 24 trio-sonatas, 6 violin sonatas, and other European art-music works.

Nevertheless, McGibbon's settings were nearly always vastly superior to those from which he started. In *Leith Wynd* he shuffled the order of Craig's variations, rebuilding the tune so that it progressed from simple decorations to complex ones with an effortless flow. The lengthy permutation of the notes D, E, F sharp, G and A which he inserted into strain

D

6 (bar 2 note 11 to bar 4 note 9), in particular, has a clarity and sense of purpose quite beyond Craig's power. Similarly, the corrections that he made to Disblair's *Three good fellows* seem so natural and obvious, in retrospect, that one could easily take McGibbon's version for the original and Disblair's for a corrupt copy. No fiddler who once played McGibbon's version could ever have wanted to play Disblair's again.

With *When she cam ben* McGibbon had even less need to do original work. Oswald's existing setting was excellent; so was McLachlan's related earlier one (no. **15**), which McGibbon probably also knew. In addition, the tune was so firmly wedded to the *passamezzo antico* chord sequence that the main lines of the harmonisation were already laid down for him. McGibbon's main concern here was to rid the tune of its antique, 16th-century flavour and give it a sprightly modern flavour instead. One good idea he thought of was to take the descending arpeggio figure from strain 4 of the tune and use it as part of the bass line for strains 1–2.

Around 1742 McGibbon's rivals disappeared from the scene, leaving him undisputed master of the drawing-room style. Forbes of Disblair died in 1740; Craig died in 1741. (McGibbon may well have waited tactfully for Craig to die before publishing a collection which cannibalised the older man's work, for Craig had known him since his childhood, and was probably his first violin teacher.) Oswald left Edinburgh for London in 1741; Barsanti went back to London in 1743. McLean's name disappears from the records after 1740; he may have gone back to the north-east of Scotland then — he had come to Edinburgh from Aberdeen in 1738 — or he may have died. Munro and Stuart are not known to have made any new settings after 1740.

McGibbon published two more books of Scots tunes in 1746 and 1755, but these were consolidations of his 1742 collection rather than advances upon it. Other composers did, however, develop the drawing-room style in one or two new directions. Oswald, after his arrival in London, invented a type of European art-music sonata with a Scots accent, which was a direct result of the pioneering work which had gone on in Edinburgh in the 1730s. John Reid also wrote sonatas in this adapted drawing-room style.

Oswald also made experiments in harmonising Highland types of tune which McGibbon had not attempted. His *Rory Dall's port* (**22**), dating from about 1756, is one of these. Nathaniel Gow followed this idea up when arranging Highland tunes for his father's collections, such as *Robaidh dona gòrach* (**24**) and *The Duke of Argyle's strathspey* (**51**).

John Reid discovered another application of the drawing-room style: he introduced it into the regimental marches that he composed. Shortly after that, Bremner published an army song with drawing-room accompaniment in his *Curious Collection of Scots Tunes* (1759), so developing this military angle further. The army song was *Will you go to Flanders?* (**23**), and it is likely that Bremner made the setting himself. It is stylistically similar to McGibbon's settings, but again uses a type of tune which did not appear in McGibbon's collections.

By 1780 the drawing-room style had reached its limits and its possibilities, never immense, had been fully explored. Meanwhile, in circles where European art-music was enjoyed, the Italian style of Corelli and Handel had become old-fashioned and a new German style — shortly to be associated in particular with the symphonies and chamber music of Franz Josef Haydn — was in the ascendant. During the 1780s a few attempts were made to update the drawing-room idea by crossing Scots tunes with the new Haydnesque style: two examples of this are Nathaniel Gow's variations on *Duncan Davidson* (in Niel Gow's *Strathspey Reels* vol.i, 1784) and James Clark's variations on *Willie was a wanton wag* (in Robert Riddell's *Scotch, Galwegian and Border Tunes,* 1794). None of these attempts, however, was particularly successful. By the end of the century most Scots-fiddle composers had lost interest in the drawing-room style, and had turned their attention to more contemporary forms of expression.

With or without accompaniment?

The drawing-room pieces were printed in the same format as Corelli's and Handel's violin sonatas: they were notated as a fiddle line and a bass line, and the bass was intended not only to be played on a cello but also to be realised on a harpsichord by a player who could read figured-bass symbols. (See the facsimile of McGibbon's *When she cam ben, she bobbit.*) The frontispiece to Stuart's collection of *c.*1728 gives us further evidence as to the kind of performance that composers of drawing-room pieces envisaged, for it shows what is evidently Stuart's actual book on the harpsichord desk. The musicians in the picture are about to start playing; when they do, they will both read off the printed copy.

Once the drawing-room pieces circulated beyond literate musicians in Edinburgh to a wider group of players, however — and McGibbon's settings did this quite rapidly — many of their 'refin'd' characteristics must have been lost. Many fiddlers in country districts would have played them with cellists who vamped, rather than read. Some would have played them without any accompaniment at all. Indeed, there are written texts of pieces in Chapter II in existence where the bass lines are omitted (nos. **17, 21** and **22** in *The Caledonian Pocket Companion,* nos. **18** and **23** in the Trotter MS., and no. **19** in the Brown MS., for example). Drawing-room pieces must quickly have reverted to a 'wild' state in outlying parts of Scotland.

'When she cam ben, she bobbit' (**20**) in McGibbon's *Scots Tunes,* 1742 (National Library of Scotland).

'The East Neuk of Fife' (**34**) in Bremner's *Scots Tunes,* 1759 (National Library of Scotland). Note the handwritten fingerings on this copy.

This situation is, however, reversed when we come to the long variation sets in Chapter III. Long variation sets work superbly on unaccompanied fiddle; accompaniments to them are usually just an encumbrance and an embarrassment. Notwithstanding this, long variation sets were often printed with accompaniments in 18th-century collections. These basses were generally very rudimentary, no better than something a dance-band cellist could have improvised during performance, and publishers seem to have provided them mainly for appearances' sake and to impress middle-class purchasers of the collections. (See the facsimile of *The East Neuk of Fife.*)

It is likely, however, that long variation sets were sometimes performed with accompaniment, just as drawing-room pieces were sometimes performed without accompaniment.

16. Johnnie Faa

set by FRANCESCO BARSANTI (*c.* 1690-1772)

17. Leith Wynd

set by WILLIAM McGIBBON (c. 1695-1756)

[Allegretto]

repeat accompaniment for strains 3 - 4 and 5 - 6

42

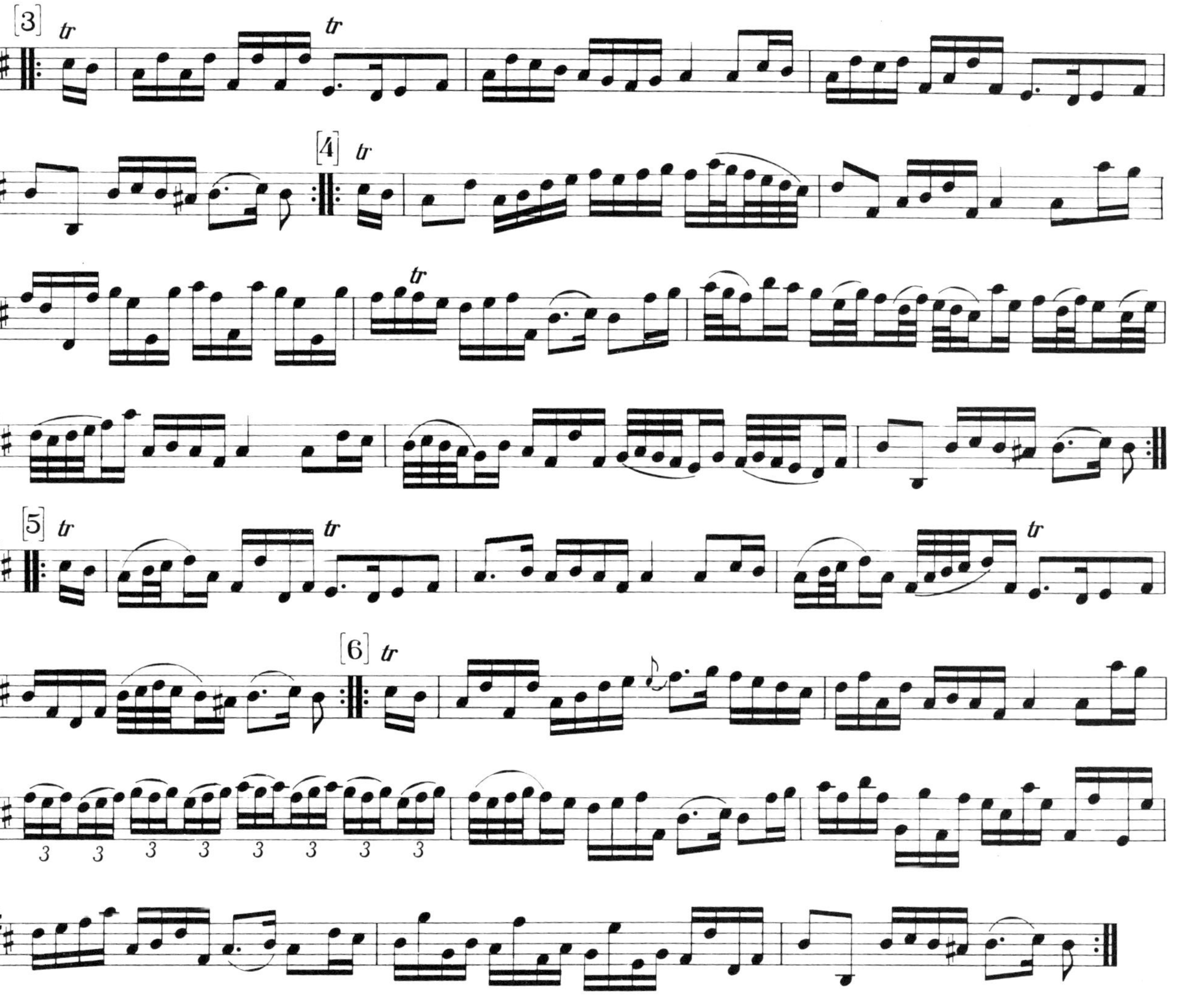

[D.C. strains 1 and 2]

18. There's three good fellows ayont yon glen

set by WILLIAM McGIBBON

Brisk

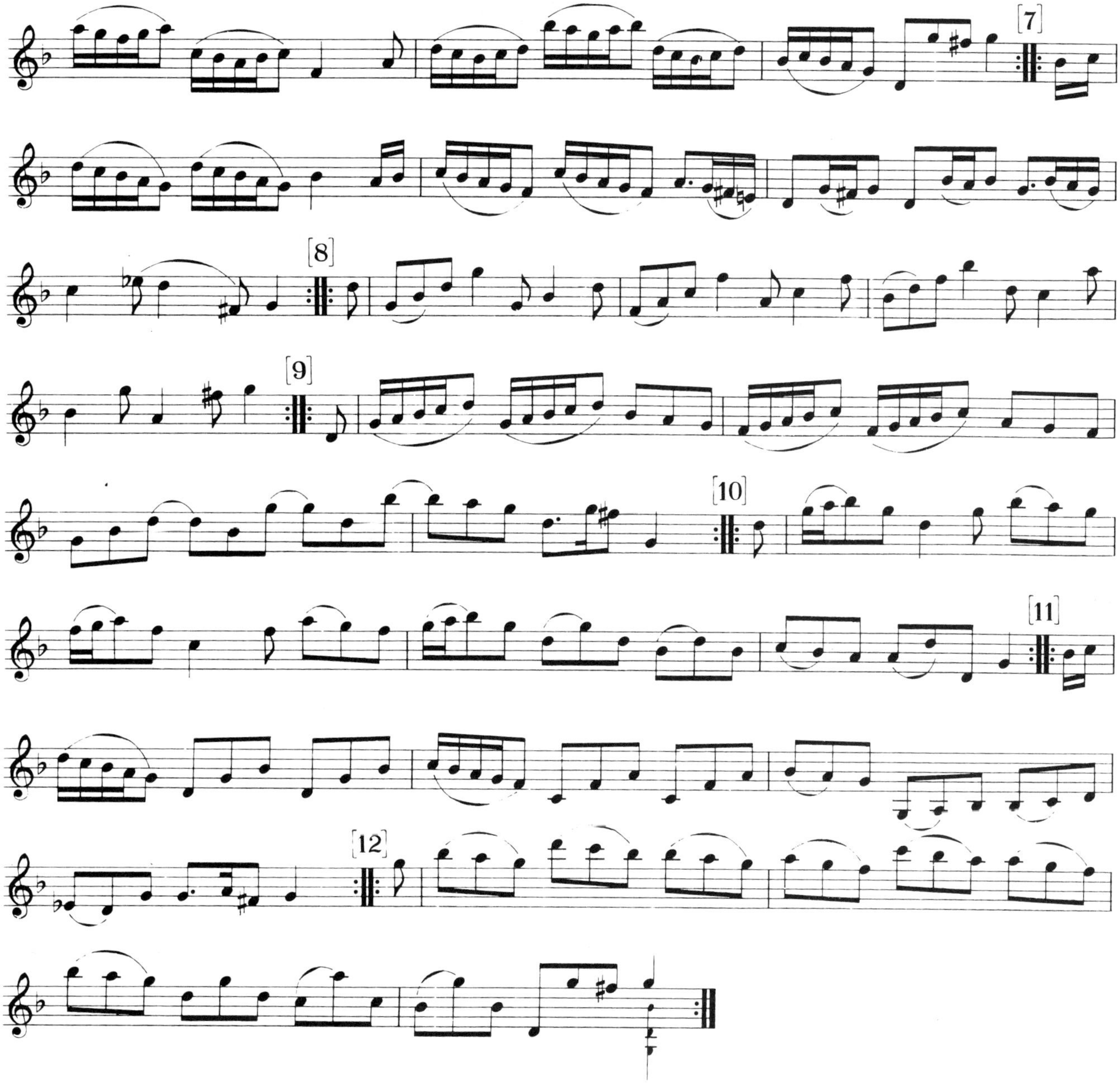
[7]
[8]
[9]
[10]
[11]
[12]

19. Through the wood, laddie

set by WILLIAM McGIBBON

repeat accompaniment for strains 3 - 4

20. When she cam ben, she bobbit

set by WILLIAM McGIBBON

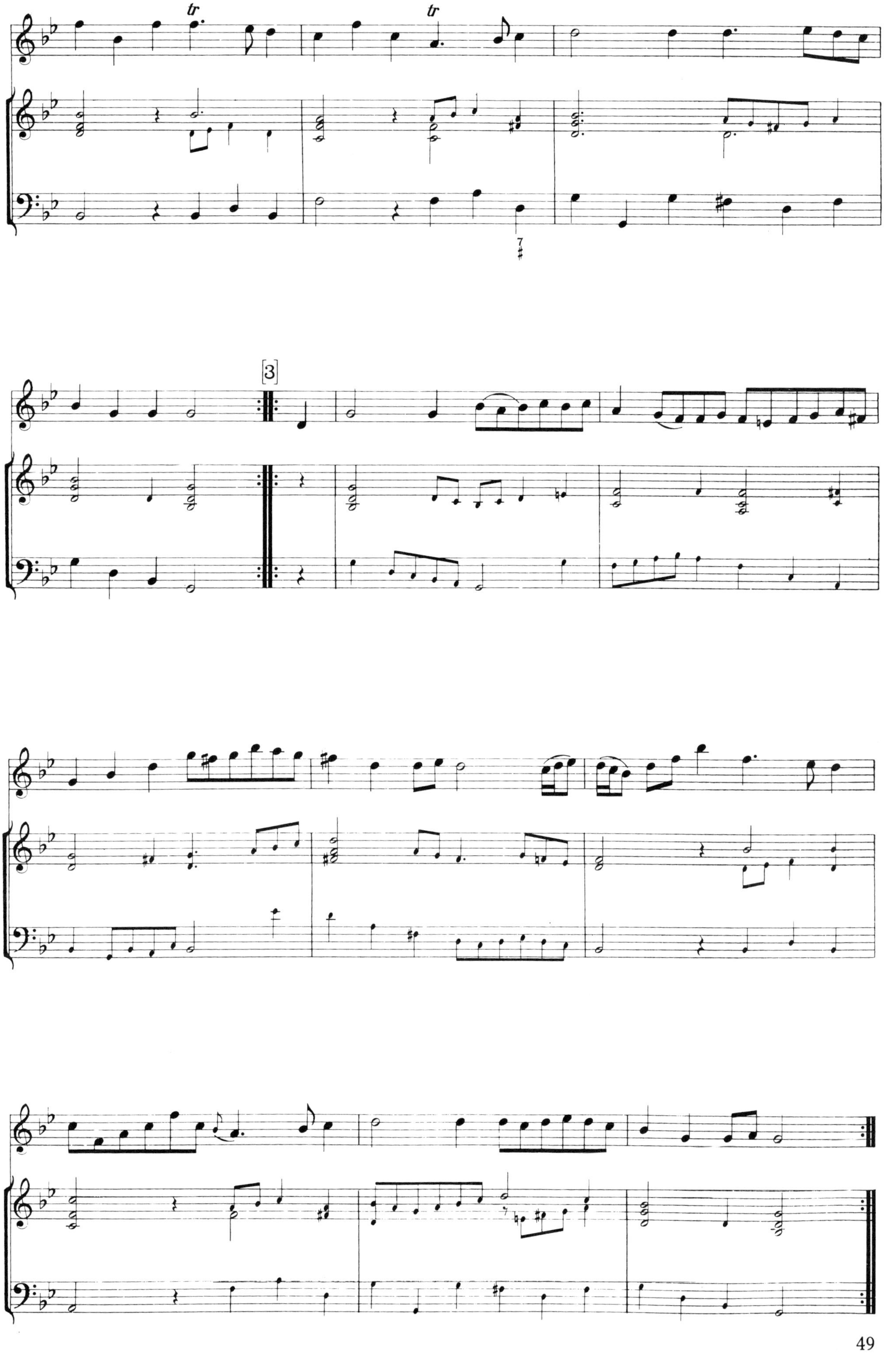
tr
tr
7
3

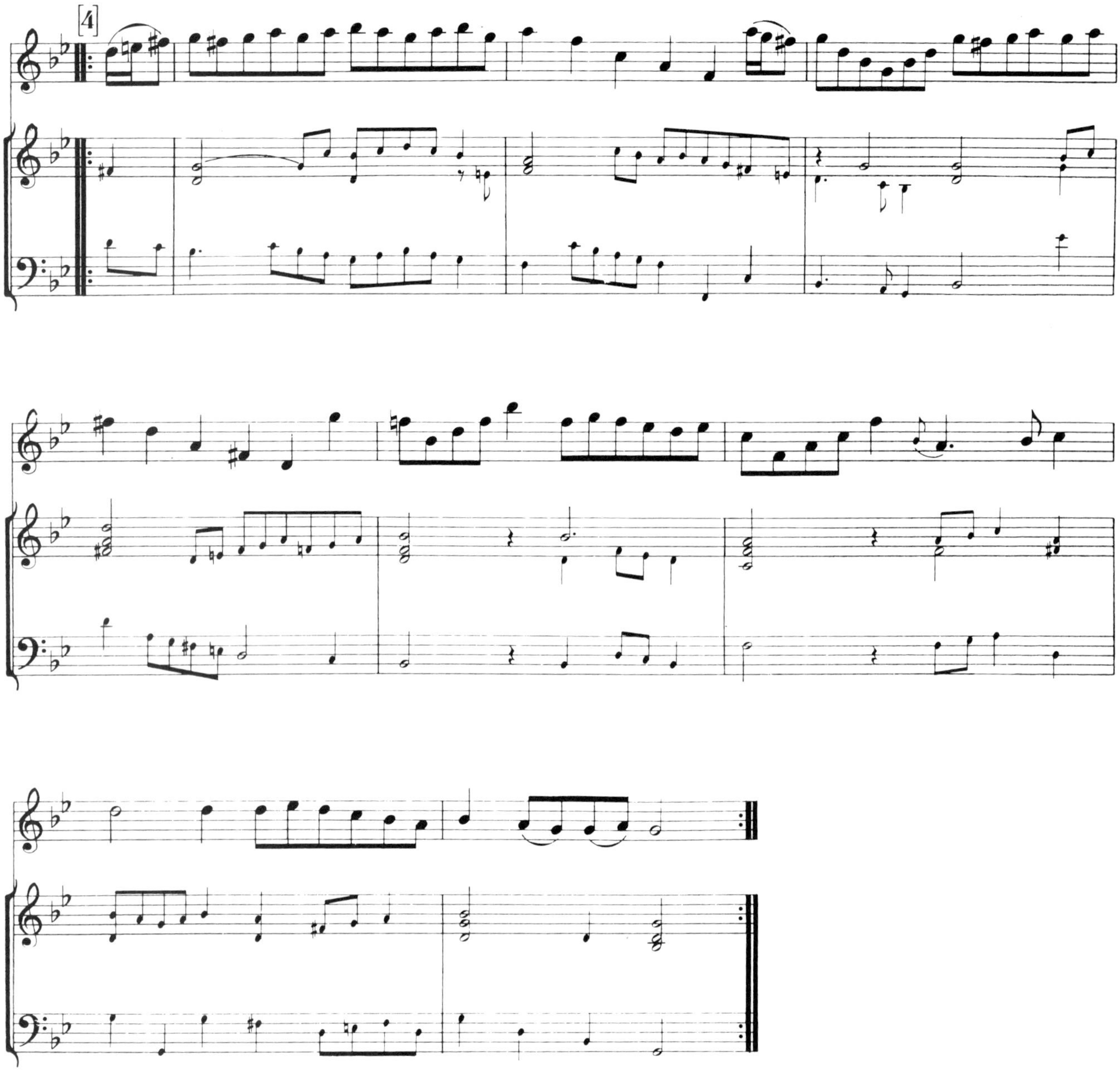
[4]

21. Pentland Hills

JAMES OSWALD (1711-69)

[Andante]

*repeat
accompaniment for
strains 3–4*

22. Rory Dall's port

JAMES OSWALD

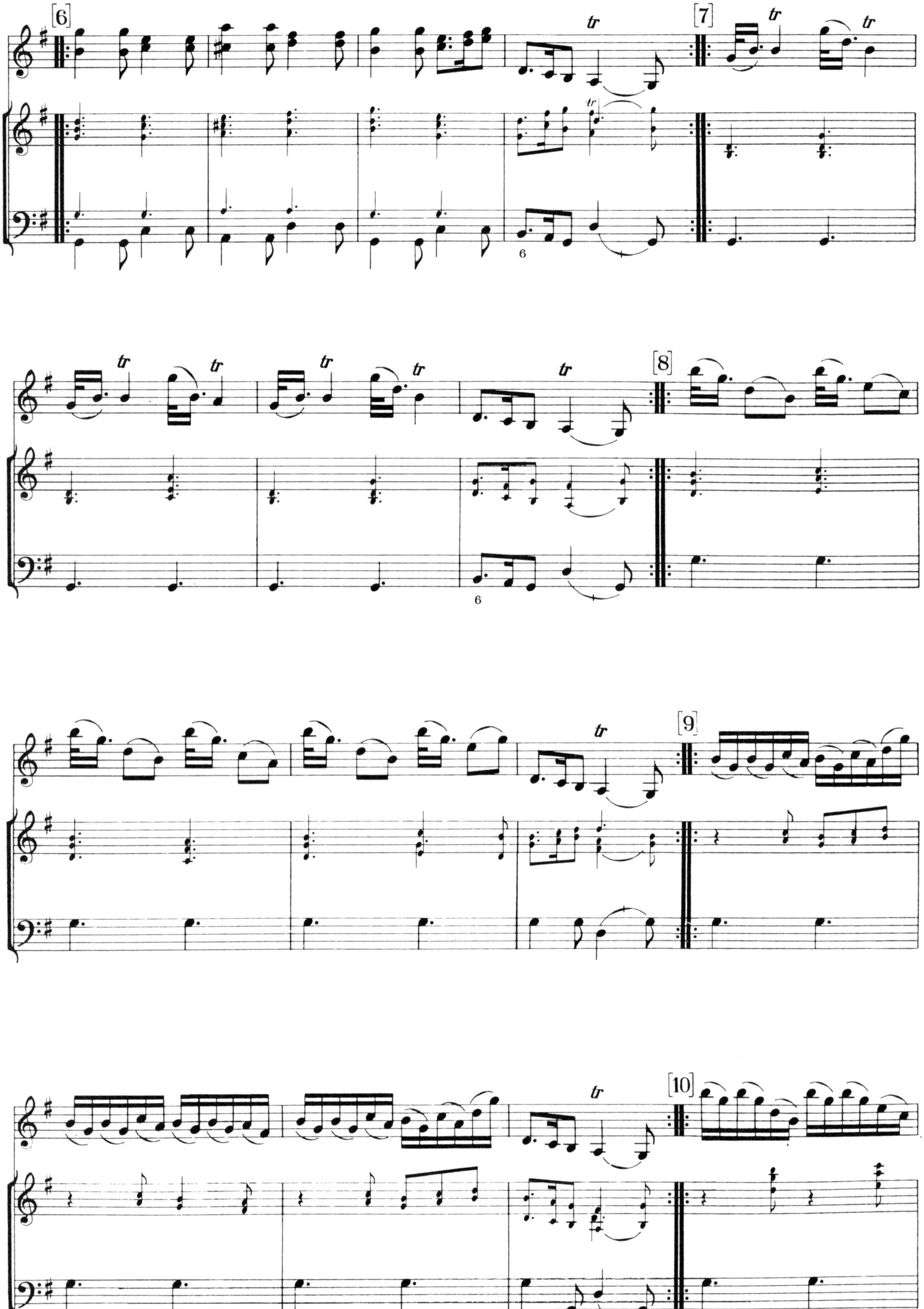
[6]
[7]
[8]
[9]
[10]
tr
6

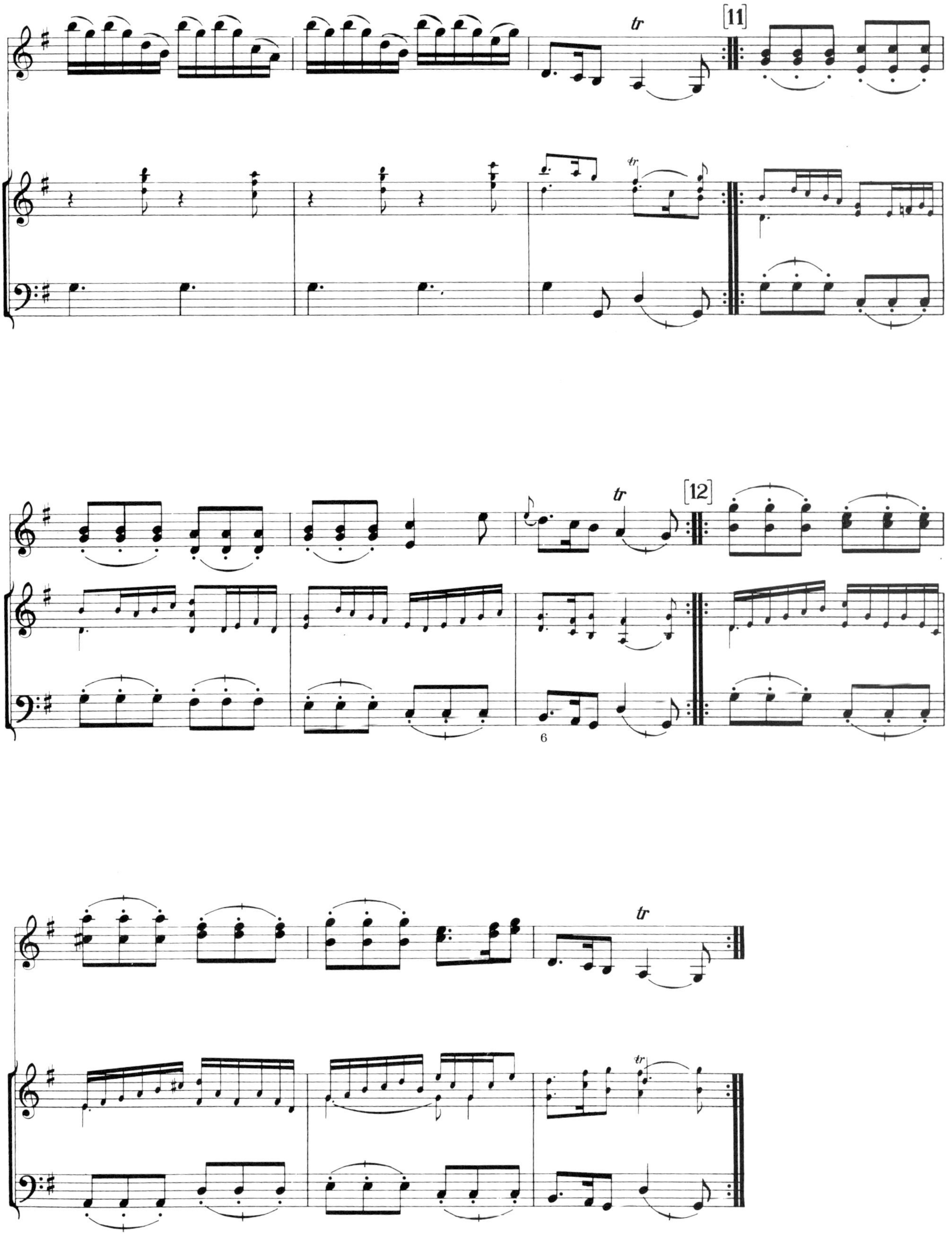
tr
[11]
tr
[12]
6
tr

23. Will you go to Flanders?

? set by ROBERT BREMNER (*c.* 1713-1789)

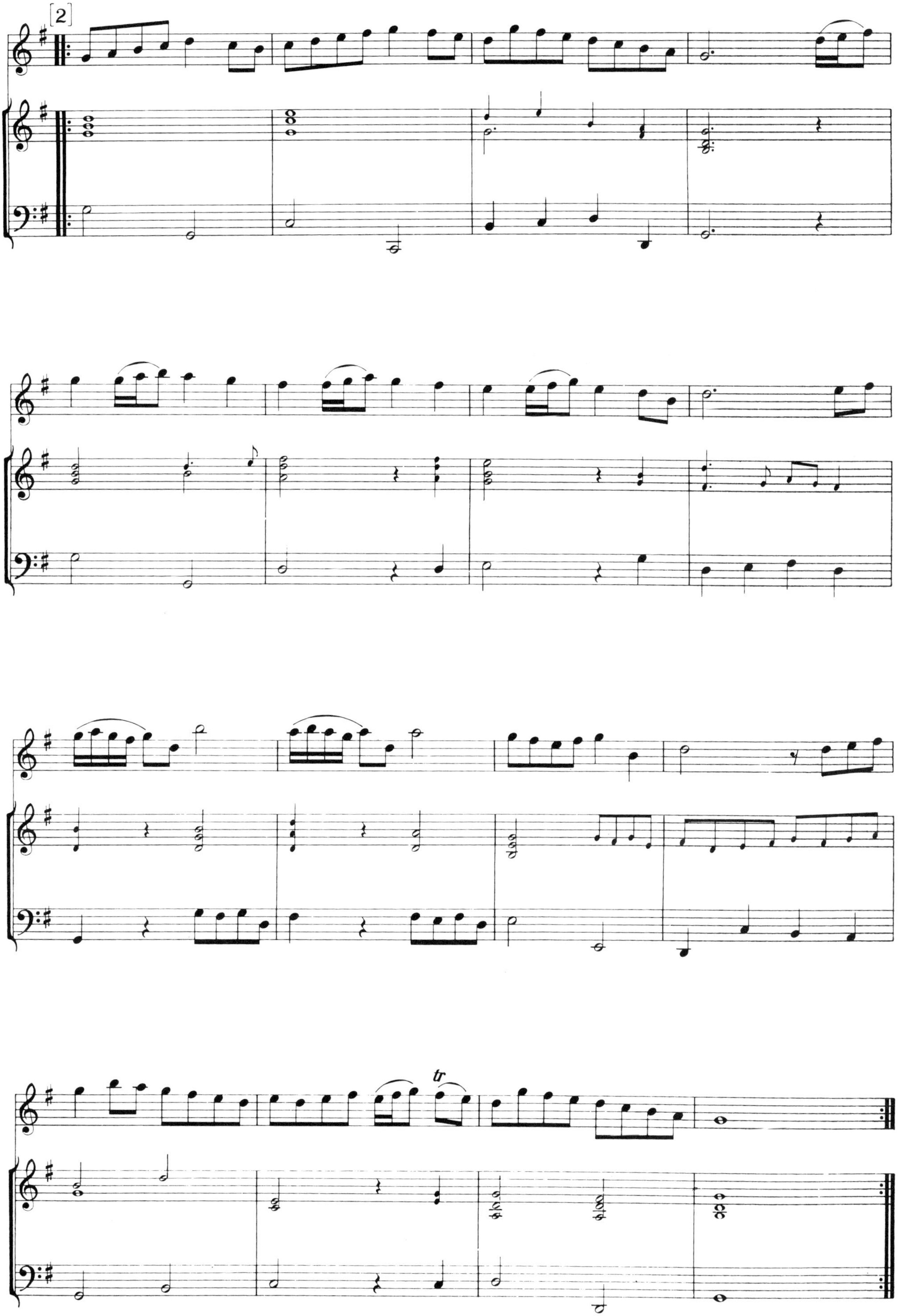
2

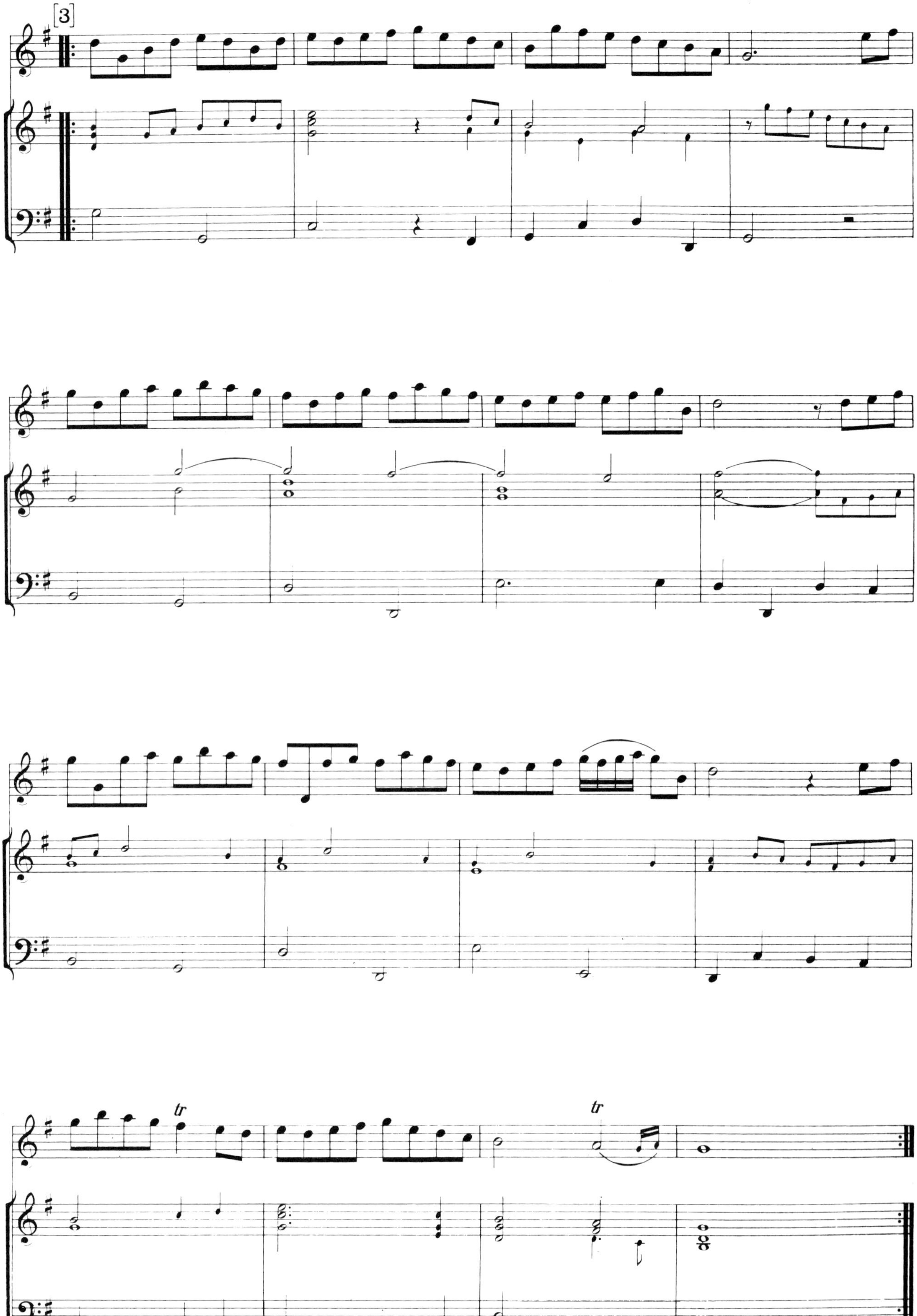
[3]
tr
tr

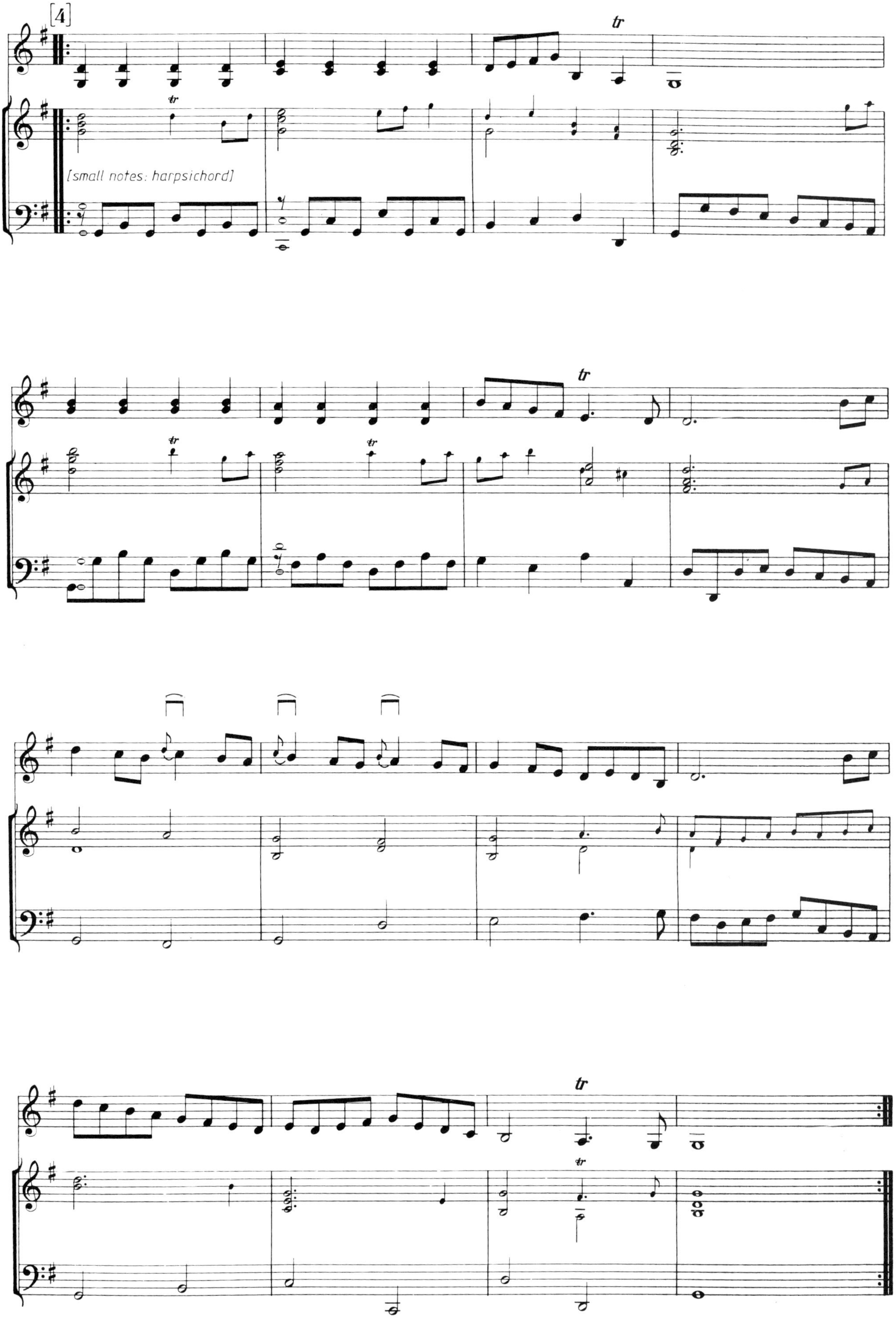
[4]
[small notes: harpsichord]
tr

[D.C. strain 1]

24. Robaidh dona gòrach
(Daft Robin)

set by NATHANIEL GOW (1763-1831)

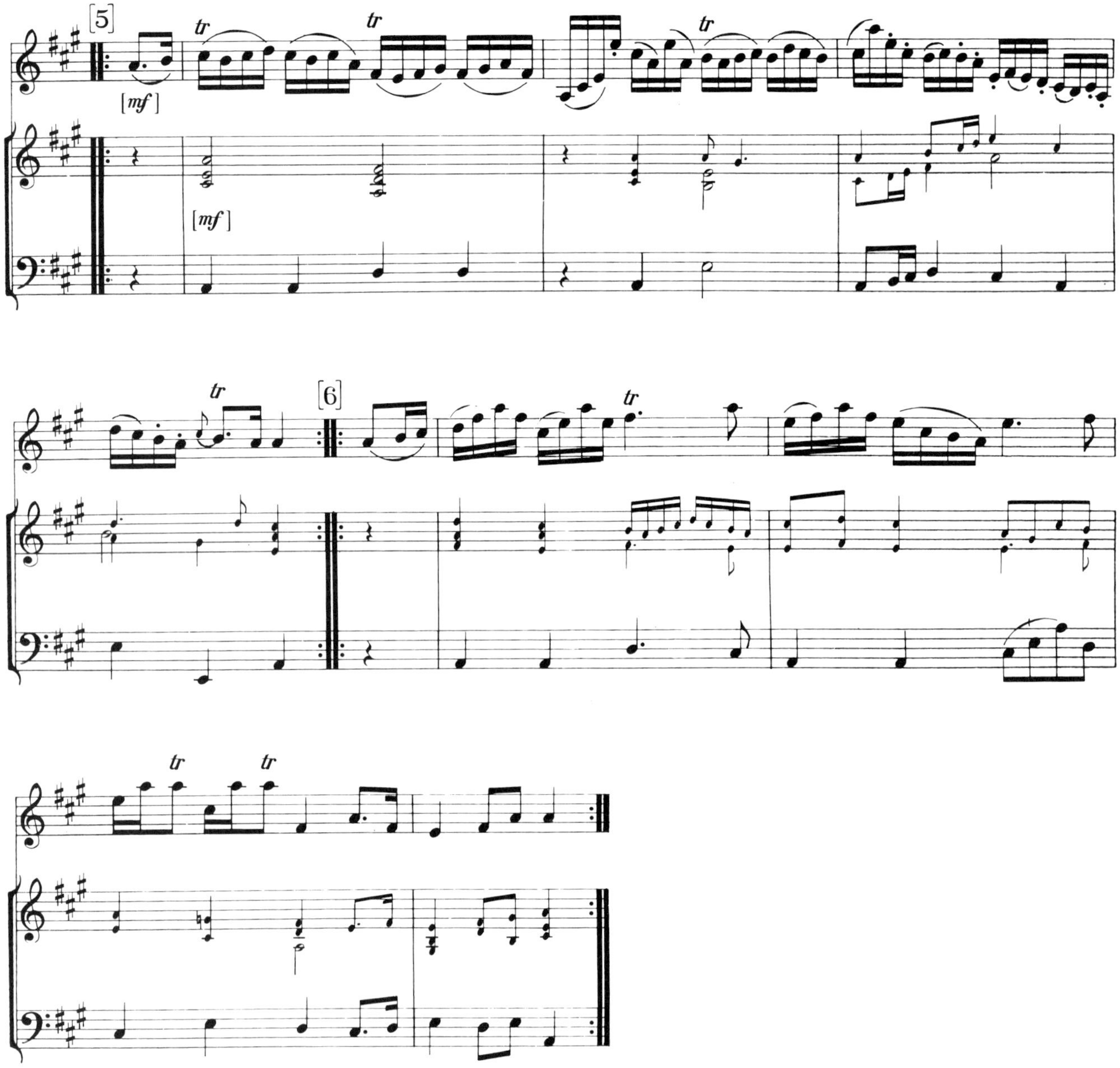

5
tr
tr
tr
[mf]
[mf]
tr
6
tr
tr
tr

NOTES ON THE MUSIC

16 *Johnnie Faa*
Source: Barsanti's *Old Scots Tunes*, p.6.
This is the first written-down text of the tune, apart from a version in the Skene mandora-book of *c*.1620 entitled *Lady Cassilles Lilt,* which Barsanti is unlikely to have known. Glen suggests that Barsanti notated the tune himself from aural tradition (*Early Scottish Melodies*, p.120); perhaps his Scottish wife taught it to him. The words were printed in vol.iv of Ramsay's *Tea-table Miscellany* (*c*.1737).
Revisions: a few slurs realigned in the violin part.

17 *Leith Wynd*
Source: McGibbon's *Scots Tunes,* vol.i. p.11.
This setting is closely based on Craig's (cf. Craig's *Scots Tunes*, p.16). Leith Wynd was a steep narrow street out of Edinburgh, leading to the port of Leith and thence to the world at large. McGibbon's setting deliberately gives the tune a strong sea-shanty flavour.
Revisions: McGibbon's alternative notes for flute in the final bars of each strain are omitted.

18 *There's three good fellows ayont yon glen*
Source: McGibbon's *Scots Tunes*, vol.ii p.18.
This is closely based on Disblair's version (McFarlane MS., vol.ii no.42). The accompaniment is a truncated form of the *passamezzo antico* chord sequence: see page 19. Nothing is known about the history of the tune.
Revisions: strain 8 bar 3 note 3 could perhaps be altered to g'' to fit the accompaniment better.

19 *Through the wood, laddie*
Source: McGibbon's *Scots Tunes*, vol.ii p.6.
Ramsay's words to this tune appear in vol.i of the *Tea-table Miscellany* (1723).

20 *When she cam ben, she bobbit*
Source: McGibbon's *Scots Tunes,* vol.i p.32.
This setting is closely based on McLachlan's earlier one (no. **15**) and on Oswald's (cf. Oswald's *Curious Collection*, p.40).

21 *Pentland Hills*
Source: *Flores Musicae*, p.53. Title from Oswald's *Caledonian Pocket Companion,* vol.xii p.19; ascription to Oswald from Davie's *Caledonian Repository,* ser.2 pt.i p.37.
The Pentlands are a range of hills to the south-west of Edinburgh. This piece probably dates from Oswald's stay in Edinburgh in the late 1730s.
Flores gives the title as 'The Battle of Pentland Hills', but this seems to be a mistake; the piece is clearly a slow pastoral air, not a battle piece (though there was a 17th-century battle on the Pentlands, at Rullion Green in 1666). For Oswald in a 'battle' mood, see no. **58**.
Revisions: strain 2 bar 12 vln note 1 orig b'
    strain 4 bar 7 note 1 orig c''
    strain 4 bar 12 note 6 orig g'.

22 *Rory Dall's port*
Source: Oswald's *Collection of Scot's Tunes With Variations,* p.30. Title from the *Caledonian Pocket Companion,* vol.viii p.24.
The original title is 'A Highland Port [tune] by Rory Dall'. This perhaps refers to Rory Dall Morison, a blind Scottish harpist who worked in the Highlands in the early 18th century; or it may refer to Rory Dall O Catháin, a blind Irish harpist who visited Scotland in the early 17th century. However, the piece is almost certainly all Oswald's own work. Oswald was renowned for publishing his compositions under exotic pseudonyms; he also wrote several other imitation Highland pieces at this period (for example, no. **58**).

Burns wrote the lyric 'Ae fond kiss and then we sever' to this tune in 1790. It has no connection with an earlier *Rory Dall's port* in the Skene mandora-book of *c.*1620.
Revisions: strain 5 bar 2 bass notes 1–2 orig *e*
    strain 11 bar 4 bass notes 1–2 orig quavers.

23 *Will you go to Flanders?*
Source. Bremner's *Scots Tunes,* p.20.
This tune was an army song, probably dating from the Flanders campaign of the 1740s.

24 *Robaidh dona gòrach*
Source: Niel Gow's *Strathspey Reels,* vol.i p.36.
The tune is described in the source as 'An Old Highland Song'; its title translates literally as 'Silly naughty Robbie'. Ascription of the setting to Nathaniel Gow is from Sainsbury's *Dictionary of Musicians,* 'Niel Gow', which states that the tunes in Gow's collections 'were set and prepared for publication by his son Nathaniel'. See also no. **51**.
Revisions: a few rhythms normalised
    strain 5 bar 3 vln notes 3–4 orig *g* ♯ ", *e"*
    strain 6 bar 3 bass note 4 orig *e.*

CHAPTER III
Long Variation Sets

THE long variation set was largely a new creation of the period 1730–1800. It was based on a strong earlier tradition: variations by John McLachlan survive from the years around 1700, as we have already mentioned in Chapter I, and there are scanty bits of evidence to suggest that many fiddle variations also existed in the 17th century. But the tradition was modernised so completely from 1730 onwards that the 18th-century long variation set really counts as a new form. It was European art-music characteristics, absorbed unobtrusively into the traditional structures, that made the difference: they enabled the 18th-century variations to become much more substantial and expressive than their predecessors.

The vitality of variation-writing at this time can be shown by the newness of the tunes on which the variations were based. Out of the eighteen variation sets in this chapter, only seven are based on tunes that were 'traditional' in 1730: nos. **25** and **42** on jigs that were probably ancient, nos. **26** and **29** on 17th-century slow airs, nos. **28** and **30** on 17th-century pipe pieces, and no. **27** on an English dance-tune that had been popular since the 16th century. The other eleven sets are based on recent tunes — ones composed, or imported into Scotland, after 1700. Nos. **31–33** and **36** are based on new English country-dances, no. **34** on a new reel, nos. **35** and **40** on new trumpet marches, nos. **37** and **38** on new Scots songs, no. **39** on a new strathspey, and no. **41** on a new army song. Indeed no. **38**, *Johnnie Cope*, was a Jacobite song about the battle of Prestonpans in East Lothian, which had taken place as recently as 1745.

The long variation set was not a fully-fledged, mature 'big music' in the way that, for instance, the *pìobaireachd* of the Highland bagpipe is. Pibrochs share their themes with 'small music' genres in exactly the same way that long variation sets do. But pibrochs diverged decisively from marches, reels, and song-tunes during the 18th century. No one listening to a piper nowadays has any doubt, after the first few bars, as to whether it is *ceòl mór* or *ceòl beag* he is hearing. With fiddle music the distinction was less clear cut, as long variation sets were still being evolved at the time.

At what point did a few variations tacked on to a tune turn into a long variation set? A possible rule-of-thumb is that long variation sets should have at least 6 strains. However, an examination of the actual pieces soon makes mincemeat of any such tidy definition. *Allan Water* **(29)**, for instance, has only 4 strains, but it is such a huge piece — 64 slow bars, if played with all Young's repeats — that it can hardly be denied long-variation status.

Four of the sets in this chapter have 6 strains, nos. **25, 26, 36** and **38**. They are all quite different in weight: *A wife of my ain* **(25)** is the slightest, hardly more than something a fiddler at a dance might improvise for his own satisfaction to make the repetitions of the tune more interesting. *My Nanny-O* **(26)** is more substantial, since the tune is slow and the decorations unpredictable. *Lumps of puddings* **(36)** seems lightweight because the strains are similar in character; though the tune is pretty and the variations tasteful, it has little real musical substance. *Johnnie Cope* (38), on the other hand, feels like a big piece. The variations are so full of ideas that each is worth playing twice, and the set will easily stand a reprise of strains 1–2 at the end.

All this, however, is a matter of degree. When we turn from *Johnnie Cope* to the longest variations — the 30-strain set of *Black Jock* (32) and the 22-strain set of *The maltman comes on Monday* (33) — there is no doubt that we have crossed the frontier into a 'big music' genre.

As printed here, long variation sets give the impression of being fixed entities, to be carefully learnt and memorised by the performer. 18th-century fiddlers, however, did not always see them in this light; they tended, instead, to regard them as extensions of the basic tunes which could well vary from one performance to the next. This becomes clear when one compares different written texts.

Black Jock (32) is a good illustration. The set printed in this chapter is from Bremner's *Scots Tunes* of 1759, and has 30 strains. But there are also texts in the McFarlane manuscript of 1740 (vol.ii no. 207), with 18 strains; in a flute manuscript of *c.*1770 (NLS Adv. MS.5.2.20, f.32r), with 10 strains; and in the Sharpe manuscript of *c.* 1790 (p.140), with 18 strains. Each text has some strains that are unique as well as some that are common; and the common ones do not always appear in the same order. Nevertheless, it is clear that these are four different versions of the *same* set of variations, not four different sets that happen to be based on the same tune.

Many more versions of the *Black Jock* variations must have been played, which were never written down and are now lost. We cannot, unfortunately, go back 200 years with a tape-recorder to find out exactly how fiddlers performed them; but by studying the surviving texts we can at least reconstruct a fairly accurate picture of what happened.

Many fiddlers would have had firm ideas about how many strains each set contained; but these ideas would have varied from one district to another, and few performances would have agreed with the theories in any case. Repeats and *da capos* would have been played, or not played, according to the mood the fiddler was in at the time. Some fiddlers would habitually have left certain strains out because they couldn't play, couldn't remember, or didn't like them, while others would have composed new strains and added them to the sets. Strains would often have been shuffled in order, both accidentally and deliberately. A few very talented fiddlers probably had the knack of improvising new strains during performance.

One anecdote about an improvisation on *The East Neuk of Fife* (34) has fortunately come down to us.

One day in about 1805, the fiddler Peter (Pate) Baillie of Loanhead, near Edinburgh, was on his way to play at a ball in Fife. The journey involved crossing the Firth of Forth by ferry, and when Baillie boarded the boat at Leith the other passengers noticed the violin that he was carrying. As everyone had an hour to kill before the boat reached Burntisland, Baillie was soon holding an impromptu musical session on deck, with the other passengers calling out requests for tunes:

A gentleman asked Pate if he could play the 'East Neuk o' Fife' with the ten variations, to which the minstrel replied in his homely way: 'Weel, sir, I'll try it'.

Off Pate set at a brisk pace with both theme and variations, till the number bargained for was completed. But Pate did not stop here. He dashed into fresh variations of his own improvising, more wonderful than the first, and went on, and on, and on, the gentleman looking at him with astonishment, till at last the fiddler did make a halt.

'Well, I declare!' said the gentleman. 'Every one of the variations must have turned out twins since last I heard them!'

(The story is told in Murdoch's *Fiddle in Scotland*, p.59; Murdoch learned it from Peter Baillie's grandson.)

Long variation sets, then were generally the work of several hands. They were arrived at by a process of trial and error, and composed partly on paper, partly on the instrument, and partly through improvisations that were later remembered and transmitted. Before the reader is misled, however, into seeing this as a free-wheeling communal activity like those fashionable in avant-garde circles in the 1960s, I should point out that the most worthwhile contributions to the long variation set came from a fairly small handful of individuals.

Some of these individuals obligingly left their names on record and are, in fact, composers whom we have met already: William Forbes of Disblair, who wrote the variations on *My Nanny-O* (26) and *Up tails a'* (27), and Charles McLean, who wrote parts of *Black Jock* (32). Another important variation composer was David Young, who was born in the Aberdeen area in about 1707. Young studied at Marischal College, Aberdeen, and then moved to Edinburgh, where he taught copper-plate handwriting and made musical manuscripts to patrons' orders. Two of his manuscripts which survive are the Duke of Perth's (1734) and the McFarlane (1740). A specimen page of the McFarlane manuscript is reproduced below. Young later returned to Aberdeen, where he helped to found the Aberdeen Musical Society in 1748. He composed the variations on *Cailleach odhar* (28) and *Allan Water* (29), and parts of *The reel of Tulloch* (30).

There seems also to have been a first-rate composer of variations in the Perth area in the 1760s, who wrote the settings of *Duncan Gray* (35), *The lea rig* (37), and *Johnnie Cope* (38). These settings are very similar to each other in style, and all three appear for the first time in the Gillespie manuscript, made in Perth in 1768. Gillespie almost certainly got the sets from someone local. Niel Gow (*b.* 1727), Daniel Dow (*b.* 1732) and Robert Mackintosh (*b.c.*1745) are possible candidates, since they all lived in villages about fifteen miles north of Perth at this time; only none of them is known to have composed in quite this polished, lyrical style. Whoever this composer was, his work was excellent.

James Oswald was also an important figure in the development of variations. Most of his contributions to long variation sets were made semi-anonymously, as a by-product of his publishing business.

Oswald's *Caledonian Pocket Companion* (London, 15 volumes, *c.* 1747–69) was one of the century's best-selling, most heavily used collections. Oswald marked a few of the tunes in it as his own work, but the element of original composition in the book was actually much larger than this: Oswald was ahead of his time, and as early as the 1730s realised that

McFarlane manuscript: 'A wife of my ain' (**25**) in David Young's handwriting (National Museum of Antiquities of Scotland).

to present one's work to the public as 'traditional' gave it an automatic authority and acceptability. He probably also wished to disguise how much of the book he had written himself, rather than collected from traditional players. Not all members of the public were fooled by this tactic, and Walter Scott had some bitter things to say about it many years later. Among the characters in Scott's novel *Redgauntlet* (1824) is a blind fiddler called Willie Steenson, who comments on Oswald's compositions as follows:

'It's no' a Scots tune, but it passes for ane. Oswald made it himsell, I reckon — he has cheated mony ane, but he canna cheat Wandering Willie.'

This seems to be pure spite on Scott's part, for there is no logical way of dismissing Oswald's work as fake. He was entitled to write new pieces in traditional styles if he wanted to, as much as any other Scottish fiddle-composer.

Many of Oswald's variations in *The Caledonian Pocket Companion* are rather perfunctory. They did, however, provide fiddlers with an immense amount of new material to work on, and many of them turn up in later manuscripts in slightly different forms, showing that they had been circulating actively in the meantime. One example is *Lumps of puddings* (36), from volume vii of the collection. Oswald probably got strains 1–3 of this from aural tradition, and wrote strains 4–6 himself in a matching style. After circulating for a few years, the set reappears in the Gillespie manuscript with a number of detailed improvements.

Finally we come to Robert Bremner, whose *Curious Collection of Scots Tunes* (1759) contained the first substantial long variation sets to appear in print. Nos. 30–34 are taken from this collection.

Bremner did not advertise his talents as a composer; he was basically in business as a publisher. But it cannot be coincidence that so many of the sets in his 1759 collection are so good — over half of them having a cohesion and artistic unity markedly superior to that of all known earlier versions. The implication is that Bremner put a lot of personal work into the variations he published, rejecting, rewriting, and rearranging with a masterly hand. Though the collection was slender, containing only 14 pieces, many of the variations in it circulated for the next two generations. Fiddlers who wanted a definitive text to learn, in preference to concocting one of their own, nearly always went to Bremner's *Scots Tunes* for it. When the gentleman on the ferry asked Peter Baillie to play *The East Neuk of Fife* 'with the ten variations', it was almost certainly Bremner's set that he had in mind. (See no. 34. It has 12 strains; but the gentleman probably regarded strains 3–12 as the variations and strains 1–2 as the theme.)

Three main methods of variation were used by 18th-century fiddle-composers: I have named them respectively decorative, replacement, and chordal variations. The three types overlapped to some extent, and it was not unknown for all three to occur in the same piece. They will be most easily understood, however, if I begin by describing them separately.

Decorative variations

This method of variation consisted of decorating the tune with short extra notes, while keeping its general outline unchanged. It was frequently used for variations on slow airs. There are good examples of it in *Sour plums of Galashiels* (8), *Through the wood, laddie* (19), *Pentland Hills* (21), and *Allan Water* (29): all these pieces consist of a statement of the tune (strains 1–2) plus a decorative variation (strains 3–4).

Replacement variations

The replacement method, on the other hand, involved discarding some portions of the tune and replacing them with new material. Often the new material was simply conventional figures like the following:

F

These figures turn up in so many different pieces that it is clear that they were clichés known to every fiddle-composer in Scotland. The last one is specially ubiquitous; it occurs in *Old Sir Symon the king* (**31**; strains 7 and 10), *Black Jock* (**32**; strain 20), *Lumps of puddings* (**36**; strain 2), and *The hare among the corn* (**42**; strains 2 and 6), and large parts of the Dixon fiddle-book of 1733 live on it almost as a staple diet.

It was usually the opening phrases of a tune that were replaced in this way; closing phrases tended to be repeated unchanged, as a sort of anchor to stop the variations drifting too far from base. In *The East Neuk of Fife* (**34**), for example, each strain ends with the phrase:

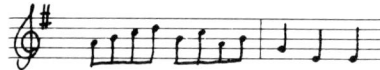

taken unaltered (or virtually unaltered) from the theme, though the theme's opening phrases are changed radically as the set progresses.

Variations sometimes occur which are arguably both decorative and replacement in type. This happens when a strain introduces a new figure which sounds unrelated to what has gone before, though it can in fact be analysed as a derivation from the theme. Whether such variations are predominantly decorative or replacement depends on how the listener hears them.

Black Jock contains some good examples of this. It begins as follows:

(This extract and the following ones are written at pitch; see no. **32** for the original scordatura notation.) These five bars have a melodic outline A — B — C sharp — B — A, which is followed by nearly every odd-numbered strain in the piece. In most later strains, however, the listener misses the connection because other aspects of the music are much more interesting. Strain 3, for instance, introduces a sketchy drone-bass on the lowest string of the fiddle:

strain 13 rough broken chords:

strain 21 grinding double stops:

strain 23 a brilliant E string figure:

and strain 25 a rich G string figure:

Each strain makes a novel and striking effect, and the listener's attention is deflected from the fact that they are all related to strain 1. Interestingly, however, strain 27 has the effect of a return to the opening. This is because strain 27 is a purely decorative variation of strain 1, and contains no significant new material:

The theme is therefore suddenly recognisable at that point, after being heavily disguised for several previous strains.

Strain 29 of *Black Jock*, in contrast, is a chordal variation.

Chordal variations

This method of variation consisted of outlining the tune's supporting chord-progressions in arpeggio form. The tune itself was entirely discarded apart from its closing phrase, which might be reproduced unchanged to round off the strain neatly.

Obviously, chordal variations were only possible for tunes which had a strong sense of supporting harmony in the first place. They were often used for tunes based on Italian chord-sequences (see page 19). Thus the jig set of *Greensleeves*, no. **84**, has a chordal variation as its strain 3 which outlines the *passamezzo antico* progression:

Similarly, strains 4, 5, 7 and 8 of *Sweden's march* **(40)** are chordal variations; this tune is based on the *passamezzo moderno* progression. Chordal variations could also be created on double-tonic tunes: two examples are *The East Neuk of Fife* **(34**: strains 7, 9, 10 and 11 outlining the chords G and A) and *Cailleach odhar* **(28**: several strains outlining the chords D and C).

Strain 29 of *Black Jock* is another chordal variation. Though the *Black Jock* tune does not fit into any standard harmonic scheme, its opening three bars could well be harmonised by the chords A, E7, and A; and strain 29 goes ahead on that idea and presents those chords as arpeggios:

However, this variation is not purely chordal in type. Its arpeggios are of an unusual kind and could perhaps be regarded as a new figure, in which case it would also count as a replacement variation; and it retains some traces of the tune's original outline, so it might possibly count as a decorative variation as well.

The decorative, replacement, and chordal methods were all ways of making *individual* variations. The order in which the variations were arranged in a set was left to chance or worked out separately in each case; there were no rules governing variation sets' overall forms. Some sets saved the most brilliant, technically difficult variations till last, but even this was not a universal practice. On the contrary, many 18th-century fiddlers seem to have liked sets to have a certain formal waywardness. The drone accompaniments in *Black Jock* **(32)**, G string effects in *Duncan Gray* **(35)**, and fast quaver passages in *Old Sir Symon the king* **(31)** are examples of such waywardness: in each case the idea is toyed with, discarded, and resumed in a quite unsystematic way.

The last example is particularly significant, for the fast quaver passages in *Old Sir Symon the king*, which occur in strains 7, 10, 12 and 15, seem originally to have been grouped together. In an earlier harpsichord setting by Henry Purcell, published in London in 1689, they appear consecutively as strains 5–8. It seems that these strains were gradually separated by fiddlers to give the set a more random, open-plan character.

European influences on variation sets

The 'Scots drawing room' pieces were created, as we saw in Chapter II, by a deliberate welding together of Scottish and European styles. Long variation sets also had a European connection, but it came about in a much less self-conscious way: from 1720 onwards, various European elements infiltrated themselves into variations, gradually and almost imperceptibly. Some of the tunes which 18th-century fiddlers used for variations were new ones, and in up-to-date styles even before the arrangers got to work on them: army songs and trumpet marches, for example. The procedures for making variations were also gradually updated as one decade followed another. Decorative variations began to use Italianate kinds of decoration as well as Scottish ones. Replacement variations enlarged their stock of useful clichés with melodic figures taken from European art music. Even chordal variations took advantage of the new kinds of arpeggio that were being developed in Baroque flute sonatas. In this way the scope of fiddle variations was vastly increased, without the framework of the tradition being broken at any point. By 1760 it was possible for a fiddler to write variations on an old tune like *The hare among the corn,* and make them sound thoroughly modern (see no. **42**).

Some European musical elements turn up frequently in variation sets. The reader may be interested to have a list of these.

G string effects. The rich, sonorous sound of the violin's G string seems still to have been a novelty in Scotland in 1720; the medieval fiddle had a gruff G string, rebecs usually possessed only D, A, and E strings, and even the cultivated treble viol, which could play lower than the violin, had a weak tone at the bottom of its compass. Fiddle-composers tended to reserve this new sound for special effects, featuring it only in certain strains of pieces. Examples are: *The reel of Tulloch* **(30),** strain 12; *The East Neuk of Fife* **(34),** strains 5, 7, 9 and 11; *Duncan Gray* **(35),** strains 3, 5 and 9; *Johnnie Cope* **(38),** strain 3; *The Highlander's farewell* **(39),** strains 1, 3 and 5.

High E string effects. These were also a novelty, since before 1720 it was unknown for Scots-fiddle tunes to shift out of first position. Passages on the E string above the limits of first position were also usually reserved for certains strains of a piece. Examples: *Black Jock* **(32),** strains 23–24; *The maltman comes on Monday* **(33),** strains 15 and 20; *Duncan Gray,* strains 7–8.

Skips across two strings. This effect was probably imitated directly from Corelli's violin sonatas. Examples: *Up tails a'* **(27),** strain 7; *Black Jock,* strain 22; *The hare among the corn* **(42),** strains 7–8.

Double stops with both notes fingered. These were almost certainly unknown in Scots-fiddle music before 1720. Examples: *Black Jock,* strains 25–26; *The hare among the corn,* strain 9.

Slurred bowing in fast passages. This was a product both of European violin technique, and of the type of phrasing natural to the German flute. Up to 1720 Scots fiddlers mostly played fast passages in single bows, as many of them do still. Examples: *Duncan Gray,* strains 6, 8 and 10; *The lea rig* **(37),** strains 9–10; *Mount your baggage* **(41),** strains 3–4.

Wide-ranging arpeggios. These were imitated from German-flute pieces; arpeggios in earlier Scots-fiddle pieces rarely cover a range of more than a 6th. Examples are *Duncan Gray,* strain 8:

Johnnie Cope, strain 6:

Continental bagpipe imitations. There was a vogue in European art-music in the early 18th century for imitations of Continental bagpipes, based on the idioms of the French *musette* and the Italian *zampogna,* and characterised by *(a)* a drone bass on the tonic or dominant; *(b)* a tune gently meandering around adjacent notes of the scale; and *(c)* a middle part, doubling the tune a 3rd or 6th lower. Pieces in this style always had an effect of idealised, pastoral innocence. The most famous examples were the finale of Corelli's *Christmas Concerto* (published 1714) and the Pastoral Symphony of Handel's *Messiah* (composed 1741).

It was possible to obtain this effect from a single violin by using the open strings as drones. Examples: *Black Jock* (many strains, particularly 13–15 and 23–26); *The lea rig* and *The hare among the corn* (almost throughout, the drones being supplied by the reverberance of the re-tuned G and D strings). There is a particularly delightful example in a variant text of *The hare among the corn* in Riddell's *Scotch, Galwegian and Border Tunes,* where the tune is played on the A string accompanied by a drone on the open E:

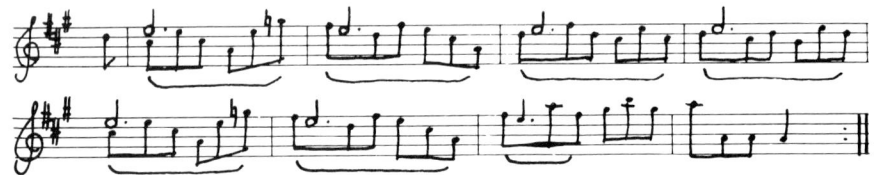

It is still unclear at the time of writing how extensive a genre the long variation set was. Less than a hundred pieces survive from the 18th century which can be classified as long variation sets, and many of these are inelegant, or incomplete in one way or another. However, we must bear in mind that some of the finest sets have reached us through only a single text. It may well be that more first-rate variation sets will turn up, once further manuscripts are available for study.

25. A wife of my ain

26. My Nanny-O

set by WILLIAM FORBES of DISBLAIR (*c.* 1662-1740)

[Slow]

27. Up tails a'

WILLIAM FORBES of DISBLAIR

[Andante con moto]

28. Cailleach odhar
(The sallow-faced hag)

set by DAVID YOUNG (*c.* 1707-*c.*1770)

[Alla marcia]

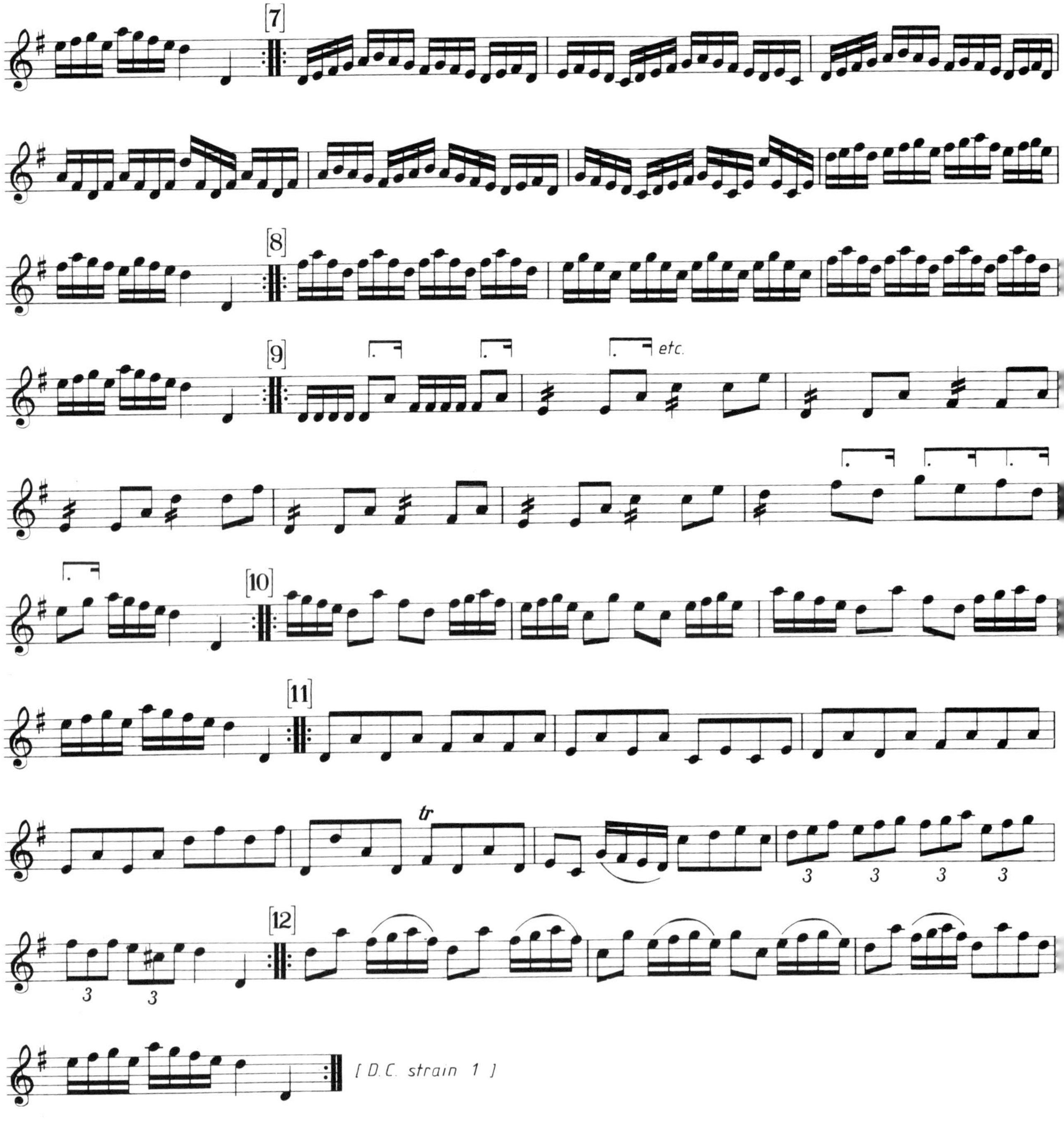
7
8
9
etc.
10
11
tr
12
[D.C. strain 1]

29. Allan Water

set by DAVID YOUNG

30. The reel of Tulloch

after DAVID YOUNG

[Vigorous, rhythmic]

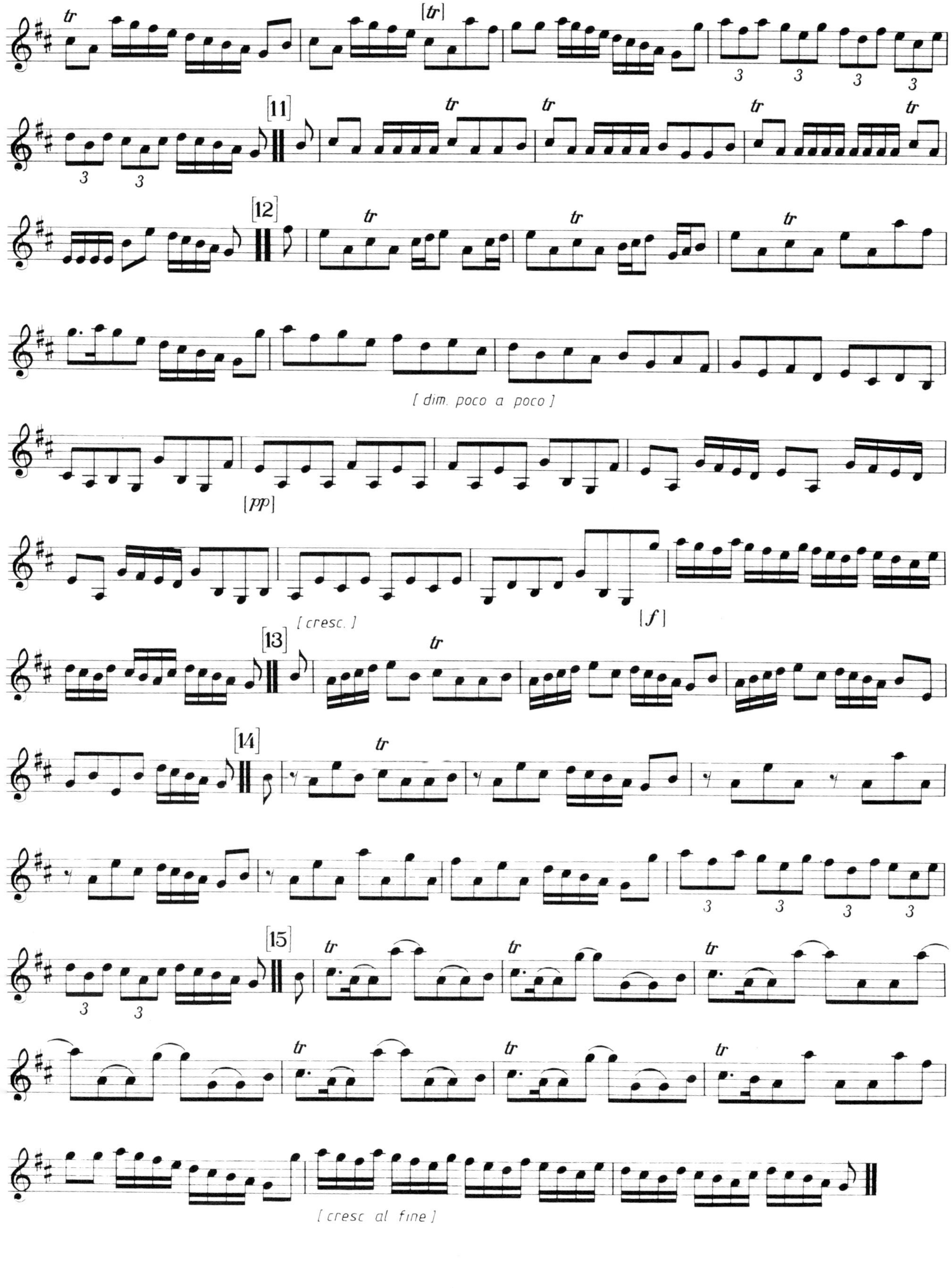
[11]
[12]
[dim. poco a poco]
[pp]
[cresc.]
[f]
[13]
[14]
[15]
[cresc al fine]

31. Old Sir Symon the king

after HENRY PURCELL (1659-95)

G

32. Black Jock

after CHARLES McLEAN (*fl.* 1736-40)

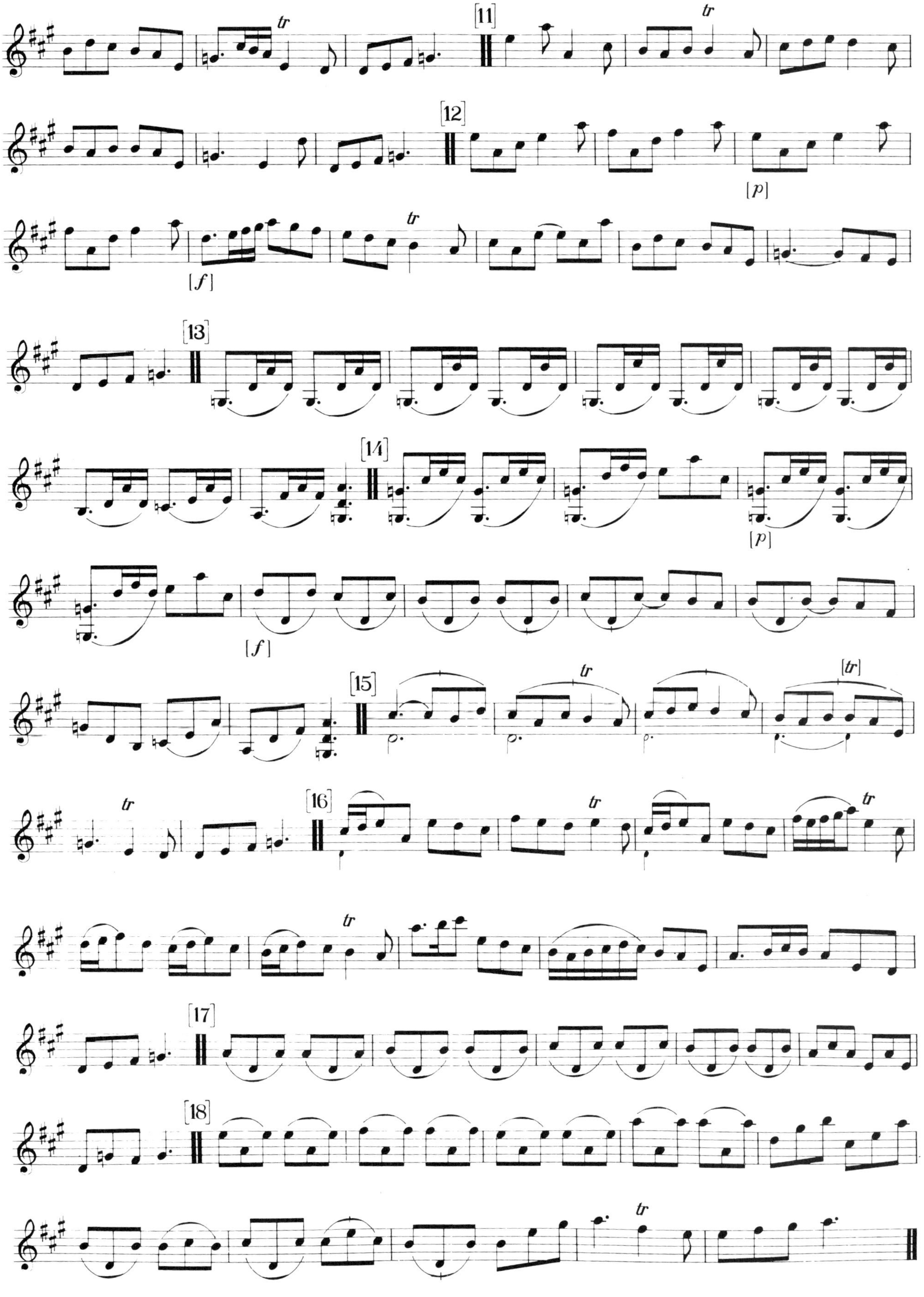
tr
[11]
tr
[12]
[p]
[f]
tr
[13]
[14]
[p]
[f]
[15]
tr
[tr]
tr
[16]
tr
tr
tr
[17]
[18]
tr

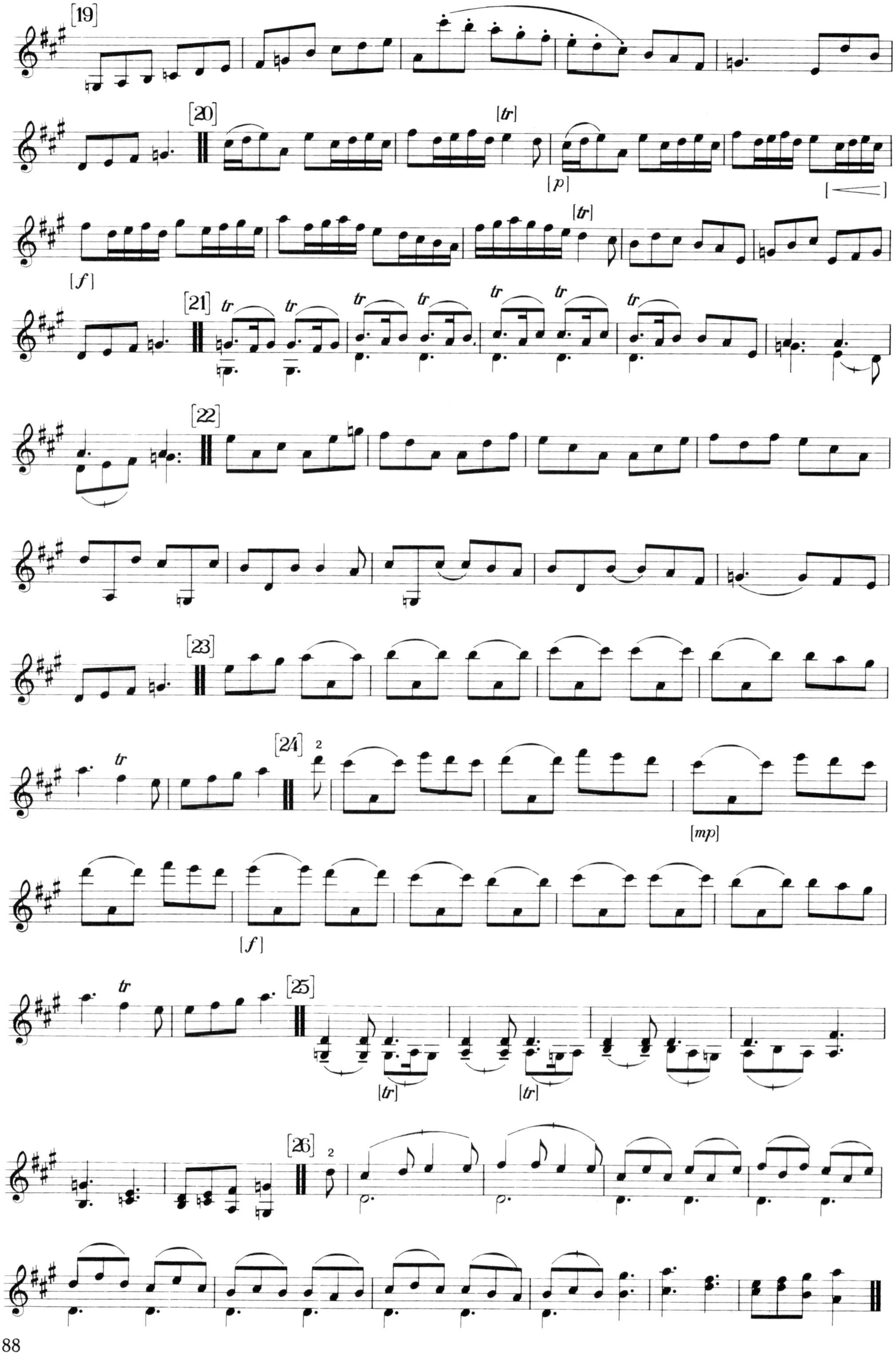
19
20
[tr]
[p]
[f]
[tr]
21
tr
22
23
24
tr
[mp]
[f]
25
tr
[tr]
26

33. The maltman comes on Monday

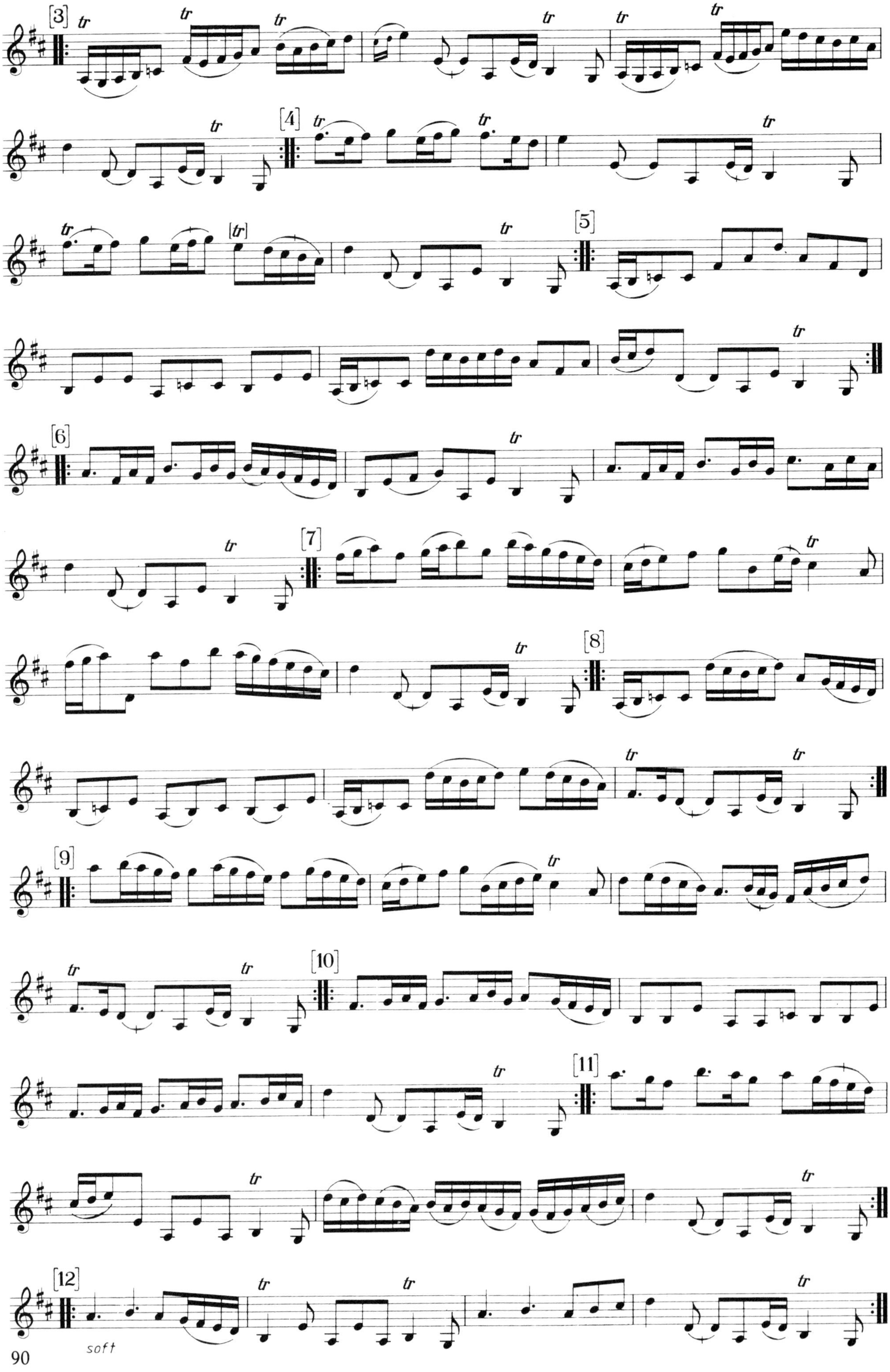
[3]
[4]
[5]
[6]
[7]
[8]
[9]
[10]
[11]
[12]
soft

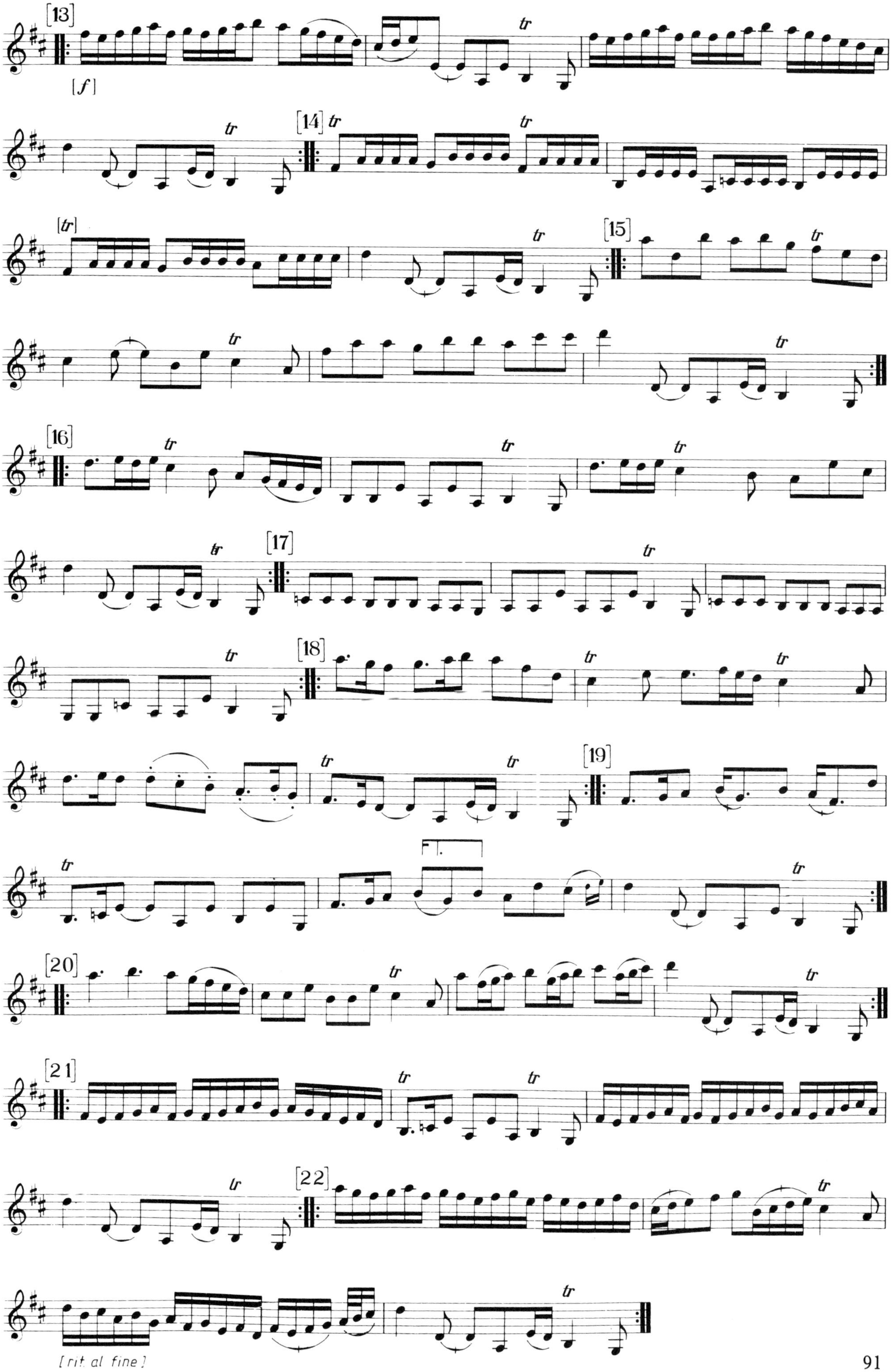
[13]
[f]
[14]
[15]
[16]
[17]
[18]
[19]
[20]
[21]
[22]
tr
[tr]
[rit. al fine]

34. The East Neuk of Fife

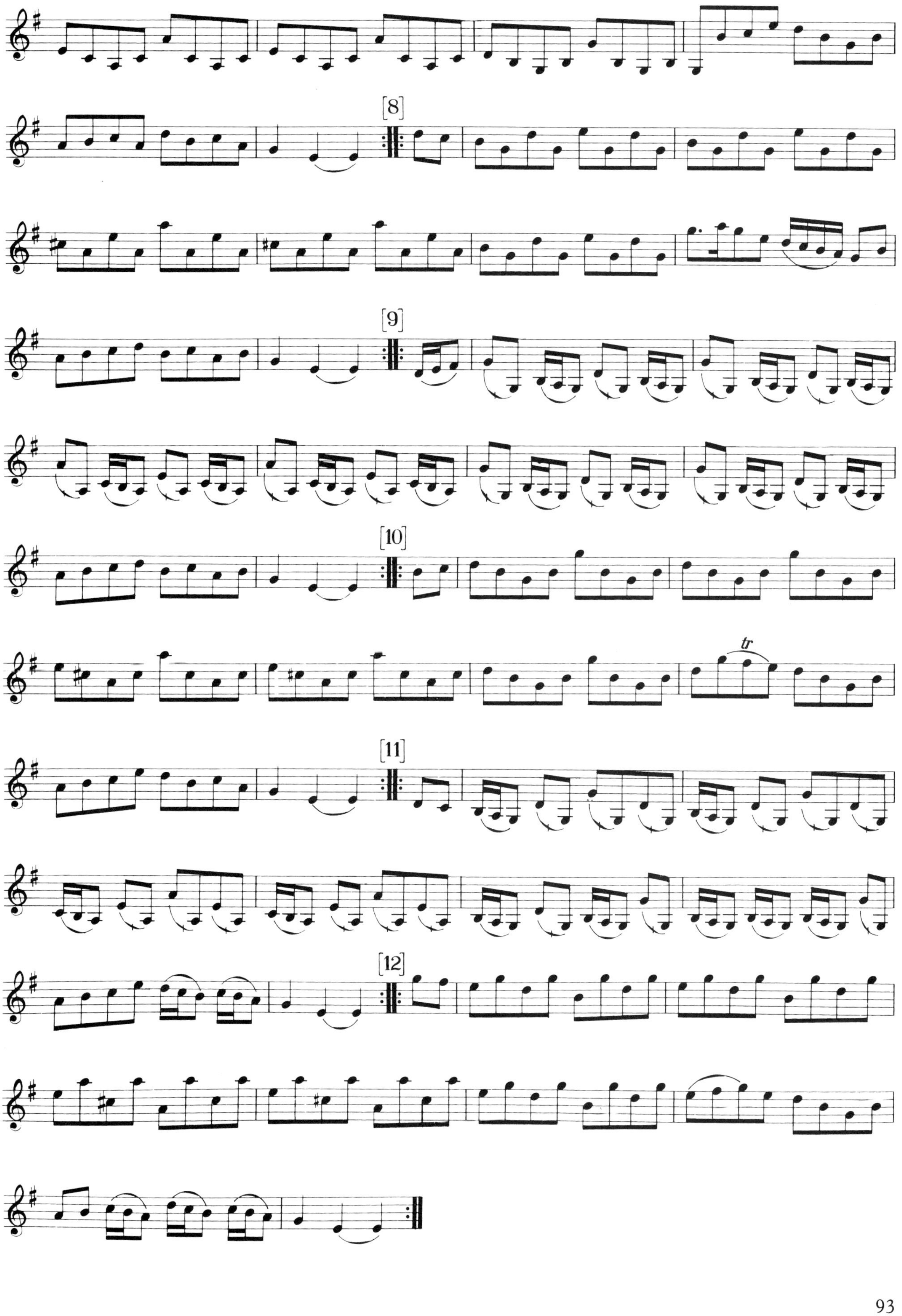
[8]
[9]
[10]
tr
[11]
[12]

35. Duncan Gray

36. Lumps of puddings

set by JAMES OSWALD (1711-69)

37. The lea rig

38. Johnnie Cope

[Brisk]

[D.C. strains 1 and 2]

39. The Highlander's farewell

40. Sweden's march

41. Mount your baggage

42. The hare among the corn

H

NOTES ON THE MUSIC

25 *A wife of my ain*
Source: McFarlane MS., vol. ii no. 28. Title supplied from the McFarlane index.
The words to this jig began 'I'll hae a wife o' my ain'; Burns rewrote them slightly at the end
of the 18th century.

26 *My Nanny-O*
Source: McFarlane MS., vol.ii no. 108.
The tune on which these variations are based was a 17th-century slow air, to which Allan
Ramsay wrote new words in 1718. The variations were later printed in the *McLean* collection
(1772).
Revisions: the paper has disintegrated in the source, so the following portions of text have had
to be supplied from an anonymous flute MS. of *c.*1770 (NLS Ing.12, p.10): strain 2, bar 2
notes 6–8, bar 5 notes 1–3, and bar 7 notes 12–13; strain 3 bar 2 note 7; strain 6, upbeats and
bar 1 note 1
   strain 3 bar 2 note 4 ♯ from NLS Ing.12
   strain 5 'Giga' heading from NLS Ing.12.

27 *Up tails a'*
Source: anonymous fiddle MS. of *c.*1770 (NLS Adv.MS.5.2.25), p.11.
This ornate setting is a far remove from the simple 16th-century English version of the tune
(cf. Simpson, p.727). The Giga section has only one strain, and does not balance the Andante
very well: there may originally have been a second Giga strain which is now lost. This can be
compensated for by playing strain 11 twice and strains 1–10 only once.
Revisions: the final notes of strains 1–7 are editorial (cf. strains 8–10)
   strain 2 bar 2 notes 11–12 orig *c*♯*"*, *b'*
   strain 2 bar 4 note 2 orig *b'*
   strain 5 bar 4 × orig at note 7
   strain 7 bar 2 note 12 orig *b'*
   strain 11 bar 6 notes 1–3 orig a tone higher.

28 *Cailleach odhar*
Source: McFarlane MS., vol.ii no. 4.
This march is quite possibly of bagpipe origin (see Chapter V). However, David Young's
variations are considerably acclimatised to the fiddle. They were later printed in the *McLean*
collection (1772).

29 *Allan Water*
Source: McFarlane MS., vol.ii. no. 103.
These variations are to be played rather slower than the simple set of the tune, no **3**. For the
work of a literate composer in 1740 they are extremely old-fashioned, and keep the tune's
pentatonic mode almost intact.

30 *The reel of Tulloch*
Source: Bremner's *Scots Tunes*, p.4. Bass omitted.
This was originally a bagpipe piece, as can be seen from its range (mostly between *g'* and *a"*),
key (A major with flattened 7ths), and extended birls; see Chapter V. It is still played on the

pipes at the present day. David Young's name is attached to an earlier text of this fiddle setting (McFarlane MS., vol.ii no. 115), which differs from the text given here in the order of the strains and in some other details; but Young probably composed the three finest sections of this version — the repeated notes in strain 6, the downward scale in broken thirds in strain 12, and the syncopations in strain 15.

I have left the source's notation of strain 15 unaltered, in case the ties (or slurs) indicate repeated notes in one bow. However, Young's notation of the strain clearly indicates syncopations:

These variations survived to the end of the 19th century, and were reprinted in a similar form in Skinner's *Harp and Claymore* Collection.

Revisions: strain 1 bar 2 note 8 orig *f*♯ "; *g*" from McFarlane

strain 5 rhythmic variants from the Webster MS., p.53

strain 5 bar 2 note 7 orig *a'*

strain 5 bar 3 notes 1–2 orig quavers

strains 5, 6, 10, 14 cadences: triplet slurs deleted

strain 12 bar 5: editorial 'dim poco a poco' based on dynamics in Skinner's *Harp and Claymore*

strain 15 bars 3, 5 and 6 notes 1–2 orig quavers.

31 *Old Sir Symon the king*

Source: Bremner's *Scots Tunes*, p.2. Bass omitted.

These variations are based on an English harpsichord set in Purcell's *Musick's Handmaid Part II* (London, 1689).

Revisions: heading orig 'Brisk'.

32 *Black Jock*

Source: Bremner's *Scots Tunes*, p.14. Bass omitted.

The theme of these variations was a popular English dance-tune entitled *Black Joke*. It was known as 'Black Jock' in Scotland from about 1735. The title may have been altered accidentally, or it may have been done in purpose to try to rid the tune of its associated words, which were extremely obscene. On the evidence of the McFarlane MS. (vol.ii no.207), Charles McLean composed strains 19 and 23–24 of the text given here.

Note that all written *a'*s are to be played open on the A string, not stopped on the re-tuned D string.

Revisions: initial key-signature orig with an extra ♯ on the *g'* line

drone notes orig written as dotted minims at strain 7 bars 1–2, strain 21 bars 1–3, strain 25 bars 1–3, strain 26 bars 3–7

fingering over upbeats to strains 24 and 26 is Bremner's

strain 30 bar 7 note 1 orig a semiquaver

33 *The maltman comes on Monday*

Source: Bremner's *Scots Tunes*, p.18. Bass omitted.

These variations are based on the 17th-century English tune *Sir Roger de Coverley*. The title given here is the first line of Ramsay's words to the tune *(Tea-table Miscellany* vol.i, 1723).

Revisions: strain 13 bar 1 note 12 orig *f* ♯ ".

34 *The East Neuk of Fife*
Source: Bremner's *Scots Tunes*, p.17. Bass omitted.
The East Neuk is the part of Fife that juts out into the North Sea, and contains the towns of St. Andrews, Crail and Anstruther. The tune was first recorded in Oswald's *Caledonian Pocket Companion* (vol.iv, *c*.1751) as *She grip't at the greatest o't*. It is still frequently played by Scots fiddlers today.

The tune is a double-tonic one, based on the chords G and A. Early 18th-century tunes of this kind are often uncertain whether their upper chords should be major or minor (see page 18), so it is interesting to see this uncertainty built structurally into the variations here: for the odd-numbered strains alternate G and A minor, and the even-numbered ones G with A major.
Revisions: ticked slurs in strains 9 and 11 from the Little MS., p.22.

35 *Duncan Gray*
Source: Gillespie MS., p.56.
An earlier text of this tune (McFarlane MS., vol.iii no.116) suggests that it was originally an English march in trumpet style. By 1760 it had local Scottish words, telling the story of a rough country wooing. Several sets of variations were written on it; the most famous were Oswald's *(Caledonian Pocket Companion* vol.iii, *c*.1750) and McGibbon's *(Scots Tunes* vol.iii, 1755). The set given here did not reach print in the 18th century. See page 31 for suggestions as to which repeats should be played.
Revisions: strains 8 bar 3 note 8 orig *f*♯ ".

36 *Lumps of puddings*
Source: Gillespie MS., p.58.
This tune was probably a 17th-century English country dance; it appears in the Sinkler MS. (1710) as 'Sweet pudding'. These variations are derived from Oswald's *Caledonian Pocket Companion* (vol.vii, *c*.1756), but do not follow Oswald's text exactly.
Revisions: key-signature originally three sharps (a mistaken afterthought on the copyist's part: the spacing shows that Gillespie began to copy the piece with only one sharp — cf. nos. **60** and **70**)
   strain 1 bar 3 note 6 orig *f*♯ ".

37 *The lea rig*
Source: Gillespie MS., p.55. Title from *Flores Musicae*, p.28.
The title in the source is 'My Own kind Dearie'. I have used the tune's alternative title, *The lea rig*, to conform to the variation sonata on the same tune (no. **67**). Both titles derive from words to the tune which began:

> I'll lay thee o'er the lea rig,
> My ain kind dearie O.

These variations were first printed in the *McLean* collection (1772), four years later than the Gillespie MS.
Revisions: Gillespie got muddled between crotchet and quaver notation, and wrote this piece out in a mixture of the two. I have rationalised the text by halving note-values of the following portions: strain 5, all except upbeats, bar 1 notes 3–6, bar 2 notes 3–6, and bar 3 notes 3–6; strains 6, 7, and 8, all except upbeats; strain 9, upbeats, bar 2 notes 5–15, and bar 4; strain 10, all except upbeats and bar 2 notes 12–13
   strain 1 bar 2 notes 10–11 orig quavers
   strain 9 bar 3 notes 1 and 9 orig *a*
   strain 10 bar 4 note 2 orig *g'*.

38 *Johnnie Cope*
Source: *McLean* collection, p.23. Bass omitted.
The words to this tune are a satirical account of the battle of Prestonpans, fought between General Sir John Cope's army and Bonnie Prince Charlie's on 22 September 1745; they were written by Adam Skirving, an East Lothian farmer across whose fields the armies marched on the day of battle. Skirving may also have composed the tune, since it is not known earlier than the 1750s (see Stenhouse, pp. 220, *189 and *305; Glen, *Early Scottish Melodies*, p.137).
   Despite the title of the source, it is unlikely that McLean had any hand in this setting. The piece is printed low down on a right-hand page in the collection, and was obviously regarded as a space-filler item by the editor.
Revisions: heading orig 'Slow'
   strain 2 bar 4b: the 2nd-time bar was originally placed at the end of strain 4. It does not fit there, but makes a good conclusion to the piece if strains 1–2 are played as a *da capo*
   strain 5 bars 1 and 3: semiquavers orig bowed in pairs.

39 *The Highlander's farewell*
Source: Ross's *Scots Reels*, p.10. Bass omitted.
This strathspey was composed in a close imitation of bagpipe style. It was also known as *The Highland Watch's farewell to Ireland*.
Revisions: repeats of strains 2 and 4 orig written out in full, with a few detailed differences.

40 *Sweden's march*
Source: Shiels MS.
The full title of the tune is *The King of Sweden's march*. These variations are derived from a set in Bremner's *Airs and Marches* (p.94), but have been considerably altered in detail. Bremner's text shows that the tune was originally in Baroque-trumpet style.
Revisions: strain 1 upbeat orig a quaver
   strain 6: editorial trills from the Gillespie MS., p.30.

41 *Mount your baggage*
Source: Trotter MS., p.30.
This army song was also known as *The Soldier's Lady* and *Mount and go*. It is phrased in three-bar units, so that strain 1 contains six bars and strain 2 twelve. However, the variations confuse this scheme: from strain 3 onwards the strains alternate between 8 and 15-bar lengths, rather than 6 and 12. Other texts of the variations (*Flores Musicae*, p.74; Gow's *Strathspey Reels* vol.ii, p.16) have similar confusions.
Revisions: strain 5 bar 7 notes 1–2 orig quavers
   strain 8 bar 7 a few rhythms normalised.

42 *The hare among the corn*
Source: Trotter MS., p.44.
This jig was probably a very ancient one; there is a short set of it in the George Skene MS. (1717). The variations given here have a strong flavour of European pastoral, however, so they are unlikely to have been composed earlier than 1760.
Revisions: the following portions of the text were originally a tone lower, owing to mistakes in scordatura notation: strain 7 bar 7 notes 1–3; strain 9 bar 7 notes 5–8.

CHAPTER IV

Scordatura

SEVERAL pieces in scordatura have already been presented (nos. **9, 32, 33, 37** and **42**), and it is time we looked at this way of playing the fiddle in more detail.

Scordatura (Italian for 'mis-tuning') indicates that the fiddle strings are not to be used at the standard pitches of *g, d', a'* and *e"*, but that one or more of them are to be re-tuned. Three different kinds of scordatura were current in 18th-century Scotland; they are shown in Table III.

Table III

SCORDATURE IN 18th-CENTURY SCOTS FIDDLE MUSIC

1.	*a d' a' e"*	Raise G string to A
2.	*a e' a' e"*	In addition, raise D string to E
3.	*a e' a' c♯"*	In addition, lower E string to C sharp

Pieces in scordatura are normally written with a prefatory stave showing the tuning. After that, the music is notated as if the fiddle had *not* been re-tuned, i.e. showing the notes that would have been produced if the fiddle-strings had been left at the usual pitches. This makes reading easy for fiddlers, but difficult for anyone trying to play the music on another instrument such as the piano; for notes on re-tuned strings will, obviously, be written down transposed. In scordatura no. 3, for example, notes on the re-tuned G and D strings will be written a tone lower than they sound; notes on the re-tuned E string will be written a minor 3rd higher than they sound; and only notes on the A string will be written at pitch. Thus the opening of no. **44**, sounding:

will be notated:

I have arranged the pieces in this chapter in a way which will, I hope, encourage fiddler-readers who are unfamiliar with scordatura to have a go at it. The first four pieces are in scordatura no. 3: two 'practice pieces' — a tune in nursery-rhyme style (**43**) and a short march (**44**) — a lullaby, *Black Sloven* (**45**), and a strathspey, *Willie Wink's testament* (**46**). The last of these can be made up to a substantial length by playing all the repeats and a *da capo* of strains 1–2.

Then follow three pieces in scordatura no.2: a slow air, *The fox lamentation* (**47**); a jig, *Donald McIntosh* (**48**); and a fiddle setting of a drawing-room song by Allan Ramsay, *Wat ye wha I met yestreen* (**49**).

The last two pieces are in scordatura no.1: a strathspey, *The miller's wedding* **(50)**, the tune later used by Burns for his song 'Coming through the rye'; and *The Duke of Argyle's strathspey* **(51)**, set by Nathaniel Gow. No. **51** is exceptional in having a harpsichord and cello accompaniment: scordatura was usually used only for unaccompanied fiddle-tunes.

The origins of scordatura in Scots fiddling are somewhat obscure. Varied tunings were used on plucked-string instruments (lute, cittern, mandora) in Scotland throughout the 17th century, and there was a fashion for re-tuning bowed-string instruments (violin, viol, cello) in England and on the Continent, roughly between 1670 and 1730. Scots fiddlers may have taken their varied tunings from the mandora, or from foreign violin music, or perhaps a bit of both.

The 17th-century instruments were re-tuned for a straightforward technical reason: to make it possible to finger chords in particular keys. This rationale continued in 18th-century Scots fiddling, for scordatura fiddle pieces had a much higher incidence of chords, double stops, and drone-notes than pieces in standard tuning, and the re-tunings were also tied to particular keys. Pieces in scordatura no.1 were always in D major; pieces in nos. 2 and 3 always in A major.

Over and above reasons of fingering, re-tuning the strings gives the fiddle a quite novel resonance. The open G string in particular, when re-tuned to A, has a tendency to reverberate in sympathy with any notes that are played above it. As the fiddler Alastair Hardie remarked recently, scordatura gives one a whole new instrument to work on. The difference in timbre cannot be heard to advantage in large concert halls; but it is easily noticed in intimate surroundings, and the person most aware of it, of course, is the player himself. Many fiddlers in the 18th century must have re-tuned their instruments simply because they liked playing with that particular sound.

During the first half of the 18th century scordatura-playing was largely an underground activity. Very few scordatura pieces were written down in manuscripts, mainly because of the difficulties of notating them, and none at all appeared in print. It is possible that some pieces written down in ordinary notation were intended to be played in scordatura, but the evidence for this is not clear.

Scordatura's position changed dramatically, however, in August 1759, with the publication of Bremner's *Scots Tunes* in Edinburgh. This collection included two pieces with re-tunings — *Black Jock* in scordatura no.2 and *The maltman comes on Monday* in scordatura no.1 — both of them using prefatory staves and transposed notation. Bremner had evidently gone to European music of a generation or two earlier for models of the notation system; under *Black Jock,* he printed a useful footnote to explain how the system worked.

James Oswald in London was not a man to let rival publishers' good ideas go to waste. He promptly went one better by inserting a whole string of pieces in scordatura no.3 into his *Caledonian Pocket Companion* and, so as not to imitate Bremner too obviously, used the word 'Acord' (for *accordatura,* 'tuning') above his prefatory staves in place of Bremner's 'Scordatura'. These pieces appeared in volume x of the collection, which was published *c.*1760.

By 1761 hundreds of fiddlers all over Scotland had Bremner's and Oswald's collections in front of them, and scordatura notation was a baffling secret no longer. Almost

Brown manuscript: f.9 containing 'The fox lamentation' **(47)** and 'Donald McIntosh' **(48)** (National Library of Scotland).

Reverse of the same leaf (f.9v.) containing 'Black Sloven' **(45)**, 'Practice piece II' **(44)**, 'Practice piece I' **(43)** and three further tunes (National Library of Scotland).

immediately, large numbers of scordatura pieces began to be written down in fiddlers' manuscripts, as though vast pent-up energies for transcribing them had suddenly been released.

Many of these pieces had never been set down on paper before. The Gillespie (1768) and Trotter (1780) manuscripts contain some fine ones, but the most exciting set is in the Brown manuscript, made in Elgin around 1775. Nos. **43–48** in this chapter are taken from the Brown manuscript, and by an odd chance, all of them except no. **46** occur on a single leaf of the book (folio 9).

Other editors of printed collections followed Bremner's and Oswald's lead. As a result, a large corpus of scordatura pieces was recorded between 1760 and 1800; and the word 'scordatura' entered Scots dialect as an accepted technical term.

Scordatura after 1800

After 1800 scordatura once more went underground, due to a growing demand for fiddle-books from amateur pianists: such players were, of course, unable to cope with scordatura notation. *The Duke of Argyle's Strathspey* (**51**) was an early casualty to this trend. The tune is given in scordatura in the first edition of Niel Gow's *Strathspey Reels* (vol.i, 1784). By the second edition (1792), however, Nathaniel Gow had realised that scordatura was discouraging to pianists and was tending to reduce sales; so he deleted the drone-notes in strain 1 and re-wrote the piece in ordinary notation, commenting in a footnote: 'This pretty Tune as it stands in the first Edition can not be played upon the Piano Forte'. The Gows' example was copied by other editors, so that by 1820 scordatura had entirely disappeared from printed collections. It also disappeared from manuscripts, for without printed texts to guide them, fiddlers once more forgot how the notation worked.

Actual playing with the strings re-tuned seems, however, to have continued unabated during the 19th century. The 'Scordatura' article in the first edition of *Grove's Dictionary* (vol.iii, 1883), for example, says that re-tuning 'is frequently employed by Scotch reel-players, and in their hands has a singularly rousing effect', and goes on to cite *Kilrack's Reel, Anthony Murray's Reel*, and *Appin House* as tunes commonly played in scordatura no.2. James Scott Skinner's books also contain references to scordatura. His *Guide to Bowing* (c. 1905) dismisses it as 'trick fiddling'; his *Harp and Claymore* collection (1904), on the other hand, recommends scordatura no.2 for one of his most famous compositions, the strathspey *The Laird o' Drumblair*.

During the early part of the 20th century scordatura declined, and finally died out, on the Scottish mainland. However, it is still used by players in the Shetland Isles; and the publicity which Shetland fiddling has attracted recently, coupled with the influential teaching of the Lerwick fiddler Tom Anderson, has caused a few scordatura pieces to appear in print once more in Anderson's *Haand me doon da Fiddle* (1979) and Hardie's *Caledonian Companion* (1981). It seems likely that this fascinating and worthwhile way of playing the instrument will be revived throughout Scotland in the near future.

43. Practice piece I

44. Practice piece II

45. Black sloven

46. Willie Wink's testament

[Strathspey]

[D.C. strains 1 and 2]

47. The fox lamentation

[Slow]

48. Donald McIntosh

49. Wat ye wha I met yestreen

50. The miller's wedding

51. Duke of Argyle's strathspey

set by NATHANIEL GOW (1763-1831)

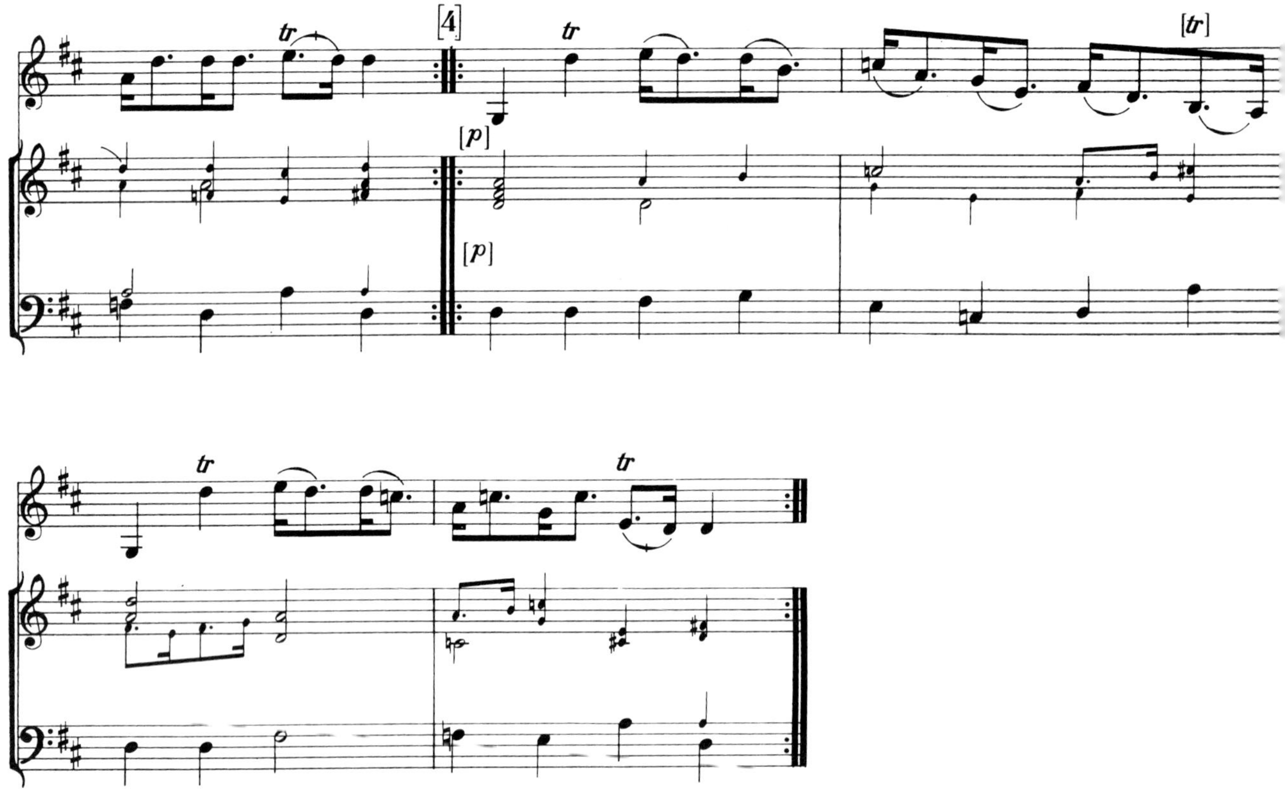
[4]
tr
[tr]
[p]

NOTES ON THE MUSIC

43 *Practice piece I*
Source: Brown MS., f.9v. Title editorial.
I have been unable to identify this piece, which seems to be otherwise unrecorded.
Revisions: Scordatura wrongly given as *a e' a' g ♯"*
 key-signature orig *c ♯ ", g ♯ "*
 1st and 2nd-time brackets omitted in orig
 strain 2 bar 4b orig a minim.

44 *Practice piece II*
Source: Brown MS., f.9v. Title editorial.
This march seems also not to be recorded elsewhere.
Revisions: Scordatura wrongly given as *a e' a' g♯ "*
 key-signature orig three sharps.

45 *Black Sloven*
Source: Brown MS., f.9v.
This lullaby is also not known in other texts.
Revisions: Scordatura wrongly given as *a e' a' g♯"*
 key-signature orig *c ♯ ", g ♯ "*
 strain 1 bar 5 upper note orig a dotted minim; ♮ orig ♭
 strain 2 bar 3 lower notes orig written as a dotted minim.

46 *Willie Wink's testament*
Source: Brown MS., f.5v.
The tune is a strathspey version of the reel *Greig's Pipes* (also frequently played in *a e' a'*
c ♯ " tuning in the 18th century). There were other tunes called *Willie Wink's* (or *Winkie's*)
testament (e.g. McFarlane MS., vol.iii no.60; *Caledonian Pocket Companion,* vol.vi p.5), but
they are only distant relatives of this strathspey.
Revisions: Scordatura wrongly given as *a e' a' g (?♮)"*
 the source has dots above the sixth notes of strain 1 bars 1–3, probably indicating that notes
6–8 of each bar are to be played with separate bows.

47 *The fox lamentation*
Source: Brown MS., f.9r.
This lament is not otherwise recorded in this form. However, two jig versions of it appear in
the Sharpe MS. (both on p.222, in B flat and D respectively). These are entitled *The Highland
Hunt*, and are in standard tuning. Note that the repeated As in strain 5 are to be played as
open strings. The dots over these notes probably indicate separate bows, rather than staccato.
Revisions: strains 2, 4 and 6: upbeats orig semiquavers
 strain 6 bar 8 note 1 orig *b.*

48 *Donald McIntosh*
Source: Brown MS., f.9r.
This jig is unknown in other texts.
Revisions: strain 3 bar 4 note 1 orig *f ♯'*
 strain 4 bars 5–6 are editorial (cf. strain 4 bars 1–2); orig as strain 2 bars 5–6.

49 *Wat ye wha I met yestreen*
Source: Trotter MS., p.63.
The title (in standard English: 'Guess who I met last night?') is the first line of Ramsay's lyric 'The young laird and Edinburgh Katy' (*Tea-table Miscellany*, vol.i). The tune is also given in Niel Gow's *Strathspey Reels*, vol. ii, in standard tuning.
Revisions: strain 2 bar 2 note 8 orig *g"*.

50 *The miller's wedding*
Source: Bremner's *Scots Reels*, p.41. Bass omitted.
Other titles for this tune were *The miller's daughter* (Sharpe MS., p.83; Niel Gow's *Strathspey Reels*, vol.i) and *My dear, durst I but mow you* (George Skene MS., f.3v); it was also played in standard tuning.
Revisions: editorial drone notes added on basis of the Sharpe MS.
  strain 5 bar 2 notes 1–2 orig a birl.

51 *Duke of Argyle's strathspey*
Source: Niel Gow's *Strathspey Reels*, vol.i p.32. For the ascription of the setting to Nathaniel Gow, see note on no. **24.**
This strathspey is unknown earlier than the Gow collections, and was probably composed by a member of the Gow family.

CHAPTER V
Bagpipe Pieces

PIECES proper to the bagpipes have been transferred on to the fiddle since at least the beginning of the 18th century. The earliest surviving fiddle text which is clearly of pipe origin is the rant *The gum-ga'd aiver* ('The old horse with sore gums') in the Gairdyn manuscript of *c.*1710; after that come a group of pieces in 'Bagpipe humour' in the George Skene manuscript of 1717, and a miscellaneous collection of about 30 items in the McFarlane manuscript of 1740. These are the earliest known records of Scottish bagpipe music in existence; no actual bagpipe texts were written down until 1760.

It is easy to identify pipe transcriptions, for they have certain obvious characteristics: most noticeably, a range of nine notes (*g'* to *a"*) coupled with a key-signature of two sharps. This characteristic arises from the nature of the pipes, as Scottish bagpipes have two tenor drones and one bass drone, all tuned to As, and a chanter which is restricted to a nine-note scale, thus:

The C sharp on the chanter tends to sound somewhat flat. The E drone shown in brackets in an aural illusion caused by harmonic overtones; there is no actual pipe tuned to E (despite the fact that piano pieces with names like 'Fantasie écossaise' invariably represent pipe-drones as fifths). It is also worth mentioning that most 18th-century sets of pipes would have had fewer than three drones; and that, though pipes were probably tuned to the same pitch as other instruments in the 18th century, present-day manufacturers make them a semitone higher, notated in A but sounding in B flat.

Most pipe transcriptions in the early part of the century were taken over on to the fiddle with minimal alterations. A few tunes, however, were transposed: *Mackintosh's Lament* (**56**), for example, was always played by fiddlers in A, though the pipe key for the piece is D, with the drones sounding as a dominant pedal. *Drunken wives of Carlisle* (**14**), also, appears in fiddle sets in G, though the pipe key for it would have to be A. Other tunes had their nine-note range expanded: David Young's version of *The gum-ga'd aiver* (McFarlane MS. vol.iii no.267; a later setting of the Gairdyn MS. piece already mentioned) is one example. Young's first 14 strains keep the tune within the traditional pipe range, but his strain 15 takes it down an octave on to the G string, while his strain 20 raises it an octave and uses high E string positions. Another piece where part of the tune has been transposed an octave is *The reel of Tulloch* (**30**); see strain 12.

Fiddlers were adventurous, and did not stop at merely transcribing the pipe repertory; they also wrote new tunes in 'pipe style', which have the same limited-scale characteristics. It is not always clear which ones are genuine pipe-tunes and which are fiddlers' imitations in the same style. Among the pieces in this book, *Drunken wives of Carlisle* (**14**), *The reel of Tulloch* (**30**), *Pibroch* (**52**), *Piobaireachd Dhomhnaill* (**53**) and *Mackintosh's Lament* (**56**) were originally part of the pipe repertory, while *The Highlander's farewell* (**39**) and *A Highland battle* (**58**) were made up by fiddlers. But *Cailleach odhar* (**28**), *Willie Wink's testament* (**46**) and *Donald McIntosh* (**48**) might well be either.

Scots fiddlers often attempted to sketch in the drone-sounds in pipe pieces (both genuine and imitation) by sounding open strings adjacent to the melody. Scordatura tunings were extremely helpful for this. As we have seen in Chapter IV, there were two *scordature* current at the time which involved raising the G and D strings of the fiddle to A and E. These were convenient for bagpipe pieces, since the open A corresponded to the pipes' tenor drone, and the open E to the prominent harmonic overtone. Both these lower strings could easily be touched with the bow while the tune was played on the upper strings; and they would resonate audibly in any case, even if they were not bowed. *Willie Wink's testament, Donald McIntosh,* and *Piobaireachd Dhomhnaill* are all set in scordatura for this reason. *Piobaireachd Dhomhnaill* is an especially revealing case: scordatura no. 2 is specified for it, but no notes on the re-tuned strings actually appear in the score. The player is obviously expected to add his own drone-notes alongside the written text.

Pipe pieces in scordatura no. 3 often contain a special effect, consisting of an open E string (re-tuned to C sharp) in unison with the same note stopped on the A string, the stopped note being trilled. The effect is written:

It has a peculiar grating sound, and was perhaps intended to suggest the 'out of tune' quality of the C sharp on the pipe chanter. For examples, see *Willie Wink's testament,* strain 2; *Mackintosh's Lament,* strain 8.

Birls are another effect which should be discussed here. The *birl* is a melodic decoration which is common to both fiddle and pipes, though it takes a slightly different form on each instrument. (Birls are still going strong at the present day. The name derives from an everyday Scots word meaning 'to rotate rapidly'; one can speak, for instance, of spin-dryers and taxi meters birling round.)

On the pipes, a birl is a short cluster of grace-notes of different pitches, played so fast that the ear cannot pick out the constituent parts. On the fiddle, it consists of three repeated notes, written as   ♫   but played as rapidly as possible (e.g. as   ♫.   ). A fiddle birl is taken in separate bows near the point, the bow moving less than a centimetre each way. As with the bagpipe birl, the listener hears it not as individual notes, but as a kind of ripple.

Fiddle and pipe birls are certainly historically connected, though it is not clear which instrument copied the effect from which. It is noticeable, however, that fiddle birls occur almost exclusively in 'pipe style' pieces up to 1750 or so. One of the pieces in 'Bagpipe humour' in the Skene manuscript of 1717, for example — *Cauld Kail in Aberdeen* — is given with three different versions of the 2nd strain, and two of these contain birls. Skene's comments between the lines of music suggest that fiddlers were still experimenting with birls at that time:

A way in stead of The gatherings in the second measure

Anoy^r [another] way of the 2^d measure w^t [with] gatherings

(*Gatherings* means clusters of grace-notes; *gr* is short for 'graces', meaning the same thing. The sign ⟋ indicates a short trill; see page 31.)

From 1750 onwards, birls were used more generally in fiddle music, and began to appear in large numbers in pieces which had no connection with bagpipes at all. *Miss Admiral Gordon's strathspey* (**80**) is a good example of a late 18th-century piece full of birls; it was composed by Marshall *c.*1775, and is not in pipe style.

A longer form of birl also existed at this time. This *extended birl* contained four, six or more repeated notes; it was the violin's equivalent of the long chains of grace-notes in pibroch. Extended birls were written as groups of semiquavers (𝄢 etc.) and were played in strict time.

In terms of the player's technique, extended birls are identical to orchestral violin tremolo, as used (e.g.) in 18th-century German symphonies. Aesthetically, however, the two are quite distinct, for the extended birl is a weird and exotic melodic decoration while tremolo is essentially a device for accompaniment. Extended birls occur only in pieces with bagpipe connections. For examples, see *Cailleach odhar* (**28**), strains 5 and 9; *The reel of Tulloch* (**30**), strain 6; *Donald McIntosh* (**48**), strain 3; *Pìobaireachd Dhòmhnaill* (**53**), strain 6; *Cumha Easbuig Earraghàidheal* (**54**), strain 4; *Cumha Iarla Wigton* (**55**), strain 5; and *The battle of Harlaw* (**57**), strains 15–19. An interesting point about the extended birls in *The battle of Harlaw* is that they are of two different kinds: those in strains 18–19 have to be played 1½ times as fast as those in strains 15–17.

This is about as far as we can go with generalisations about pipe-style fiddle pieces; further investigation is hampered by the fact that so little is known about 18th-century piping. Two different types of bagpipe were in use in Scotland at the time, the Highland pipes, which were mainly played in Gaelic-speaking areas of the country, and the Lowland (or Border) pipes, which were played only in the south. Lowland pipes were smaller-toned than Highland pipes, and were inflated by bellows where the Highland pipes were blown with the mouth. But they seem to have been tuned identically, and their repertories of tunes probably overlapped to a much greater extent than is generally realised. *Drunken wives of Carlisle* (**14**), for example, is clearly a Lowland-pipe tune from its title (anyone writing a satirical piece about women in Carlisle would almost certainly have lived in the town's vicinity). But it could well have been played on the Highland pipes also, and fiddle manuscripts show that the tune did, in fact, travel north. Indeed, a companion-piece was written to it later in the century entitled *Drunken wives of Fochabers,* commenting on women in a town in the north-east of Scotland, hundreds of miles from Carlisle.

Nor is the relative importance of the Highland and Lowland bagpipes at this time exactly clear. During the 19th century the Highland pipes became the official instrument of Scots army regiments and were taken all over the world, while the Lowland pipes, back in Scotland, declined and died out; so that nowadays the Highland bagpipe seems by far the more important of the two. But they probably had a much more equal standing in the 18th century.

The pipes' great classic art-form — pibroch — seems, however, only to have been played on the Highland pipe.

Pibroch

The Highland-pipe repertory is normally regarded as being divided into two parts: *cèol beag* ('small music'), consisting of airs, marches, and dance music, and *ceòl mór* ('large music'), consisting of pibroch. It is a confusing point of terminology that the first two tunes in this chapter, nos. **52** and **53**, are *ceòl beag* pieces even though they are entitled 'pibroch'. The reason why no. **52** is so called is that the Gaelic abstract noun *pìobaireachd* has a general meaning of 'piping as an activity' as well as being the name of the specific musical form. The title of no. **52** therefore means simply 'piping' or 'pipe piece'. No. **53** is so called because the tune is the basic theme of a *ceòl mór* piece, *Pìobaireachd Dhomhnaill Dhuibh* ('The pibroch of Black Donald'). The setting given here, however, is a straightforward march; a *ceòl beag* version of the same tune. The next four pieces in the chapter, nos. **54–57**, are pibrochs in the full sense of the word.

Pibrochs are a ceremonial form. They were often written to celebrate or lament events affecting the whole of society — such as a battle, the death of a hero, or an important political meeting between clan chiefs — and though some were inspired by everyday, personal matters, they still come across as public utterances in a grand manner. Pibrochs make few concessions to the listener; they cannot easily be whistled or danced to, and are hard to memorise without conscious effort.

All pibrochs begin with an *ùrlar* ('ground', or main theme), played with what seems, to uninitiates, maddening slowness. The ground is often a pre-existing popular tune; one reason for the slowness is to rid such tunes of their common-or-garden associations. After the ground, the player proceeds to stylised variations such as the *suibhal, leumluth* and *taorluth,* leading up to the most complex variation, the *crunluth.* (A few pibrochs have an even more complex final variation, the *crunluth a mach.*) The work then ends with a reprise of the *ùrlar,* played at the original slow speed. The entire pibroch may last 15 or 20 minutes.

Pibrochs today are highly standardised. Each has a similar (though not quite identical) form, and each has only one version which is generally accepted as correct. However, Campsie is clearly right in suggesting that this extreme standardisation came about only in the mid-19th century, with the onset of printed pibroch texts, and that before that a much greater variety of forms and styles were used. Even Angus MacKay's bagpipe collection of

1838, which marks the beginning of the standardisation, shows that pibrochs were played in two distinct forms up to that time: *(a)* with the *ùrlar* appearing at the beginning and end of the work, as it does today (we might perhaps call this 'da capo form'); and *(b)* with the *ùrlar* making additional appearances at points midway (we might call this 'rondo form'). Of nos. **54-57**, *Cumha Easbuig Earraghàidheal* is in rondo form, and *Cumha Iarla Wigton* and *The battle of Harlaw* are in da capo form. *Mackintosh's Lament* could be either; it has 9 strains with strain 1 repeated at the end, but strain 7 could be regarded as an extra varied reprise of strain 1, occurring midway.

So we should not be surprised that the 18th-century fiddle versions of pibroch are less formalised, more improvisatory, than the pibrochs that are played on the pipes today. 18th-century bagpipe versions probably differed from each other considerably to start with. On top of that, fiddlers would have added many new elements while arranging the pieces for their own instrument.

But did fiddlers get all their pibrochs from the pipes in any case? It is now generally accepted that the virtuosic *ceòl mór* variation form was first developed in the Middle Ages on the clarsach (Highland harp), and was transferred to the bagpipes only at a later date. (See Collinson, pp. 150–3.) But virtuoso harping in Gaelic-speaking parts of Scotland did not die out until the beginning of the 18th century. Recent research by Alan Bruford indicates that the date for the transference of *ceòl mór* to the pipes was much later than most people realise: that it only happened towards the end of the 17th century. On this theory, all four of the pibrochs given here as nos. **54-57** would have been composed, not for the pipes at all, but for harp. *The battle of Harlaw* **(57)** was probably written immediately after the battle it commemorates, which took place in Aberdeenshire in 1411. *Mackintosh's lament* **(56)** was written, according to widespread tradition, in honour of a chief of Clan Mackintosh who died in 1526. Bruford suggests that *Cumha Easbuig Earraghàidheal* **(54)** was a lament for Donald Carswell, the 16th-century Bishop of Argyll who translated the Book of Common Order into Gaelic, and that *Cumha Iarla Wigton* **(55)** was a lament for the third Earl of Wigton, who died in 1665. All four would thus have been written before *ceòl mór* was established on the bagpipe.

It follows that there would have been a short interim period (say, 1690 to 1720) during which the Italian violin could have acquired *ceòl mór* pieces directly from the harp, without intervening bagpipe transmission. And this, in fact, is probably what happened with *Cumha Easbuig Earraghàidheal* and *Cumha Iarla Wigton*. Neither piece is known to pipers, and neither would actually fit the pipes without its melody being almost totally re-written. Both, however, are easy to play on clarsach and violin. In addition, both pieces contain melodic leaps of a seventh, from B to high A, which were probably typical of harp style at that time.

The battle of Harlaw may well have reached the fiddle via the pipes; it fits the pipe-compass with only small alterations and is, indeed, played on the pipes today under the title *The desperate battle*. *Mackintosh's lament* is clearly a pipe transcription from its trills and other decorative figures, which are highly characteristic of pipe style.

Only a few fiddle texts of *ceòl mór* pieces have come down to us (the ones presented in this chapter, plus about ten others), but they are enough to show us certain things very clearly. Fiddlers experimented with *ceòl mór* from around 1710 until the end of the century, in the Lowlands as well as in the Highlands. They regarded it as a great challenge to their ingenuity and musicianship, and decided, early on, that the best way to tackle the form was to go for the overall effect rather than the precise details. Skill in arrangement accumulated quickly and was passed from one fiddler to another, until 'fiddle pibroch' began to take off as a new genre, independent of either harp or pipes. Players started to write new pibrochs, designed specifically for fiddle. (No. **58** is one of these.) But though fiddlers had a common technique for handling the form, they were individualists when it came to performance, and were liable to play personal versions of the pieces, just as they did with long variation sets.

Mackintosh's lament seems to have been the pibroch that fiddlers liked best: no fewer than four violin texts of it are recorded. The version I have edited as no. **56** is from Macdonald's *Highland Vocal Airs*, and there are also sets in the McFarlane manuscript (vol.iii no.284), in Oswald's *Caledonian Pocket Companion* (vol.x p.18), and in Riddell's *Scotch, Galwegian and Border Tunes* (p.32). The McFarlane text was notated in 1740 by David Young, a fiddler who lived in Edinburgh but probably came from Aberdeenshire. Oswald's version was printed in London around 1760, and probably derived from performances which Oswald heard in Edinburgh in the 1730s. Macdonald's was printed in 1784, from a copy sent by a Mr Campbell of Ardchattan, on the west coast near Oban. Riddell's was edited in Dumfriesshire in 1794, and may well have been acquired from a local player even though Riddell calls it a Highland tune.

These four sets are therefore well spread out, both chronologically and geographically. They have many similar elements, such as strains in common, which show that the fiddlers concerned were all part of one tradition; but they are remarkably different in length, emotional power, and technical difficulty.

One more record of an 18th-century fiddle version of *Mackintosh's Lament* should be mentioned here. Niel Gow played the piece to Robert Burns in October 1787, when Burns visited Dunkeld, along with *Loch Erroch-side*, *Tullochgorum*, *Lament for Abercairney*, and other tunes (see Murdoch, p.46). It would be interesting to know if Gow had got his set out of Macdonald's book, which had been published only three years earlier. The chances are, however, that Gow had his own personal version of the piece.

Battle pieces

Many *ceòl mór* pieces were written to commemorate battles. The form was well suited to express society's feelings after a battle, since the opening and closing *ùrlar* could be regarded as a lament for the slain, and the variations, with their tension gradually rising up to the *crunluth*, as a description of the battle itself.

The battle of Harlaw (**57**) is one of the finest pieces of this type. A sense of occasion comes across vividly in the fiddle version given here; though neither player nor listener may know anything about the actual battle referred to, there can be no mistaking the horror and catastrophe in the piece, its sense of damage done to society which will take generations to repair. This setting may have been intended for rebec, as it does not use the violin's G string; certainly the wiry, gritty sound of the rebec suits it admirably.

'Mackintosh's Lament' (**56**) in Macdonald's *Highland Vocal Airs*, 1784 (National Library of Scotland). A bagpipe setting of the piece is given on the previous page.

Killiecrankie (**6**) may also have been a battle pibroch, describing the conflict at Killiecrankie in Perthshire in 1689. The 2-strain version of the tune given in Chapter I looks promisingly like an *ùrlar*; but if it was the opening section of a larger work, no more of it has come down to us.

Battles seem to have been on people's minds in the mid-18th century, after the 1745 Jacobite Rebellion and its terrible defeat at Culloden. This concern was reflected in many fiddle pieces of the time. *The horseman's port* **(13)**, for example, appeared in Bremner's *Scots Tunes* in 1759 with a note saying that it was 'To be begun moderately & increased in quickness to the end, As the Tune represents a Battle'. All other information about the piece, however, points to its being a song about horse-racing. *Pentland Hills* **(21)**, also, was given in the *Flores Musicae* collection of 1773 as 'The Battle of Pentland Hills', under the mistaken idea that the tune had something to do with the 17th-century battle of Rullion Green. The same fascination with battles led James Oswald to compose two new fiddle pibrochs, *The battle of Falkirk* and *A Highland battle*, in the late 1750s. Both were published in *The Caledonian Pocket Companion.*

A Highland battle **(58)** is the finer of the two. It can certainly be classed as a pibroch, though it is a most extraordinary one. To begin with, it is unusual in being blatantly descriptive, with sub-titles which give a blow-by-blow account of the action. Oswald almost certainly got this idea from 16th-century European battle pieces, in particular from a harpsichord suite entitled *The Battell* by the English composer William Byrd.

Next, not much of the music is actually derived from *ceòl mór*. The only parts of it that resemble other pibrochs are strains 7–18 (variations) and strains 26–31 (the closing *ùrlar*). Other sections are based on *ceòl beag*: strains 1–6 and 23–25 are in strathspey style, and strains 21–22 are like a Highland slow air. Strains 19–20 are an imitation of army bugle-calls, and have no direct connection with Scottish music at all.

Then there is the question of limited ranges. *A Highland battle* has a strong 'limited scale' feel to it, partly because it is pentatonic; but its actual range is d' to b'', an octave and a sixth. Oswald set himself this range because d' was the lowest note of the flute and b'' the highest note the violin could reach in 1st position; he wrote the piece to suit *The Caledonian Pocket Companion,* a collection aimed at both flautists and fiddlers. In strains 19–20 another restriction on pitches is introduced: to get the effect of bugle-calls, the tune uses only notes of the natural harmonic series. This too has little to do with bagpipe scales.

Finally, there are the extended birls in strain 11, used here specifically to imitate the sound of cannon-fire: a completely original idea on Oswald's part.

Nevertheless, this is a genuine and moving work, in which Oswald's knowledge and love of Highland music are everywhere apparent. Its novel use of traditional materials is best regarded simply as an extension of what other fiddlers were doing to bagpipe pieces at this time.

52. Pibroch

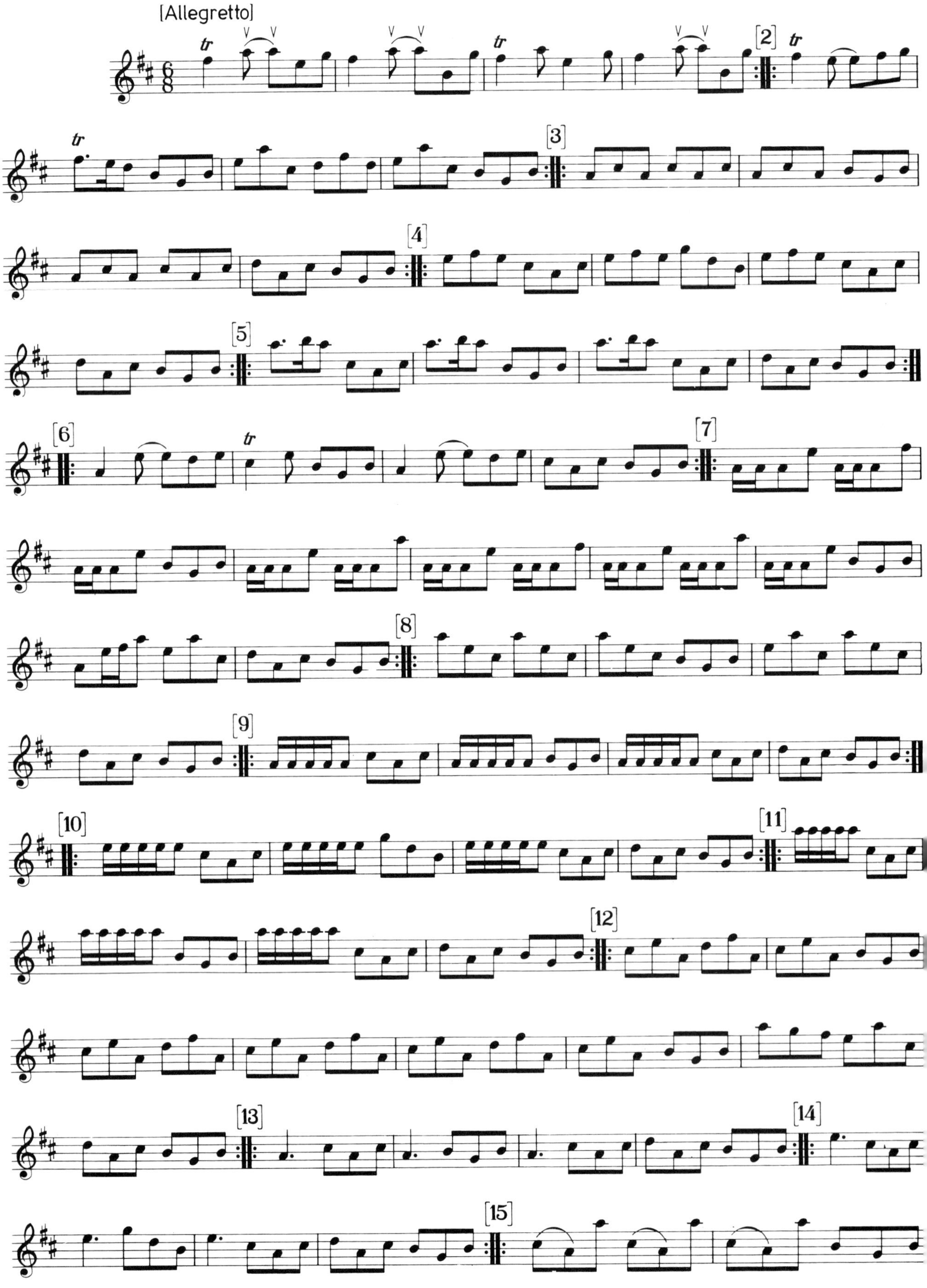

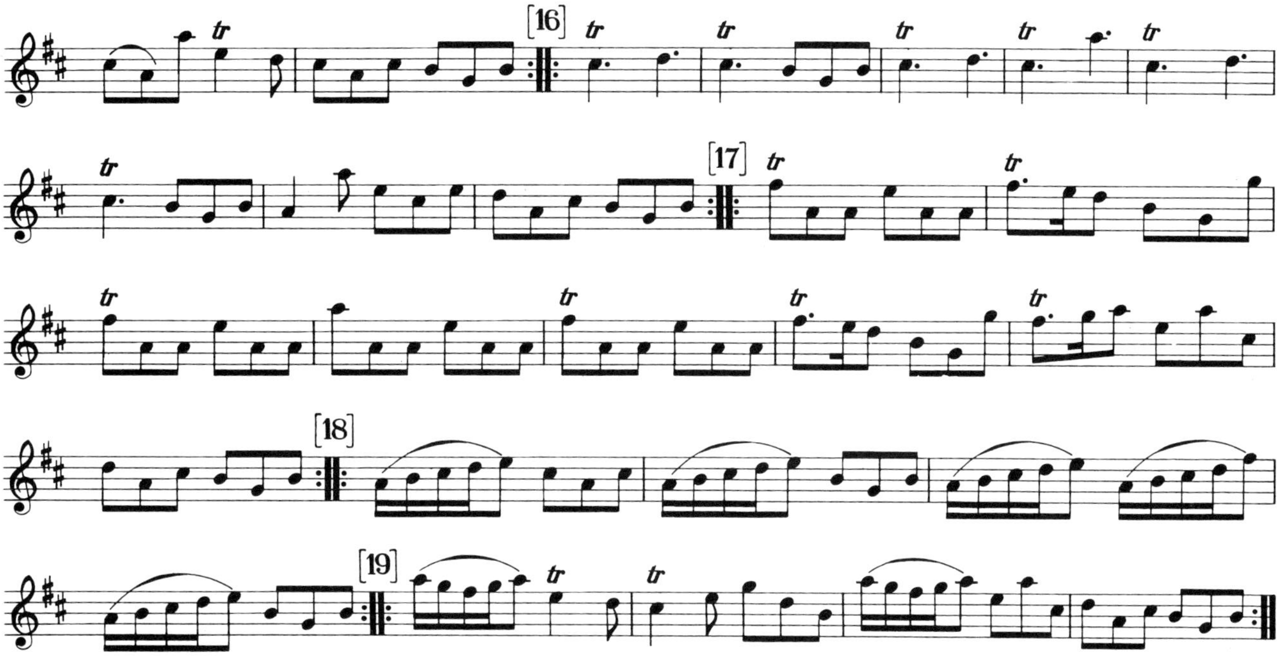
[16]
[17]
[18]
[19]

53. Pìobaireachd Dhomhnaill
(Donald's pipes)

54. Cumha Easbuig Earraghàidheal
(Lament for the Bishop of Argyll)

[repeat strain 1]

[repeat strain 1]

[rit e dim]

55. Cumha Iarla Wigton
(Lament for the Earl of Wigton)

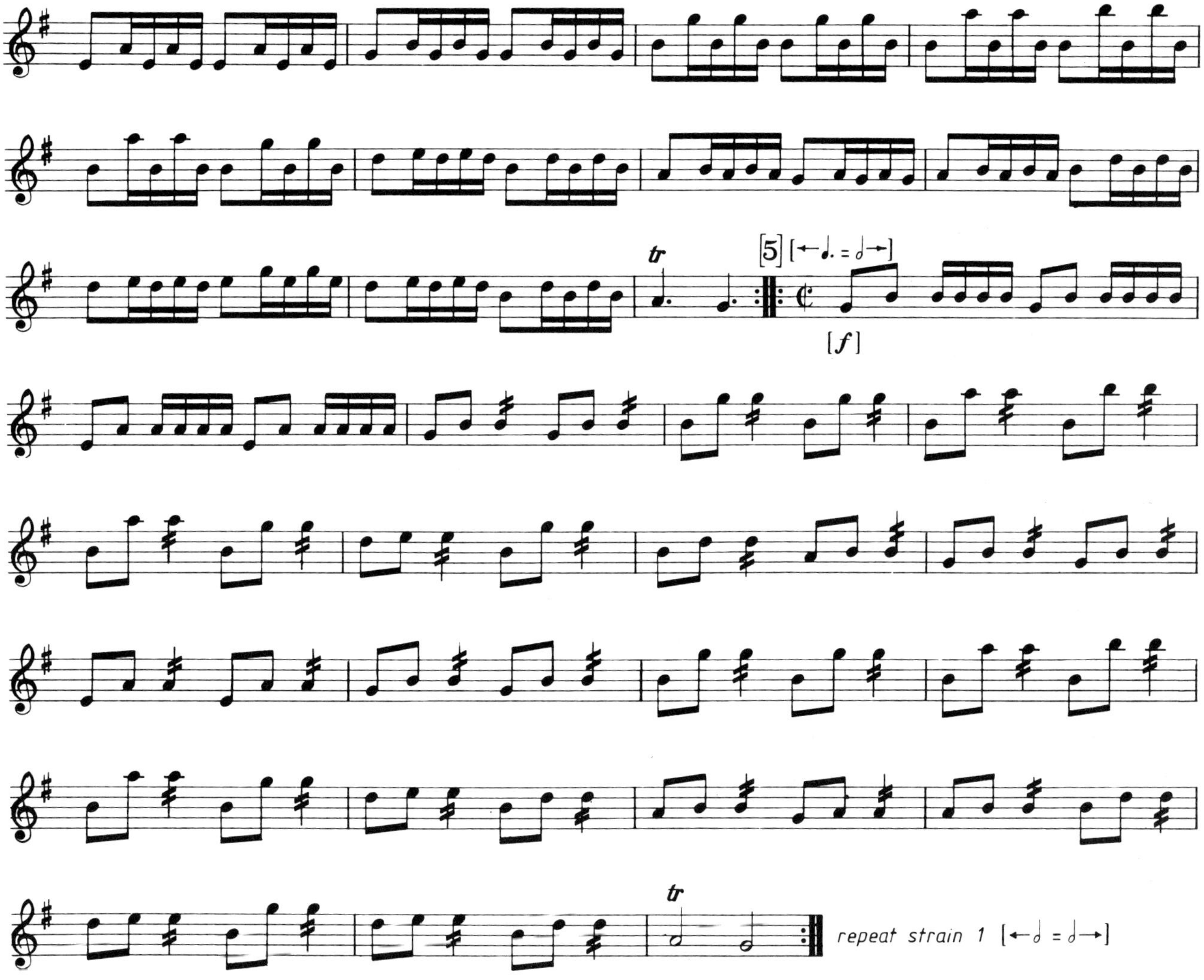
tr
[5] [← ♩. = 𝅗𝅥 →]
[f]
tr
repeat strain 1 [← 𝅗𝅥 = 𝅗𝅥 →]

56. Mackintosh's Lament

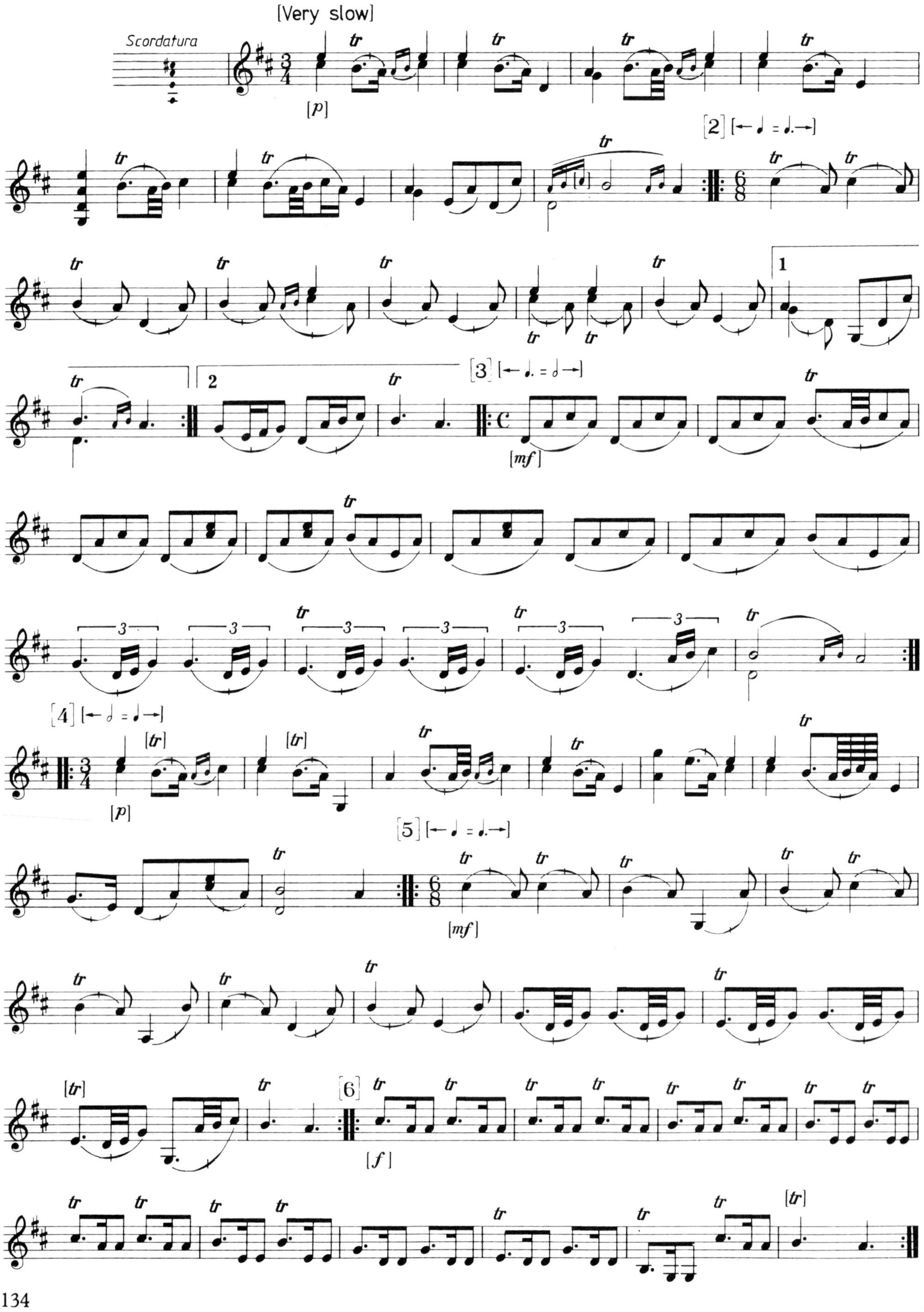

57. The battle of Harlaw

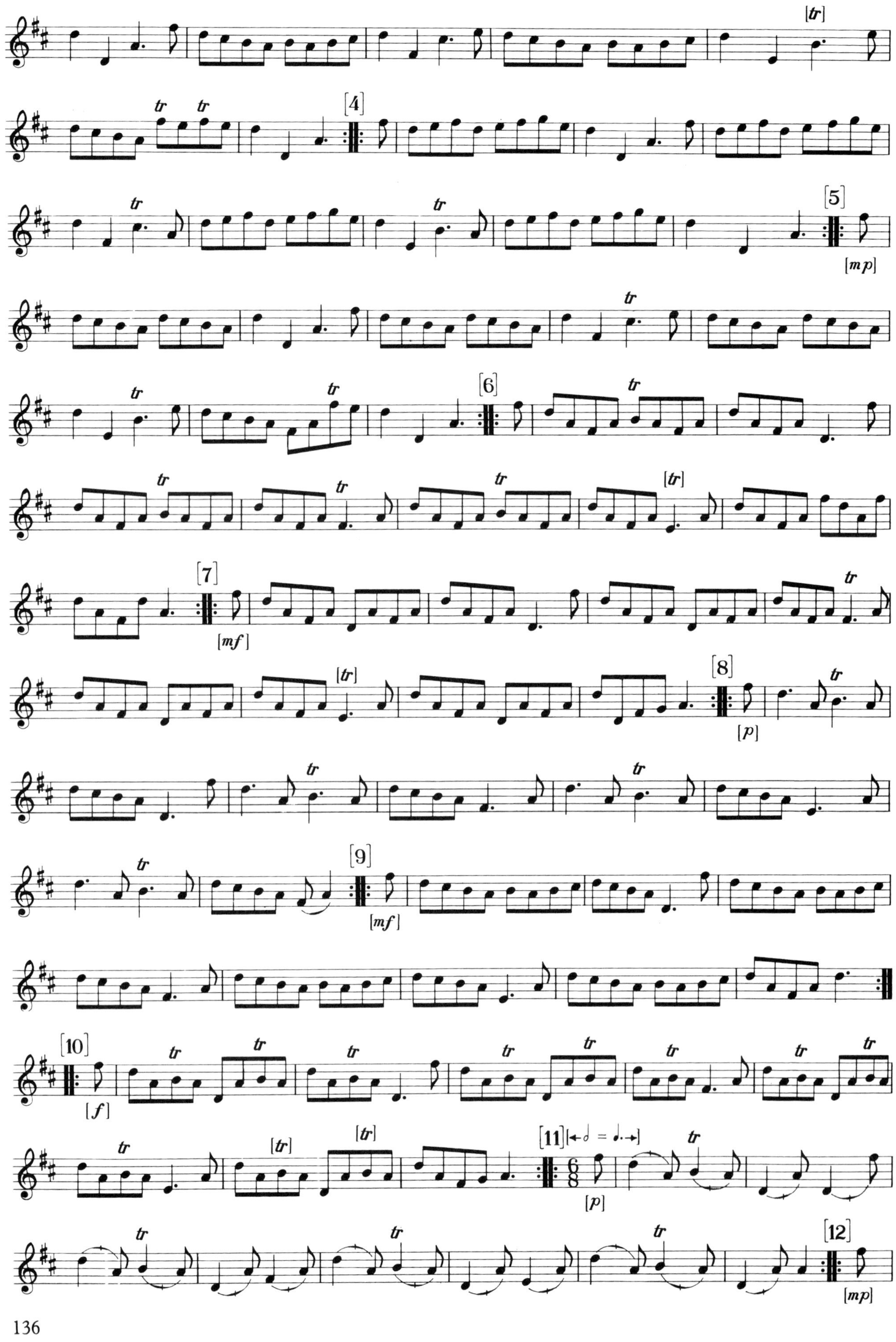
[tr]
[4]
[5]
[mp]
[6]
[tr]
[7]
[mf]
[tr]
[8]
[p]
[9]
[mf]
[10]
[f]
[tr]
[11]
6/8
[p]
[12]
[mp]

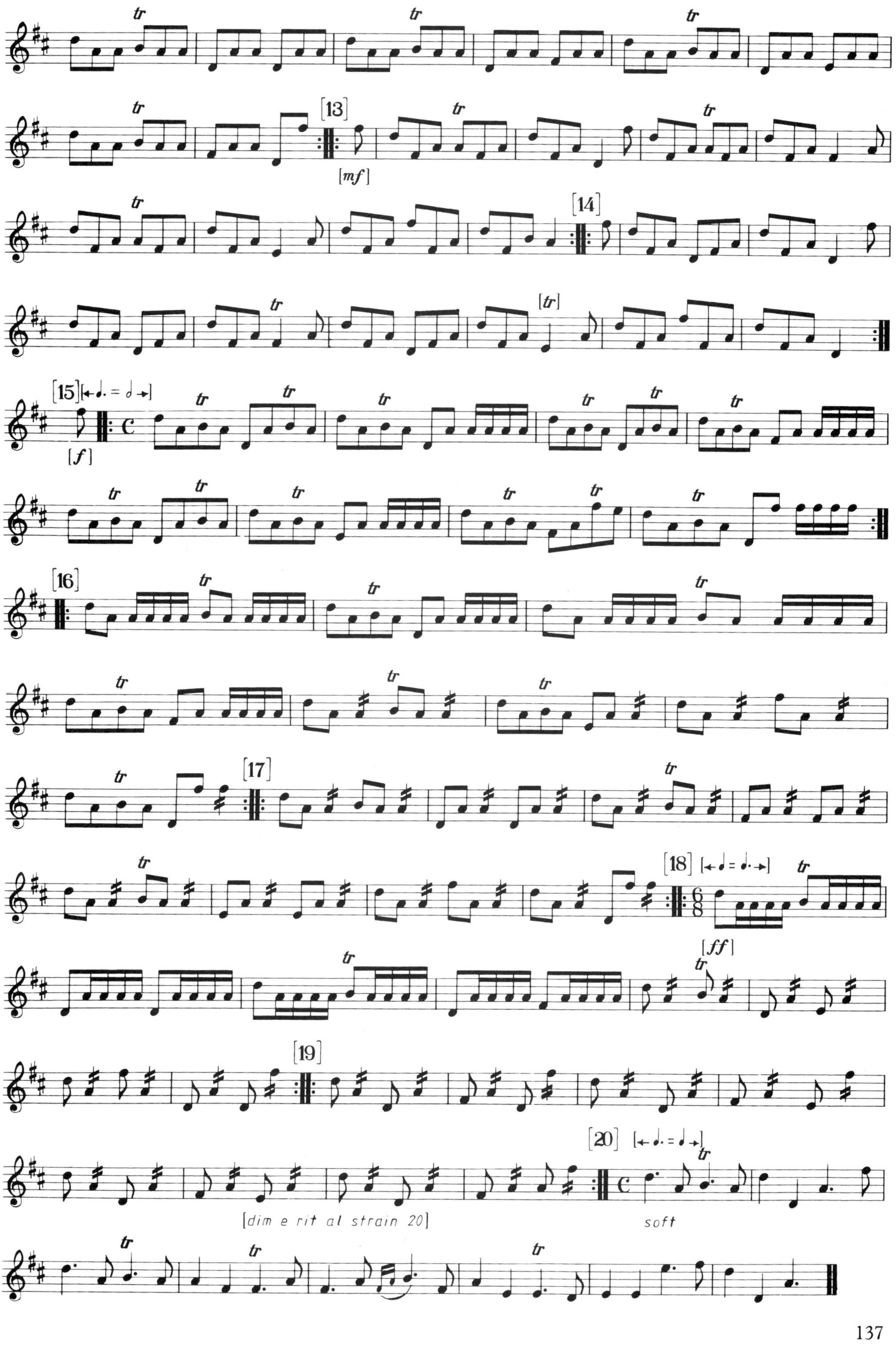

tr
[13]
[mf]
[14]
[tr]
[15]
[f]
[16]
[17]
[18]
[ff]
[19]
[20]
[dim e rit al strain 20]
soft

58. A Highland battle

JAMES OSWALD (1711-69)

The march

They mend their pace

The battle begins

The height of the battle

The preparation for a retreat

The chief is killed

The retreat

The lamentation for the chief

NOTES ON THE MUSIC

52 *Pibroch*
Source: McFarlane MS., vol.ii no.162. Title from the Little MS., p.4.
The McFarlane and Little texts are almost identical, though the piece seems not to be recorded elsewhere.
Revisions: strain 12 bar 2 note 3 as Little; source has *c* ♯ ″
   strains 18–19 separated as Little; source runs them together.

53 *Pìobaireachd Dhomhnaill*
Source: Sharpe MS., p.44.
An earlier version of this tune, *Lord Forbes' March*, is given in the McFarlane MS. (vol.ii no.7); it is still played on the pipes today in both *ceòl beag* and *ceòl mór* versions. The player is expected to add drone-notes on open strings adjacent to the tune: see page 120.
Revisions: title orig 'Pibroch-gonnel' (a Lowland attempt at phonetic transcription of the Gaelic)
   a few bowings normalised
   key-signature orig three sharps on opening line, otherwise two sharps
   strain 4 bar 4 note 4 orig *a'*
   strain 7 bar 4 note 5 orig *g'*.

54 *Cumha Easbuig Earraghàidheal*
Source: McFarlane MS., vol.iii no.34.
This pibroch was probably originally composed for harp. It is perhaps no more than a coincidence that its theme (strain 1) is strikingly similar in rhythm to the Italian *La folia* tune, on which Corelli, McGibbon and others wrote variations.
   Like no. **53**, the piece could well have drone-notes added on open strings alongside the tune, as:

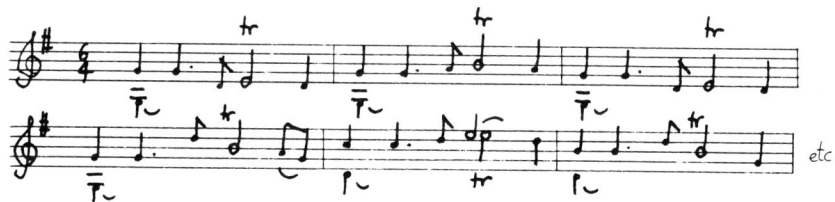

   The mathematical ratios between time-values in the different sections of the piece are an editorial suggestion only. However, they are in keeping with the general intellectual spirit of *pìobaireachd*, and they work well in performance. Similar editorial suggestions are given for nos. **55–57**.
Revisions: strain 1 bar 4 note 1 orig *e'*
   strain 3 bar 2 notes 6–7 orig *g'*.

55 *Cumha Iarla Wigton*
Source: Dow's *Ancient Scots Music*, p.2. Bass omitted.
The fiddle version of this pibroch probably dates, on stylistic grounds, from *c.*1720, though it was not published until 1776. It was probably originally composed for harp, like no. **54**.

56 *Mackintosh's Lament*
Source: Macdonald's *Highland Vocal Airs*, p.40.
This pibroch is supposed to have been written in 1526; it is still frequently played by pipers today.
Revisions: tempo marks are editorial, replacing the following original markings: strain 1, 'Slow'; strain 4, 'Slow'; strain 5, 'Quicker'; strain 7, 'Slow'; strain 8, 'Brisk, loud'
    strain 3 bars 7–10 orig twice as fast
    strain 8 bars 1–6, 9–10, upper notes orig crotchets; bars 7–8, upper notes orig semiquavers
    Macdonald has a note on how 'some of the variations may be prolonged' by inserting extra bars into them, e.g. after strain 6 bar 6 and strain 9 bar 6; for these extra bars, see the facsimile on page 125.

57 *The battle of Harlaw*
Source: Dow's *Ancient Scots Music*, p.28. Bass omitted.
This pibroch may well have been composed soon after the battle it commemorates, which took place in Aberdeenshire in 1411. It is mentioned as a song in *The Complaynt of Scotland* (1548), and as a bagpipe piece in a poem by Drummond of Hawthornden (*c*.1650). A lyric to it, with 31 verses, appears in Ramsay's *Ever Green* (1724). It is still played on the pipes today as the pibroch *The desperate battle*. See Stenhouse, p.445; Cannon.
    This fiddle version was probably made *c*.1720. It should be played with as many open strings as possible to maximise resonance, the end of strain 1, for example, being fingered:

Revisions: strains 6 and 7, bar 4 note 3 orig *g'*.

58 *A Highland battle*
Source: Oswald's *Caledonian Pocket Companion*, vol.ix p.6.
Ascription of this novel fiddle pibroch to Oswald is editorial; it ties in closely, however, with other quasi-traditional Highland pieces which he wrote at this time (e.g. no.**22**).
Revisions: strain 8, 2nd-time bar editorial
    strain 14 bar 2 note 5 orig *g'*
    strain 21 bar 4 note 3 orig *c"*
    strain 22 bar 4 note 1: sharp from a MS. copy of *c*.1780 (NLS Glen 228(3)).

CHAPTER VI

Minuets

SO far in this book we have discussed music which was either unique to Scotland, or at any rate had very strong regional characteristics. When we turn to minuets, however, we are suddenly faced with an international scene. The minuet dance originated on the Continent, and its music was firmly rooted in mainstream European styles. Minuet tunes hardly varied from one part of Europe to another, so that Kelly's *Capillaire minuet* (composed *c.*1762 in Edinburgh) and the minuet in the ballroom scene of Mozart's opera *Don Giovanni* (composed 1787 in Prague), for example, are in the same rhythms, go at the same speeds, and use the same international clichés of melody and harmony. It does not seem likely, at first sight, that minuets ever had much to do with Scots fiddle music.

Minuets certainly began the 18th century as a self-conscious foreign import, so far as Scotland was concerned. Up to 1750 or so, only upper-class people who lived in the Edinburgh area appear to have danced them, and fiddlers who were on hire for the parties and balls of the very rich seem to have got most of the music they needed from collections printed in London. One Scottish minuet-book was published at the time, James Oswald's. But only a few copies of it seem to have been run off (none survive today), and it was extortionately expensive; it can have made no impression at all on the general run of fiddlers.

After 1750, however, the dancing of minuets spread downwards socially into the lower middle classes. Formal dancing lessons became cheaper; dancing-masters set up practices in towns remote from Edinburgh; and it was not long before minuets became so widespread that even those who could not afford lessons had a good chance of picking up the steps. Fiddlers who played for ordinary dances, as well as those engaged for posh dances, started to find that the job required a knowledge of minuet tunes.

One sign of the minuet's changing status was that in 1760 Neil Stewart, Edinburgh's no. 2 music publisher, decided to bring out a low-price, hopefully big-circulation, minuet book. No collection like this had been done in Scotland before. Stewart first issued his *Collection of the Newest and Best Minuets* as a cautious 8-page pamphlet. But his hunch was right: the market was there. The collection sold well for the next twenty years, gradually being enlarged until it reached 92-page size about 1778. Edinburgh's no.1 publisher, Robert Bremner, followed suit with a rival *Collection of the Best Minuets,* and that sold well too. Stewart's and Bremner's books travelled considerable distances from Edinburgh; one copy of Stewart's (a 64-page edition) is known to have been purchased by Kilravock Castle, Nairn, in about 1772, and much handcopying was done from both books into fiddlers' manuscripts.

By 1780 minuet tunes were an accepted part of nearly every Scots fiddler's repertory. A high proportion of the tunes in circulation by then were new ones, written by local composers; Scotland had become practically self-sufficient in the production of them, and was no longer dependent on tunes imported from other countries. How Scottish composers got organised to write their own minuets is a fascinating story.

Minuets by Scottish composers

Only a few minuets were written in Scotland during the first half of the century. Besides the ones in James Oswald's minuet-book of 1736, which were probably all original compositions, there are records of two by John McLachlan, two by Sir John Clerk of Penicuik, two by Charles McLean, and one by Lorenzo Bocchi, an Italian who worked briefly in Edinburgh in the 1720s. William McGibbon probably also wrote dance-minuets at this time; he certainly wrote a number of recital-minuets, including his *Minuet in A, with variations* (59).

Two minuets by Sir John Clerk of Penicuik, *c.*1720, in the composer's hand (Scottish Record Office GD18/4538; by kind permission of the Clerk family). Clerk was a landowner, advocate, Baron of Exchequer, and one of the signatories of the 1707 Treaty of Union.

None of these pieces, however, can have reached a very wide audience. It was not until the 1760s that a real impact was made on the public by a Scottish minuet composer: Thomas Erskine, Earl of Kelly.

Kelly was born at his family's country seat, Kellie Castle in Fife, in 1732. He was an excellent violinist, and was known locally in Fife by the nickname 'fiddler Tam', which suggests that he was keen on Scots-fiddle music in his youth. One of his first compositions seems to have been the dance-tune *Lord Kelly's Reel*. However, he conceived a passion for European art-music, and around 1752 went to Germany to study violin and composition with Johann Stamitz, the leading composer in the avant-garde Mannheim orchestral style. He returned to Scotland in 1756, and within a few years had established himself as the finest modern composer in the country. Bremner published his first set of symphonies in 1761, and issued several more later in the 1760s. Kelly also wrote at least 24 minuets at this time, including *Mrs Grant of Arndilly's minuet* **(63)**.

It was fortunate for Kelly that his working life coincided with the only boom period for music-publishing in Edinburgh's entire history. His minuets were written at exactly the right time. Six of them were included in Bremner's minuet-book and nine more in the later editions of Stewart's book, so putting 15 of Kelly's minuet tunes into fiddlers' hands almost the moment they were written.

Up and down the country, fiddlers were impressed. Lingering doubts which some of them had as to minuets being a foreign art-form, not to be mastered by Scottish composers, were dispelled overnight. Kelly was a hundred per cent Scottish, yet his minuets were first-class, and in the latest German style. Kelly also had connections with traditional music (*Lord Kelly's Reel* had been published by that time). Composing minuets suddenly became an acceptable thing for a fiddler to do, a natural complement to composing reels and strathspeys; even the prospect of handling European musical idioms well enough to write 16-bar tunes seemed less daunting than it had been.

The first fiddle-composer to follow in Kelly's steps was John Riddell. Riddell spent his whole life in Ayr, having gone blind in early childhood. He published a *Collection of Scots Reels and Minuets* around 1770; it contained 10 minuets, 27 reels, 23 jigs, 1 strathspey, 1 hornpipe and 2 slow airs, all of his own composition.

Daniel Dow brought out *Twenty Minuets and Sixteen Reels* shortly afterwards, in 1773. This collection also consisted entirely of original pieces, and included *Lady Jean Lindsay's minuet* **(62)**. Dow came from Perthshire, but moved to Edinburgh in the 1760s, where he played violin in the Musical Society's orchestra.

J. G. C. Schetky also wrote minuets at this time. Schetky was a German musician who came to Edinburgh in 1772 to become the Musical Society's principal cellist. He seems never to have written dance-music before he set foot in Edinburgh; however, he found that minuets were in demand and composed 12 of them, all dedicated to upper-class girls. *Miss Kinloch's minuet* **(64)** is one of these.

Robert Mackintosh, whom we met earlier as editor of the *McLean* collection, was another minuet composer. He was born in Perthshire around 1745, and moved to Edinburgh about 1770; like Dow and Schetky, he was a member of the Edinburgh Musical Society's orchestra. Mackintosh wrote at least 16 minuets, two of them published in Stewart's minuet-book, the others in Mackintosh's own *Airs, Minuets, Gavotts and Reels* (1783).

Many more minuets of probable Scottish provenance appear anonymously in music-books of the 1780-1800 period (e.g. the Trotter and Sharpe MSS., Campbell's *Newest and Best Minuets and Reels,* and Clarkson's *Collection of much admired Tunes).* Kelly, Riddell, Dow, Schetky and Mackintosh were clearly only the leading figures in a general trend; many lesser composers must also have tried their hands at minuets at this time.

Minuets made from traditional tunes

A different, but equally Scottish, kind of minuet seems to have evolved during the 1760s: fiddlers began to make minuets out of traditional Scots tunes.

It is not clear how extensive this practice was. Creating new minuets of this sort would not have been difficult for fiddlers with a quick ear, and they would have seemed too home-made for anyone to think of marketing them commercially; so the fact that no minuets of this kind were ever published is no guide to how many there were in circulation. The surviving records of them in fact run to only three texts, all in the Gillespie manuscript (Perth, 1768): *Miss Carmichael's minuet* **(60),** based on the fiddle-tune *Galway's Lament; Miss Faw's minuet* **(61),** based on the fiddle-tune *She's sweetest when she's naked;* and *Mary Scott,* based on the song *Mary Scott, the flower of Yarrow.*

None of these minuets is vastly different from its 'parent' tune. Out of the three, two have been re-named and one has kept its original title; two have been slightly speeded up and one slightly slowed down. No basic changes have been made to rhythms, however, as the original tunes were all in 3/4 time already.

It is likely that these minuets arose as improvisations during dances. Fiddlers in the 1760s must often have been caught out by unexpected demands for minuets from the dance-floor; knowing roughly what a minuet sounded like, but not knowing any of the proper tunes, they would have hastily racked their brains for something suitable, adjusted its tempo, altered its bowing so as to put the accents and lifts in the right places, and pressed it into service. Successful efforts of this kind could then have been re-used and passed on to other fiddlers.

Three other aspects of minuets deserve discussion here: instrumentation, the use of flat keys, and dedications.

Instrumentation

Minuets, as far as their musical style was concerned, were an offshoot of European art-music. They did their best to follow European styles of orchestration, among other things: so that Kelly's *Mrs Grant of Arndilly's minuet* **(63),** for example, was written for a small orchestra of 1st and 2nd violins, cellos, and pairs of clarinets and horns. Indeed, the minuet is in Kelly's finest symphonic style, and might well have been added to his Symphony in E flat of 1767 as an extra movement. (The symphony is scored for the same size of orchestra plus violas, two flutes, and a bassoon.)

In Scotland, however, only the most lavish balls could afford such a large band; even the aristocracy often used only a single fiddler for private dances in their homes. In any case, Kelly was almost the only Scottish composer with the technical skill to handle a large band.

From an orchestration point of view, then, Scottish minuets can be divided into four categories, as shown in Table IV:

Table IV

INSTRUMENTATION OF MINUETS

1.	Chamber orchestra	Fiddles in 2 parts, cellos, wind, horns
2.	Accomplished fiddle band	Fiddles in 2 parts, cello
3.	Run-of-the-mill fiddle band	Unison fiddles, cello
4.	Single fiddler	1 fiddle

Which category a composer wrote for depended partly on the musical resources available, partly on his own skill. Kelly wrote mainly for categories 1 and 2; Schetky for category 2; Riddell and Mackintosh for categories 2 and 3; Dow for category 3. The minuets made from traditional tunes come into category 4.

Minuets tended to descend in the scale once they began to circulate. Publishers liked to reduce minuets to category 3, as this format was attractive to amateur harpsichordists — the player taking the violin line in his right hand, the cello in his left — and increased a collection's sales. Local fiddlers helped this trend. No village fiddler would have been put off Kelly's minuets just because clarinettists, horn players, and fiddlers able to play 2nd-violin parts were in short supply in the district. He would simply have played the 1st violin part as a solo, and left the dancers to imagine the rest of the score. In this way a minuet which started out with the same instrumentation as a classical symphony could end up with the same instrumentation as a traditional reel.

The three surviving texts of *Mrs Grant of Arndilly's minuet* **(63)**, as it happens, illustrate this reduction process rather neatly. In Kelly's *Fête Champêtre* collection the piece is given in full score (category 1); and this text also shows how it can be played on a harpsichord, using 1st violin and cello lines only (category 3). In Stewart's *Newest and Best Minuets* the parts for clarinets and horns are omitted and only the string parts given (category 2). The Brown manuscript has only a 1st violin part (category 4).

The Brown manuscript text is interesting in another way. Kelly's minuet appears in it on folio 11 — only two leaves away from folio 9 on which so many splendid scordatura pieces are written out (see page 109). Here Kelly's minuets seem to have met the most traditional types of fiddle piece on equal terms.

Flat keys

Most Scots fiddlers disliked keys with more than one flat. They preferred keys where all the fiddle's open strings could be used, and where all the stopped notes could be reached easily in 1st position. Though Scottish violin sonatas were sometimes more adventurous

Brown manuscript f.llv, containing 'Mrs Grant of Arndilly's minuet' [by Kelly] **(63)**, 'Miss Stewart's minuet' [by Filtz], 'Miss Grant's minuet' [by Dow], and 'The Capillaire minuet' [by Kelly] (National Library of Scotland). Filtz was not a Scottish composer, but lived in Mannheim in Germany; several of his minuets were given spurious local titles by Edinburgh publishers.

than this — McGibbon's Sonata no. 5 (1740 set), for example, being in C minor, with a slow movement in A flat major — traditional fiddle pieces stuck to the easy keys of A, C, D, F, G, A minor, B minor, D minor and E minor.

There are occasional traditional tunes such as *When she cam ben, she bobbit* **(15, 20)**, *Johnnie Cope* **(38)**, and *Greensleeves* **(84)** which seem to be an exception to this, since they are in G minor and should properly be written in two flats. However, the 6th degree of the scale is often sharpened in such tunes, changing many E flats to E naturals and allowing the open E string to be used. These pieces also do their best to avoid the most awkward progression in the two-flat scale, the juxtaposition of E flat on the A string (close 4th finger) with F on the E string (backward-extended 1st finger).

So one can imagine fiddlers' horror when they discovered that at least half of Kelly's minuets were in E flat major: a key-signature of three flats.

E flat major was a new, fashionable key in Germany in the 1750s and 60s. Composers of symphonies liked it especially, as it was an ideal key in which to combine clarinets, horns and bassoons — instruments central to the new Mannheim orchestral style. B flat major was the second favourite key. Both keys did novel things to the violin: they reduced the number of open-string notes and often forced the fingering into higher positions, giving the instrument a veiled, suggestive quality quite different from its usual bright ring. Orchestral pieces in E flat, also, frequently opened with violin-chords containing the open G string as the third (such as or), and this effect too was completely new. Mozart's Symphony no. 39 has one of these characteristic E flat openings, and so do Kelly's *Mrs Grant of Arndilly's minuet* and Schetky's *Miss Kinloch's minuet*.

In their choice of key, then, Kelly's minuets were simply following German fashions; out of his series of 24, twelve are in E flat and two in B flat. Kelly must have realised that Scots fiddlers would not take kindly to this, and the prospect probably amused him, for he was not dependent on his compositions for a living. Fiddlers, however, rose to the challenge. They must have done, for the composers who wrote minuets immediately after Kelly used flat keys too. Seven of Dow's minuets are in E flat and one in B flat (out of 20); three of Schetky's are in E flat and three in B flat (out of 12); and three of Mackintosh's are in E flat, six in B flat, and two in F with middle sections in F minor (out of 16).

After that, surprisingly, flat keys began to catch on in traditional types of fiddle music. In 1772 Mackintosh published two variation sonatas in flat keys: *The Braes of Ballenden*, in B flat, and *Jockie was the blythest lad*, in C minor. Reels and strathspeys in flat keys appeared shortly afterwards, in Campbell's collection (*c.*1780), Marshall's (1781), and Gow's (1784). Two examples of such pieces are Nathaniel Gow's *Earl of Dalhousie's reel* **(74)**, in E flat, and Mackintosh's *Mrs Fordyce of Ayton's strathspey* **(81)**, in B flat.

In the long run it was William Marshall who used flat keys most fruitfully. His *Scottish Airs* (1822) is sectionalised according to key, and the B flat and E flat sections are both substantial. Many fiddlers complained to Marshall of the difficulty of these pieces. Marshall replied tartly that 'all the tunes *could* be played, and that those performers must learn to play better, as he did not write for bunglers'.

Scots-fiddle pieces in flat keys have continued to the present day, Hardie's *Caledonian Companion* (1981) even containing a special chapter on them. All this development stems indirectly from Kelly's minuets in the 1760s.

Dedications

It was normal practice in Scotland for minuets to be dedicated to patrons, the titles of the pieces taking the form '. . .'s Minuet' (insert patron's name). Most dedicatees were upper-class girls in their late teens or early twenties. A few minuets were also dedicated to men, and a few to corporate bodies. (Kelly's *Capillaire Minuet*, written for the Capillaire Club in Edinburgh, is one example of a corporate dedication.) The practice was useful to composers for basic financial reasons.

L

The first result of writing a minuet for an upper-class girl was that her family would feel obliged to buy multiple copies of the composer's forthcoming music collection, in which the piece would be published. For example, the 20 minuets in Dow's 1773 collection all have dedications – 18 to girls, 1 to a married lady, 1 to a gentleman – and each dedicatee, or their relatives, may well have subscribed for three copies. The resulting 60 advance orders would have covered the book's entire printing costs.

After that there could be valuable spin-offs. The girl's mother might invite the composer to become music tutor at the family's country estate for the summer. Her father might engage the composer's dance-band to play at a row of hunt balls, of which he happened to be the convener.

Scottish composers seem to have been business-like about dedications. Dow evidently wrote his minuets first and selected the patrons afterwards, for two of the pieces in his 1773 book – *Miss Babie Gray's minuet* and *Lady Jean Lindsay's minuet* **(62)** – are given earlier in the Gillespie manuscript (1768) simply as 'A New Minuet'. Schetky and Mackintosh probably worked in the same way: there was a wide choice of patrons in Edinburgh. Riddell had less of a choice, as he lived in the provincial town of Ayr; all the same, his dedications show that he did some excellent self-promotion among the local Ayrshire gentry.

The practice also had a certain value for dedicatees, amounting to a kind of personal PR. A frequently-played minuet kept a girl's name before the public in the nicest possible way. Also, when a dedicatee married, minuets inscribed to her changed their names, so that Kelly's *Miss Jeanie Maxwell's minuet* (*c.* 1766) became *The Duchess of Gordon's minuet* from 1767 onwards, and Mackintosh's *Lady Sophia Hope's minuet* (*c.* 1771) became *Lady Binnie's minuet* from 1779. In both cases, the minuets informed the public of the suitable matches which the young ladies had made.

Dedications thus set up a kind of symbiotic relationship between composer and patron. Kelly's minuets, however, though they had titles of the usual sort, stood some distance back from this commercial junketing. Kelly was an aristocrat with a private income, and had no need to chase patrons; his minuets were written, instead, for his friends for fun.

His *Lady Anne Lindsay's minuet* and *Lady Margaret Lindsay's minuet* illustrate this well. The pieces were written *c.* 1768 for the Duke of Balcarres's daughters, then aged 17 and 15 respectively. The girls were Kelly's second cousins; they were also his neighbours, for the Balcarres estate was in Fife, only two miles from Kelly's own. Here composer and dedicatees were obviously social equals.

The practice of dedicating minuets was shortly afterwards extended wholesale to reels and strathspeys, with far-reaching consequences: see Chapter IX.

Minuet tunes went a considerable distance in the late 18th century towards being integrated into the Scots-fiddle tradition. This integration would probably have proceeded further, had the dance itself not suddenly gone out of fashion around 1790. After the French Revolution, dancers lost interest in it all over Europe. Minuets continued to be performed in Scotland only until 1800 or so, and by 1810 they had disappeared from the scene for ever.

59. Minuet in A, with variations

WILLIAM McGIBBON (*c.* 1695-1756)

repeat accompaniment
for strains 3-4, 5-6

60. Miss Carmichael's minuet

61. Miss Faw's minuet/
She's sweetest when she's naked

62. Lady Jean Lindsay's minuet

DANIEL DOW (1732-83)

63. Mrs Grant of Arndilly's/
General Burgoine's minuet

THOMAS ALEXANDER ERSKINE,
sixth EARL of KELLY (1732-81)

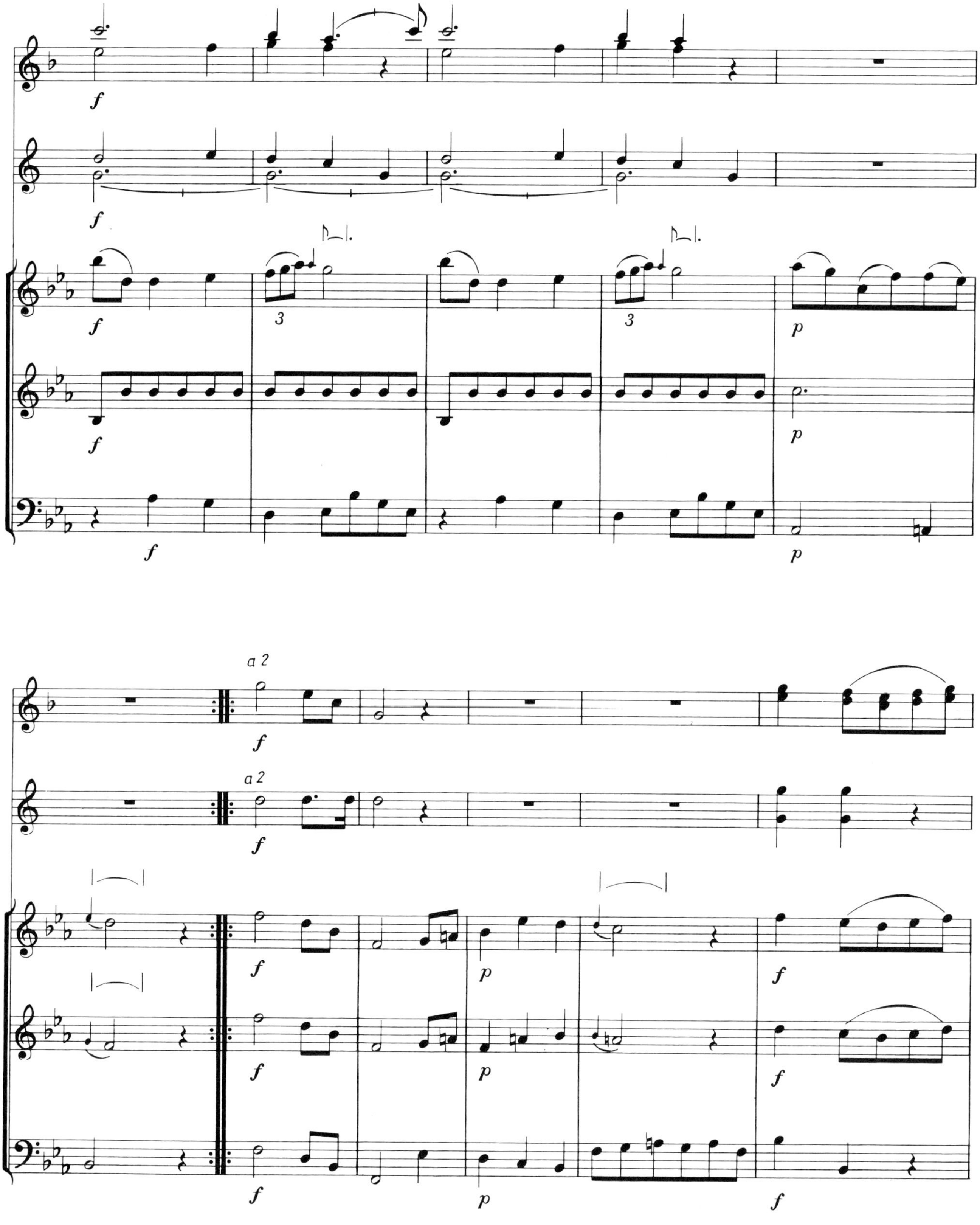

a 2
a 2
f
p
3

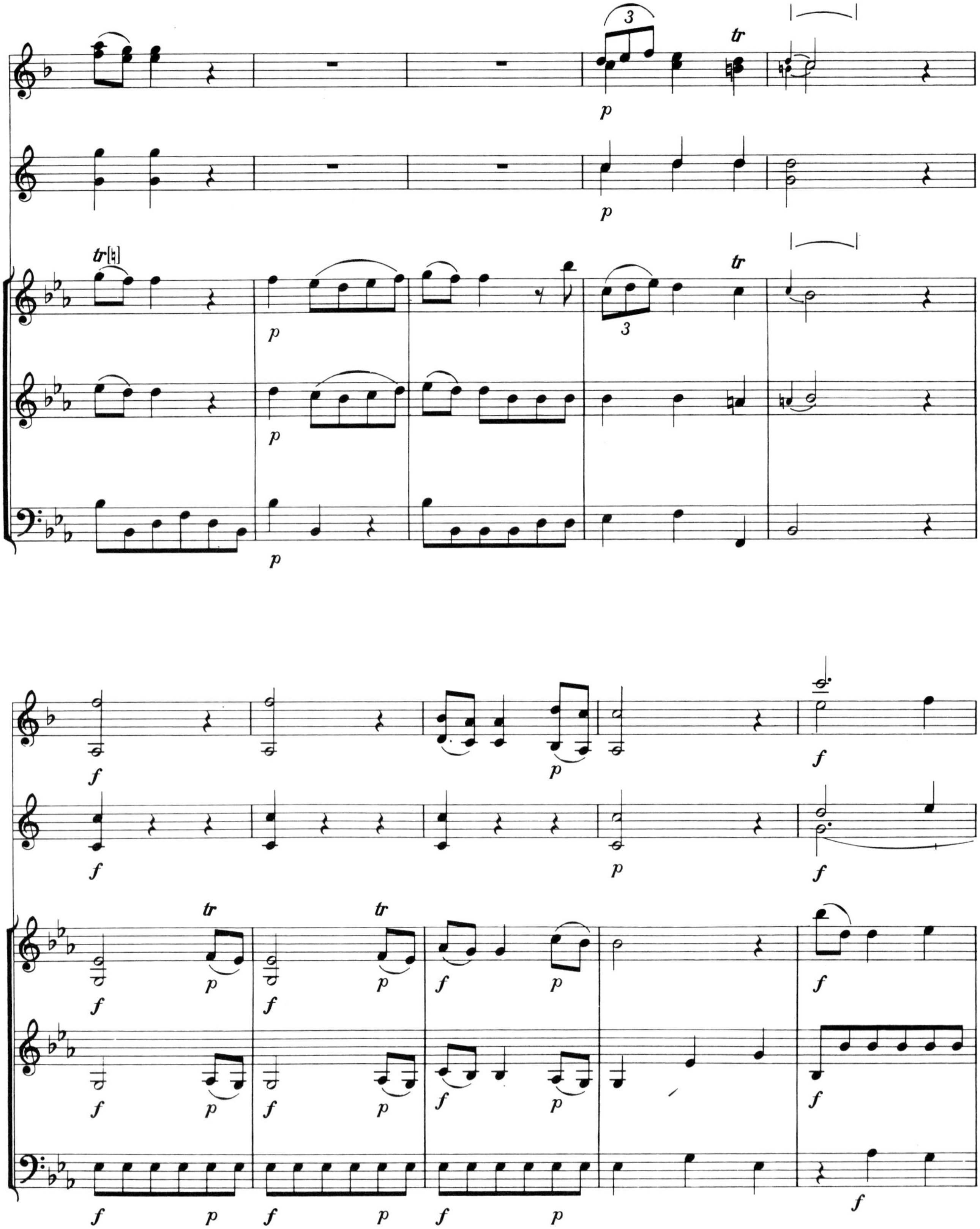
3
tr
p
tr[♮]
p
f

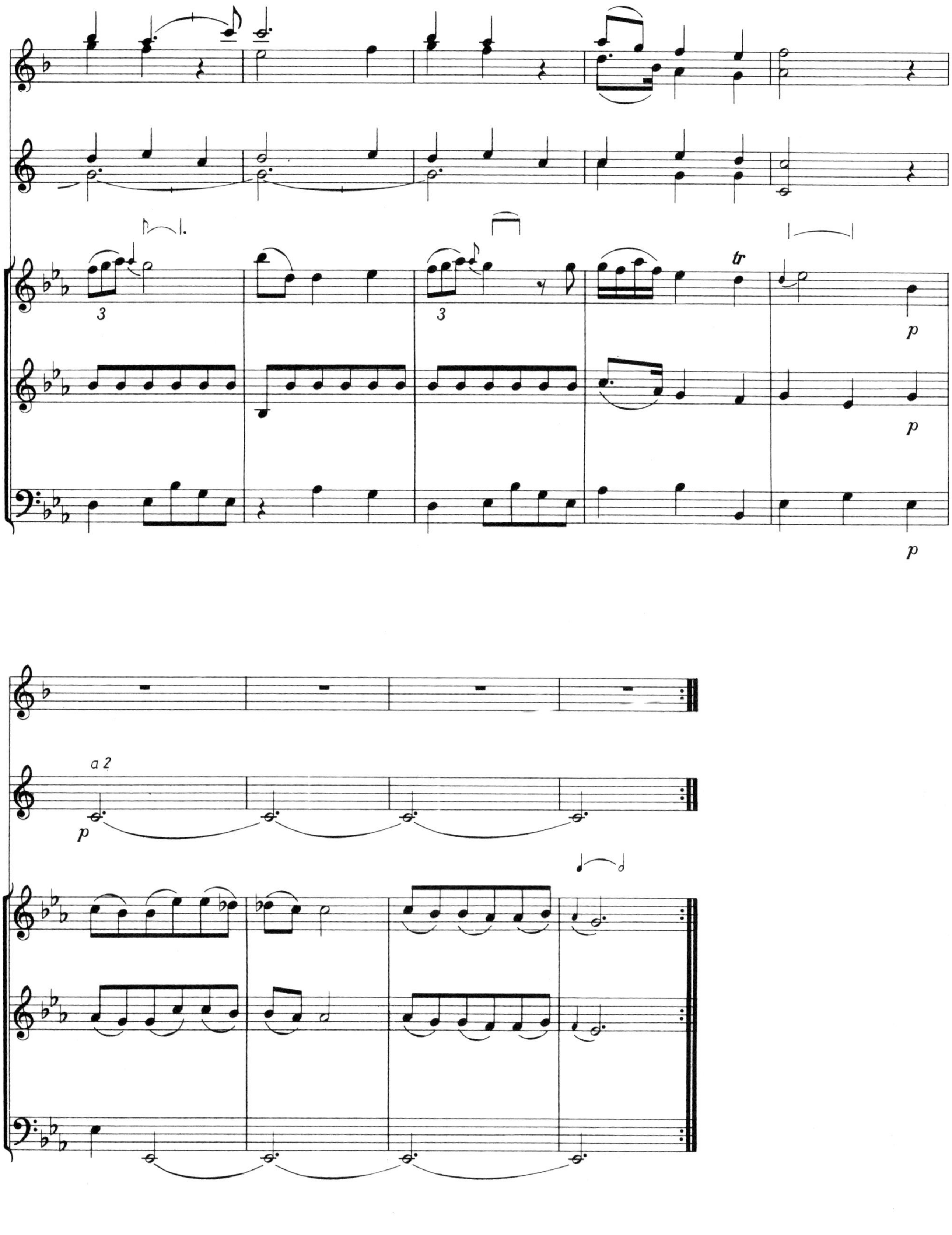
3
tr
p
a 2

64. Miss Kinloch's minuet

JOHANN GEORG CHRISTOPH SCHETKY
(1737-1824)

NOTES ON THE MUSIC

59 *Minuet in A, with variations*
Source: McFarlane MS., vol.iii no.125. Bass from Stewart's *Marches and Airs*, p.81.
This is one of three recital-minuets with variations which McGibbon composed in the late 1730s.
Revisions: title editorial; source has 'Minuet by McGibbon'
   rhythms of strain 3 bar 8b, strain 4 bar 8a, strain 5 bar 8b, and strain 6 bar 8a as Stewart
   strain 5 bar 2, bowing as Stewart
   strain 6 bar 7 notes 1–4 as Stewart; source has semiquavers.

60 *Miss Carmichael's minuet*
Source: Gillespie MS., p.75.
This minuet was evidently created from an earlier pentatonic fiddle piece, *Galway's Lament* (Sinkler MS., p.10, McFarlane MS., vol.ii no.247). The original tune went somewhat slower.
Revisions: key-signature originally four sharps (but the spacing in the source shows this was a mistaken afterthought on the copyist's part; cf. nos. **36** and **70**)
   strain 1 bar 8 note 1 orig *g'*
   strain 2 bars 3 and 5: the triplets are probably a trendy-looking notation for ♪♪♩ rhythms.

61 *Miss Faw's minuet/ She's sweetest when she's naked*
Source: Gillespie MS., p.84.
This minuet, like no. **60**, was made from an earlier pentatonic piece, *She's sweetest when she's naked* (Oswald's *Curious Collection*, p.35). The original version went slightly faster.
Revisions: strain 1 bar 8 and strain 2 bar 16 as Oswald; the source has:

in both places, which is an unmusical reading and would also have been impossible to dance to, since minuet-steps worked in 2-bar units
   strain 2 bar 5: bar orig written out twice.

62 *Lady Jean Lindsay's minuet*
Source: Gillespie MS., p.88 ('A New Minuet'). Title and ascription from Dow's *Twenty Minuets and Sixteen Reels*, p.1.
Dow's printed version has a rather ungrammatical bass line, which is omitted in the source; but most 18th-century performances were probably given with solo fiddle in any case.
Revisions: bracketed trills from Dow
   strain 2 bar 8b orig *f'* (dotted crotchet) *b♭' a' g'* (quavers).

63 *Mrs Grant of Arndilly's/General Burgoine's minuet*
Source: *Fête Champêtre*, p.10 ('General Burgoine's Minuet'). Alternative title from Stewart's *Newest and Best Minuets*, p.60; Brown MS., f.11v.
Kelly dedicated this minuet to two different people: *(a)* c.1767, to Mrs Grant, châtelaine of Arndilly House on the River Findhorn in the north of Scotland; *(b)* in 1774, to John Burgoine, the illustrious English army general. Burgoine was one of the principal guests at Lord Stanley and Lady Betty Hamilton's wedding in Surrey in 1774. Kelly had been asked to write a set of

new minuets for the occasion, dedicated to the bride and bridegroom and various guests; but he was thoroughly bored with minuets by that time, and ended up re-vamping and re-titling a lot of old ones and hoping no one would notice the difference (see Johnson, 'The Earl of Kelly's minuets'). Burgoine, incidentally, was the general who led the British army to its crucial defeat in the American War of Independence in 1776.

Revisions: dynamics orig in the 1st-violin part only

some slurs, and discrepancies between ♪♩ and ♩.♩ groups, standardised.

64 *Miss Kinloch's minuet*

Source: Stewart's *Newest and Best Minuets,* p.82.

Schetky wrote this minuet soon after his arrival in Edinburgh in 1772. Despite its brevity, it has the poise and elegance of his finest chamber music.

Revisions: Stewart printed only top and bottom lines, since amateur keyboard-players could not have coped with the full score. I have supplied an editorial 2nd-violin part on the assumption that the original scoring was similar to that of Kelly's and Mackintosh's minuets

strain 2 bar 3 vln 1 dynamic orig *f*

strain 2 bar 9 vln 1 grace-notes editorial (cf. strain 1 bar 1).

CHAPTER VII

Variation Sonatas

THE variation sonata arose as an adjunct to the 'Scots drawing room' style, which we have already discussed in Chapter II. It was invented, as was the drawing-room style itself, by a small group of Edinburgh composers in the 1730s. It was an extremely short-lived form: the first developed examples appeared in Munro's collection of 1732, others were written shortly afterwards by McLean, Oswald, and McGibbon, and by 1742 the best work in the genre had already been done. Several variation sonatas of this period did, however, continue in fiddlers' repertories until the end of the century.

Thirty years later Robert Mackintosh attempted to revive the form, and wrote several variation sonatas which were published in the *McLean* collection of 1772. These have many good features. However, Mackintosh ran into a number of problems with these pieces, and he did not inspire any other composers to follow in his steps.

The variation sonata can be regarded, then, as having two creative periods, respectively from 1732 to 1742 and around 1770. The four pieces presented in this chapter were all written within these narrow time-bands. *Bonny Jean of Aberdeen* (65) comes from Munro's 1732 collection, and *Twas within a furlong of Edinburgh town* (66) from the McFarlane manuscript of 1740. *Pinkie House* (68) is also in the McFarlane manuscript, though the set presented here is the one given in the 1772 *McLean* collection with emendations by Mackintosh. The *Lea rig* sonata (67) comes from a book published late in the century, Riddell's *Scotch, Galwegian and Border Tunes* of 1794; however, there is another set of it in the McFarlane manuscript, showing that it too basically dates from the 1730s.

It is probable that variation sonatas circulated aurally to a certain extent, since they are not difficult to memorise and do not depend very heavily upon their harpsichord and cello accompaniments, which could therefore have been discarded without great damage to the music. No accompaniment has survived, for example, to *The lea rig* (67), and it seems complete and satisfying without one. *Bonny Jean of Aberdeen* (65) also works well played unaccompanied. It has not been possible so far, however, to prove that variation sonatas were transmitted by ear.

Formal structures

Formally speaking, the variation sonata consisted — like the long variation set and the fiddle pibroch — of a set of variations based on a popular tune. However, it was unlike the long variation set in that the variations were not continuous but divided into sections, each with its own character and speed. Fiddle pibrochs were also divided into sections like this; but where the different sections of a pibroch are abstract music, related only to similar sections of other pibrochs, the sections of a variation sonata are based on pre-existing dance-forms.

The roots of the variation sonata lie in the Scottish flair — which we have already noticed — for turning song-tunes into dance-tunes and vice versa. Many Scots tunes could be played on the fiddle in different ways, for example as decorated slow airs, as jigs, or as reels. Variation sonatas begin to emerge when players, instead of regarding these as *alternative* ways of performing a tune, start tacking the different versions together to form *ad hoc* suites.

This tacking-together process was known in the late 17th century. The Leyden lyra-viol manuscript (*c.*1695), for instance, contains two settings for gamba of *I wish I were where Helen lies* (2), the first a decorated slow air ('Where Hellen lays'), the second a jig ('the dance of it'). These two settings occur consecutively in the manuscript, and were probably intended to be played one after the other, making up a short suite in 'air-jig' form.

By the 1720s, certainly, air-jig suites for fiddle were fairly common: the 'air' section usually had its own decorative variations while the 'jig' section re-stated the tune at the end in a new rhythm. Adam Craig composed at least one setting of this kind (McFarlane MS., vol.ii no.13) and Forbes of Disblair wrote at least seven (e.g. nos. **26** and **27**). Later, James Oswald made many more air-jig settings for inclusion in his *Caledonian Pocket Companion*. None of these pieces, however, quite counts as a fully-fledged variation sonata; they have more the effect of long variation sets with unexpected endings in 6/8 time.

Scottish composers could well have developed such suites further with purely native materials, and extended their forms to — say — air-hornpipe-jig, air-jig-reel, or air-hornpipe-strathspey-jig-reel. But no one seems to have considered these possibilities except, rather marginally, Oswald, who made an isolated air-jig-reel setting of the tune *O dear Minny (Caledonian Pocket Companion*, vol.iii). Instead, the form was extended by having elements of the Italian *sonata da camera* injected into it. This idea was the brainchild of Alexander Munro.

Munro is one of the mystery figures of Scottish musical history. Nothing at all is known about his life, and nothing about his compositions apart from the twelve works in his *Collection of Scots Tunes* of 1732. This book, oddly, was printed in Paris, though Hawkins states that Munro was a native of Scotland. On the internal evidence of the 1732 collection, Munro was a man of enormous talent and vision, whose composition technique sometimes failed him at crucial moments, and was probably a well-to-do amateur musician rather than a struggling professional.

It is tempting to identify him with Alexander Monro *primus* (1697–1767), first professor of anatomy at Edinburgh University. Professor Monro had many Parisian connections, for Paris was a world-famous centre for surgery: this would explain the composer's choice of a French printer. Furthermore, Monro had a musical training in his youth (see Erlam). But this identification is only conjectural at present.

Munro's idea of crossing the Scottish air-jig form with the Italian *sonata da camera* form was simple but daring. *Da camera* sonatas typically consisted of a substantial first movement ('Preludio') followed by a string of dances such as Sarabanda, Corrente, Allemanda, Gavotta, and Minuetto, and ending with a Giga in 6/8 or 12/8 time. Short linking movements were sometimes added between the dances. The most famous *da camera* violin sonatas of the time were Corelli's, op.V nos. 7–10; their ground-plans are shown below in Table V (dance movements given in italics):

Table V

ITALIAN DANCE-FORMS IN CORELLI'S OP.V VIOLIN SONATAS

 7. Preludio — *Corrente* — *Sarabanda* — *Giga*
 8. Preludio — *Allemanda* — *Sarabanda* — *Giga*
 9. Preludio — *Giga* — Adagio — *Tempo di Gavotta*
10. Preludio — *Allemanda* — *Sarabanda* — *Gavotta* — *Giga*

There were slight correspondences between this form and that of the Scottish air-jig suite, for the opening Preludio could be regarded as equivalent to the air, and the concluding Giga as equivalent to the jig. (*Giga* and *jig* are actually cognate words; both dances were fast, lively ones in triple time.) It was true that in *da camera* sonatas the tunes were nearly always newly composed ones, and the different movements of the piece not thematically connected, while in air-jig suites the whole work was based on a single, pre-existing tune. But there was no particular difficulty about writing a *da camera* sonata as a connected set of variations on a traditional tune, and that was what Munro did. His pieces can therefore be taken either as Italian sonatas with their movements recast as variations on Scots tunes, or as Scottish air-jig suites with extra Italian-style dances added midway.

Table VI shows the ground-plans of Munro's four longest variation sonatas. Their similarity to Corelli's sonatas in Table V should be fairly obvious:

Table VI

ITALIAN DANCE-FORMS IN MUNRO'S VARIATION SONATAS

Bonny Jean of Aberdeen
[Air] – [*Sarabanda*] – [*Corrente*] – *Tempo di Gavotta* – *Giga*

Sour plums of Galashiels
[Air] – [*Allemanda*] – Largo – *Giga*

Corn rigs
[Air] – *Minuetto* – [*Gavotta*] — [*Allemanda*] – [*Corrente*] – Adagio – *Giga*

Fy gar rub her o'er wi' strae
[Air] – Adagio – *Corrente* – *Gavotta* – *Minuetto*

Inspired though this idea was, Munro did not always put it into practice very well. His opening 'air' sections were often taken from earlier solo fiddle settings, so that his first task was to harmonise the basic melody. His technique was not always up to this. Some of his tunes were rash choices: the double-tonic sequences in *Bonny Christy,* for instance, landed him with insuperable harmonic problems. However, his re-building of the tunes as Italian dances was generally successful, and his sonatas often improve in the later sections as they move further away from the tunes and allow his own invention freer rein.

Bonny Jean of Aberdeen **(65)** is Munro's masterpiece. It contains many delightful surprises such as this passage, where a falling pentatonic scale (Scots) is combined with a fashionable syncopated rhythm (Italian):

Tempo di Gavotta

His *Fy gar rub her o'er wi' strae* sonata is also good, with an imaginative cello part which takes the instrument up to high A and gives it a role of equal importance to the violin's.

After Munro's pioneering work, Charles McLean's variation sonatas are somewhat of a disappointment. McLean scaled the form down to only three movements: air-minuet-jig. Within their limits, however, McLean's pieces are more assured than Munro's, for he was careful to choose tunes which would harmonise easily, and whose harmonisations would bear a lot of repetition. The opening airs of *Twas within a furlong* **(66)** and *Pinkie House* **(68)**, for example, both include interesting modulations which recur as strong features of the later movements.

William McGibbon's variation sonatas are perfunctory. His best ones are *I love my love in secret*, in air-minuet form *(Scots Tunes*, vol.i), and *John come kiss me now*, in an experimental air-jig-allegro form (McFarlane MS., vol.iii no.193).

James Oswald's variation sonatas, as already mentioned, are mostly of the basic air-jig type. However, his *Curious Collection of Scots Tunes* (*c.*1739) contains a novel 'Sonata of Scots Tunes' in five sections, Largo-Adagio-Andante-Largo-Andante, set for two violins and continuo. This is unlike Munro's sonatas in that it introduces a different Scots tune in each section, the tunes used thus totalling five: *O dear Mother, Ettrick Banks, She rose and let me in, Cromlet's Lilt* and *Polwarth on the Green*. The piece is nicely turned; its *Ettrick Banks* section, for instance, opens with the tune in the violin 1 part and a creditable contrapuntal imitation of it in the cello:

Adagio

However, it is a lightweight piece compared to the sonata constructed from a single tune — a mere pot-pourri of popular melodies which might come in handy as, say, an entr'acte in a theatre show. Oswald never wrote in this form again, and his piece had no known successors in Scotland.

Before we leave the 1730s, one or two anonymous variation sonatas should be briefly mentioned. All these appear in the McFarlane manuscript, without accompaniment. They are formally interesting, even though not completely successful artistically: *John Ochiltree*, air-gavotta-minuet-jig (vol.ii no.9); *The lass of Patie's mill*, air-jig-gavotta (vol.ii no.12); *Jockie was the bravest lad*, air-minuet-jig (vol.iii no.36); and *The lea rig*, air-allemanda-corrente-gavotta-giga-reel (vol.iii no.195). The last of them is the earliest known text of no. **67**.

We must now turn to Mackintosh's revival of the variation sonata in 1772. This seems to have been a single-handed effort on Mackintosh's part: Mackintosh admired the composers who had worked in Edinburgh a generation before, particularly McLean, and decided to publish a collection of their work, especially of their variation sonatas. He also wrote several new variation sonatas of his own for the collection, mostly following McLean's format of air-minuet-jig.

Mackintosh's editorial methods for the *McLean* collection have already been discussed in the Introduction. His aim was to update the variation-sonata form and make it suitable for the 1770s: he modernised the earlier composers' work considerably, and his own variation sonatas are full of up-to-date effects like flat keys, up-bow spiccato, and quavers phrased in 'sighing' pairs.

Pinkie House **(68)**, composed by McLean, revised by Mackintosh, illustrates Mackintosh's modernisations well. Mackintosh transposed the piece down from G to E flat and completely changed its phrasing, giving it a quite new expressive impact:

McLean, *c.*1738; G major

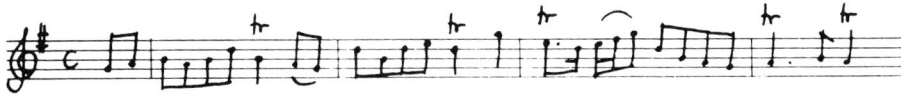

Mackintosh, 1772; E flat major

He also added one new movement of his own, strains 7–8. In this section the violin has an interesting tendency to get out of step harmonically with the accompaniment, as in the middle bar of this extract:

It sounds almost as if the fiddler had got a beat ahead of the other players; or as if the composer had had a temporary brainstorm. In fact, the un-coordinated harmony is a deliberate expressive device; the passage is exactly parallel to one in the slow movement of Haydn's F minor string quartet, op.20 no.5. Haydn's quartet was written in 1771, probably the same year that Mackintosh made his version of *Pinkie House*. So Mackintosh shows himself here as being on a level with very recent European ideas. (Note, too, the modern up-bow spiccato in the last bar of the extract.)

On its own terms, *Pinkie House* is an excellent piece. Unfortunately, however, it was modern only in its surface details; its underlying form — a large number of short movements, each with a separate character — was inescapably tied to European art music of an earlier period. By the 1770s the European mainstream had moved on, and Continental composers had begun to write sonatas with fewer but larger movements, each of which had its own built-in emotional contrasts and dramatic surprises. The dynamic use of tonality was already being explored; this was to lead to the great sonatas and symphonies of Beethoven. These developments could not possibly be reconciled with the rigid, four-square formal scheme of the variation sonata.

Mackintosh probably did not fully understand why the problem he had set himself, of modernising the variation sonata, was insoluble. But he responded to the situation by writing no more variation sonatas after 1772, and turned his attention to other types of music instead.

Alterations during transmission

It is probable that some fiddlers learned variation sonatas by ear. The texts that have come down to us have many 'aural' characteristics: composers' names are frequently lost between one written version and the next, bass lines are discarded and replaced by new ones, and strains are dropped out and other ones inserted. Interchanges were also possible between the variation-sonata and long-variation-set forms; composers seem quite often to have used a long variation set as a starting-point for writing a variation sonata and vice versa.

Once one compares texts it becomes clear that variation sonatas had fluid properties similar to those of long variation sets and fiddle pibrochs. The reader may find it interesting to look at the various texts of *Bonny Jean of Aberdeen* (65) and *The lea rig* (67).

There are six main texts of *Bonny Jean of Aberdeen*. *A* is from the Cuming manuscript of 1723 (p.62); *B* is from Munro's 1732 collection, and is the set edited here as no. 65; *C* is from the McFarlane manuscript of 1740 (vol.iii no.259); *D* is from a flute manuscript of *c.*1770 (NLS Adv.MS.5.2.20, f.59v); *E* is from the *McLean* collection of 1772 (p.8); and *F* is from the Little manuscript of *c.*1775 (p.73). Texts *A, C, D,* and *F* are unaccompanied; *B* and *E* have bass lines, but different ones.

Ground-plans of all six are given below in Table VII. Every square in the table represents one strain; they are numbered to correspond with the edited text of no. 65. (Strains a–b in text *D* do not feature in no. 65.)

It is fairly easy to work out the lines of transmission here. The fullest and best text is obviously *B*, the one made by Munro. All that the earlier *A* text shows is that Munro used

Table VII

TEXTS OF *BONNY JEAN OF ABERDEEN*

A	B	C	D	E	F
[C] 1 2 3 4	Allegro ¢ 1 2 3 4	C 1 2 3 4	Gratioso ¢ [sic] 1 2 ... a b	Slow C 1 2 3 4	Allegro ¢ 1 2 3 4
Gratioso ¾ [sic] 5 6 Vivace 3 7 8	¾ 5 6 7 8			Minuet ¾ 5 6 7 8	Gracioso ¾ [sic] 5 6 Vivace ¾ 7 8
Tempo di ¢ Gavotta 9 10 11 12	¢ 9 10 11 12	Tempo di Gavotta 11 12		Allegro ¢ 9 10 11 12	Tempo di ¢ Gavotta 9 10 11 12
Giga Allegro ¹²⁄₈ 13 14	¹²⁄₈ 13 14			Gigg ¹²⁄₈ 13 14	Giga Allegro ¹²⁄₈ 13 14

A (or something similar to it) as a starting-point for writing *B*. *C* and *F* are both copies of *B*, minus *B*'s bass line. *C* also discards *B*'s Italian headings, and runs strains 5–6 and 7–8 together into a single section. *E*, which was put together by Mackintosh, almost certainly derives from *C* rather than from *B*: it has different headings from *B* and a different bass line, and shares *C*'s concept of strains 5–8 as a single movement.

Text *D* is an oddity. It clearly derives — possibly at one or two removes — from *B*, since it has *B*'s 'Gratioso' and 'Tempo di Gavotta' headings even though they are attached to the sonata in the wrong places. But it has lost 10 of *B*'s 14 strains and acquired two new ones somewhere down the line.

The history of the *Lea rig* sonata is much more obscure. There are five main texts of this piece. *A* is from the McFarlane manuscript (vol.iii no.195); *B* is from Bremner's *Scots Reels* of c.1765 (p.76); *C* is from the Gillespie manuscript of 1768, and is the long variation set presented earlier as no. **37**; *D* is from the Sharpe manuscript of c.1790 (p.138); and *E*, from Riddell's 1794 collection, is the version edited as no. **67**. All five texts are unaccompanied apart from *B*. Their ground-plans are given overleaf.

The lines of transmission in Table VIII are by no means obvious. The simplest way to explain them is to assume that *The lea rig* was originally played on the fiddle in two different forms: as a song-tune with a short set of decorative variations (strains 1–4), and as a reel (strains 13–14). The song-tune version was extended into a long variation set, giving us text *C*, and the reel version was published, giving us text *B*. From this basis we can go on to account for texts *A* and *E*. During the 1730s, some enterprising composer such as Munro or McLean brought the song and reel versions together and wrote four new Italian-style sections to sandwich between them, so creating text *E*. Around 1740 a further composer, such as Young, took *E* and added strains a–d, e–f and g–h to it; he also

Table VIII

TEXTS OF *THE LEA RIG*

	A	B	C	D	E
Slow $\frac{3}{4}$	a, b, c, d				
Brisk ₵	1, 2, 3, 4		C 1, 2, 3, 4	C 1, 2, 3, 4	Andante ₵ 1, 2, 3, 4
	e, f				
Brisk $\frac{3}{4}$	5, 6, 7, 8		plus six further strains at the same speed, not related to any other strains in this table	Minuetto $\frac{3}{4}$ 5, 6, 7, 8	Largo $\frac{3}{4}$ 5, 6; Vivace $[\frac{3}{4}]$ 7, 8
Quick $\frac{2}{4}$	9, 10			Gavotta $\frac{2}{4}$ 9, 10	Tempo di $\frac{2}{4}$ Gavotta 9, 10
Fast $\frac{12}{8}$	11, 12			Giga $\frac{6}{8}$ 11, 12	Giga All° $\frac{12}{8}$ 11, 12
Very fast ₵	13, 14	₵ 13, 14			Presto ₵ 13, 14
	g, h				

translated *E*'s Italian titles into English and ran *E*'s strains 5–6 and 7–8 together into a single movement. The result was text *A*.

This is the simplest explanation. But it is not necessarily the correct one, and it does not fully account for text *D*. On the face of it *D* is a derivation from *E*, minus strains 13–14; except that *D* treats strains 5–8 as a single section, unlike *E* but like *A*. A further complication is caused by the fact that some of the texts (*A*, *B*, and *D*) are in standard tuning, others (*C* and *E*) in scordatura. This cuts right across the transmission lines suggested above.

The connections between these texts would probably become clearer if further versions of the piece were to turn up.

The textual changes described above can all be explained as alterations made deliberately by literate musicians. All the discards could have been made by lazy copyists who did not want the complete text, all the additions made by copyists who were creative individuals. However, this does not rule out the possibility that aural transmission also played a part in changing the texts; and indeed it is likely that other discards and additions were made aurally and that the results were not written down.

It is at any rate clear that variation sonatas were fluid in form, and subject to alteration over a period of time. This puts them into a quite different category from European art-music sonatas, for an art-music sonata is written entirely by one person and reaches a definitive state as soon as the composer decides that the piece is finished. Art-music sonatas by Scottish composers will be discussed in the next chapter.

65. Sonata on "Bonny Jean of Aberdeen"

ALEXANDER MUNRO (*fl.* 1732)

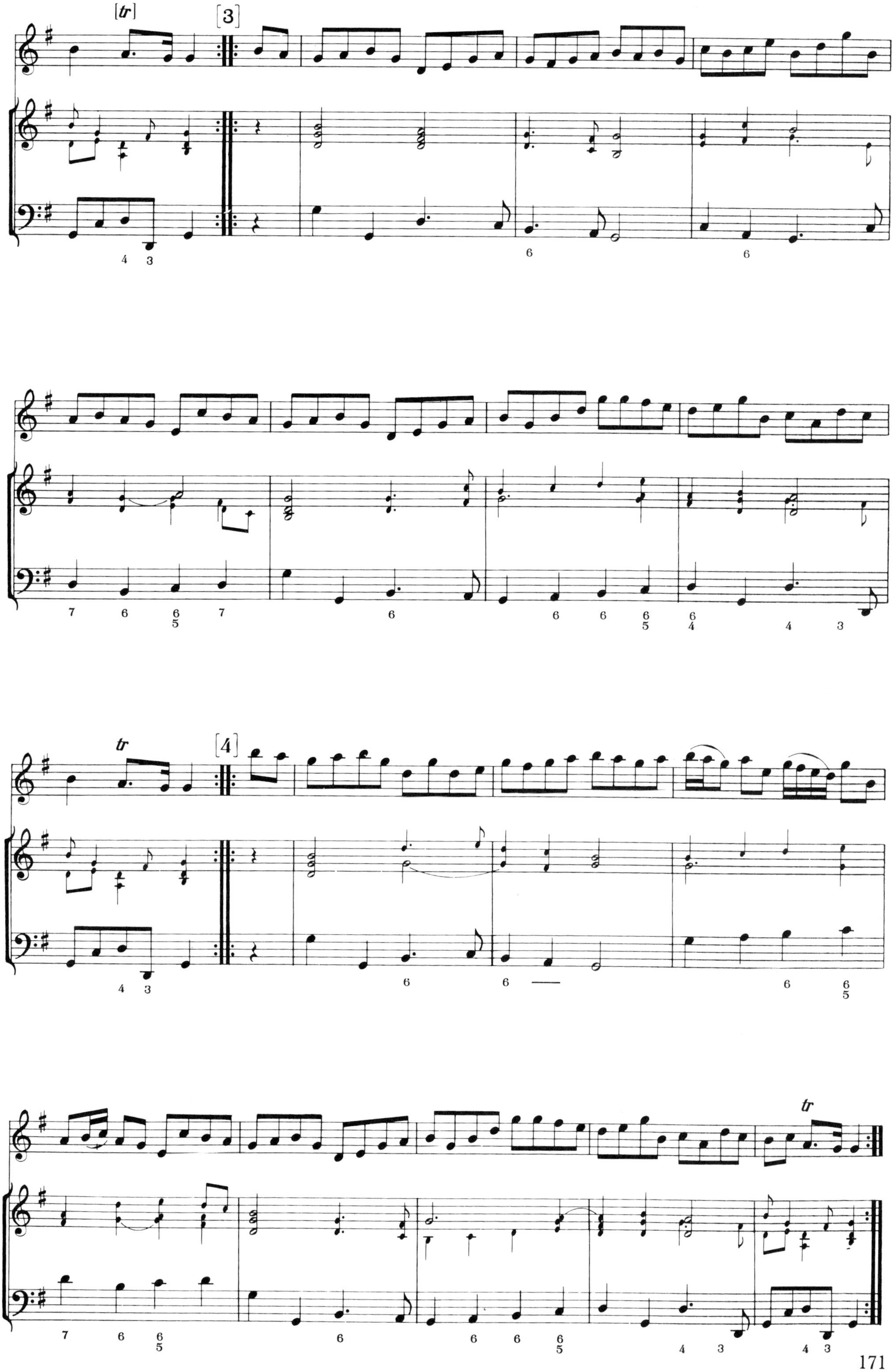
[tr]
[3]
tr
[4]
tr

[Sarabanda.] Grazioso

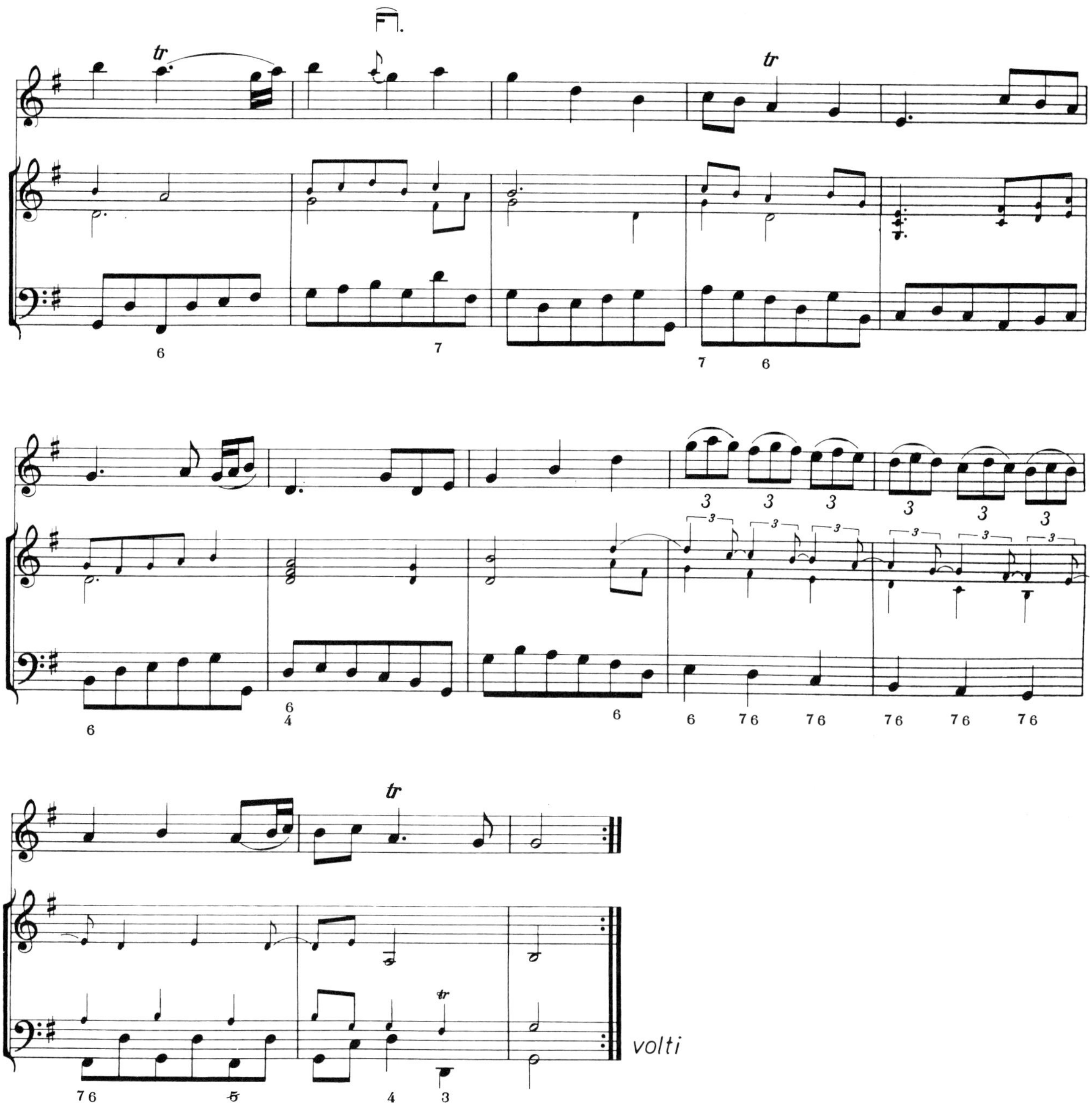
volti

174

volti

Tempo di Gavotta

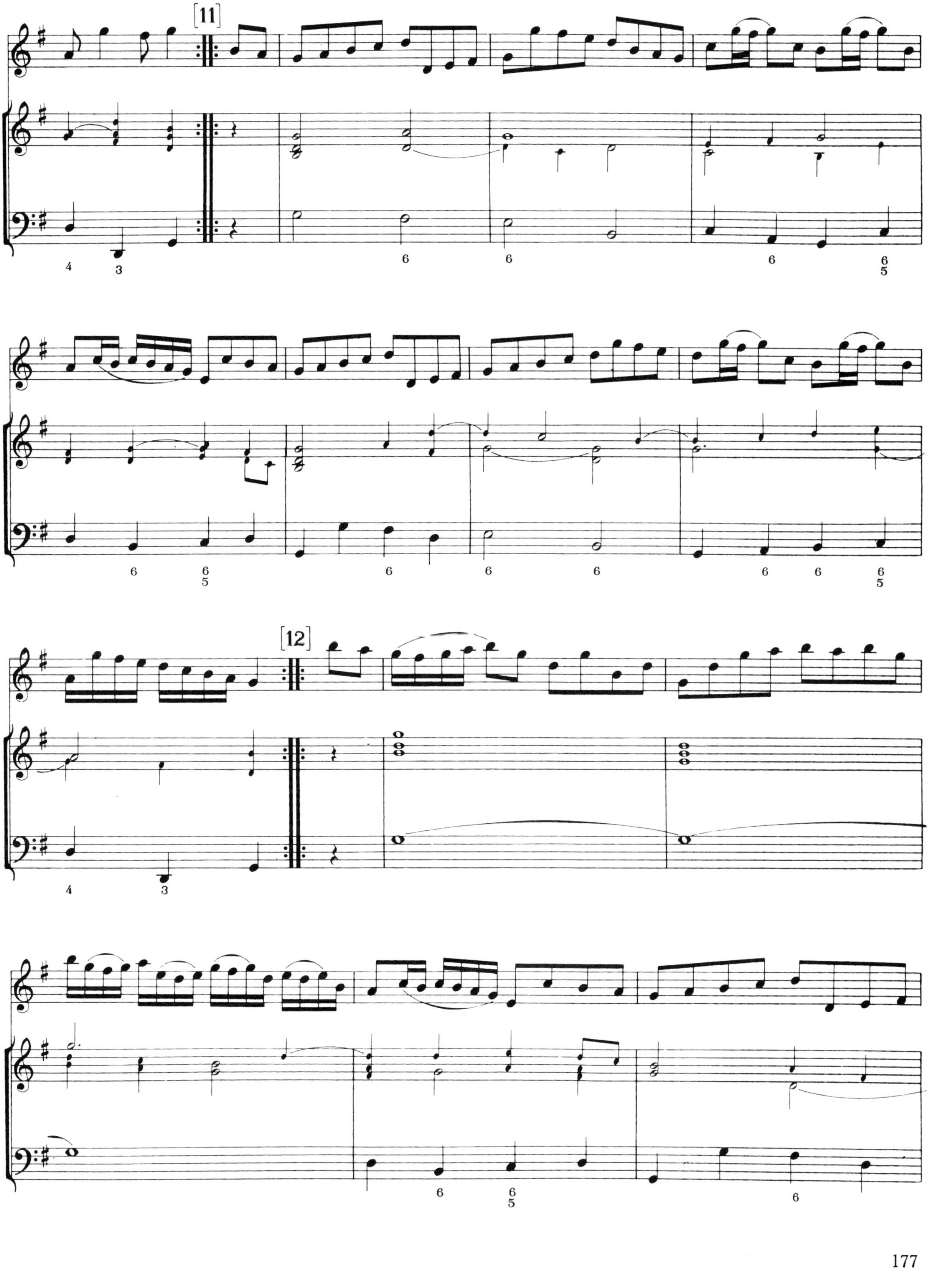
[11]
[12]

Giga. Allegro

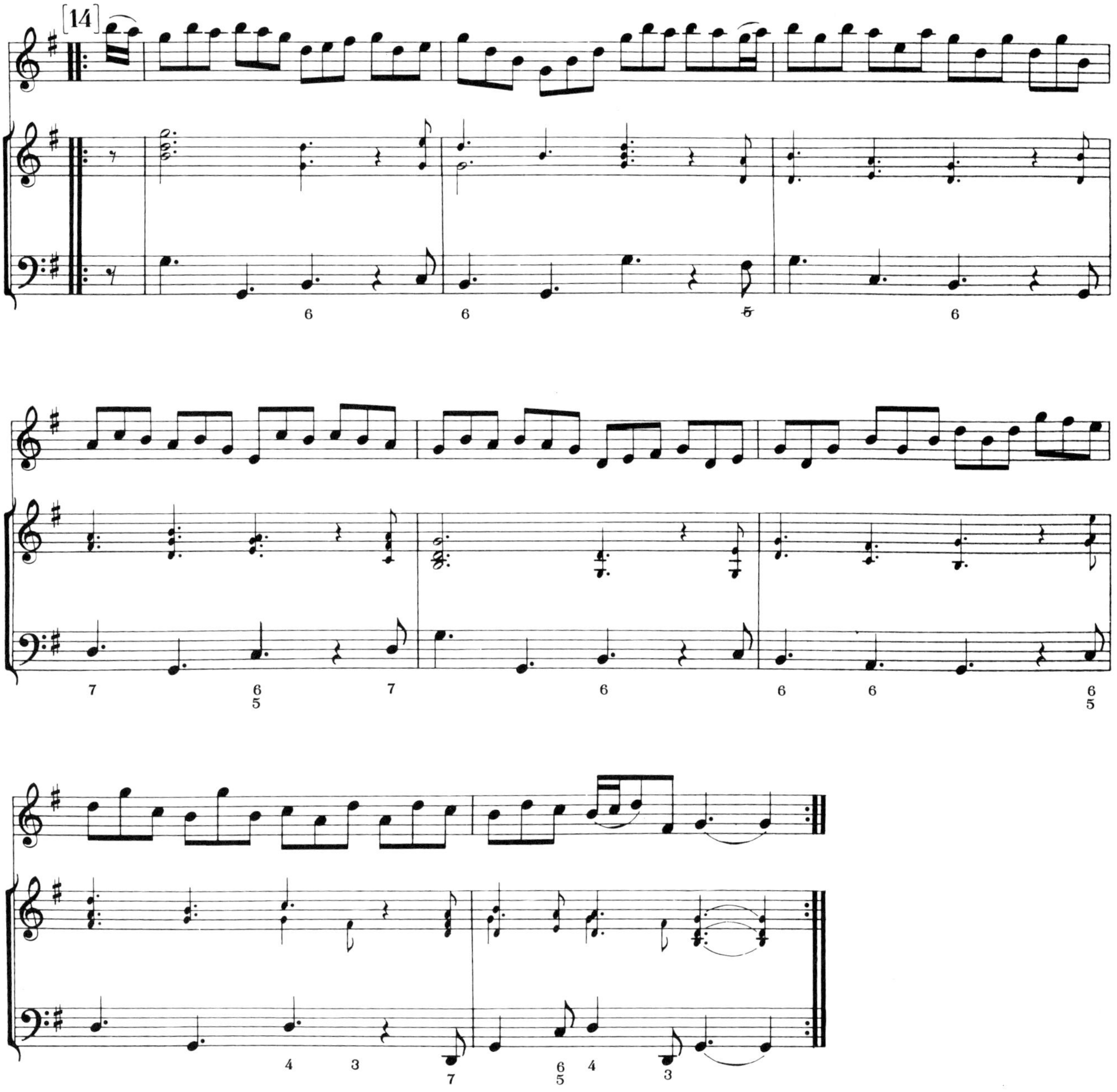
14

66. Sonata on "Twas within a furlong of Edinburgh town"

CHARLES McLEAN (*fl.* 1736-40)
after HENRY PURCELL (1659-95)

Minuet. [Allegro]

N

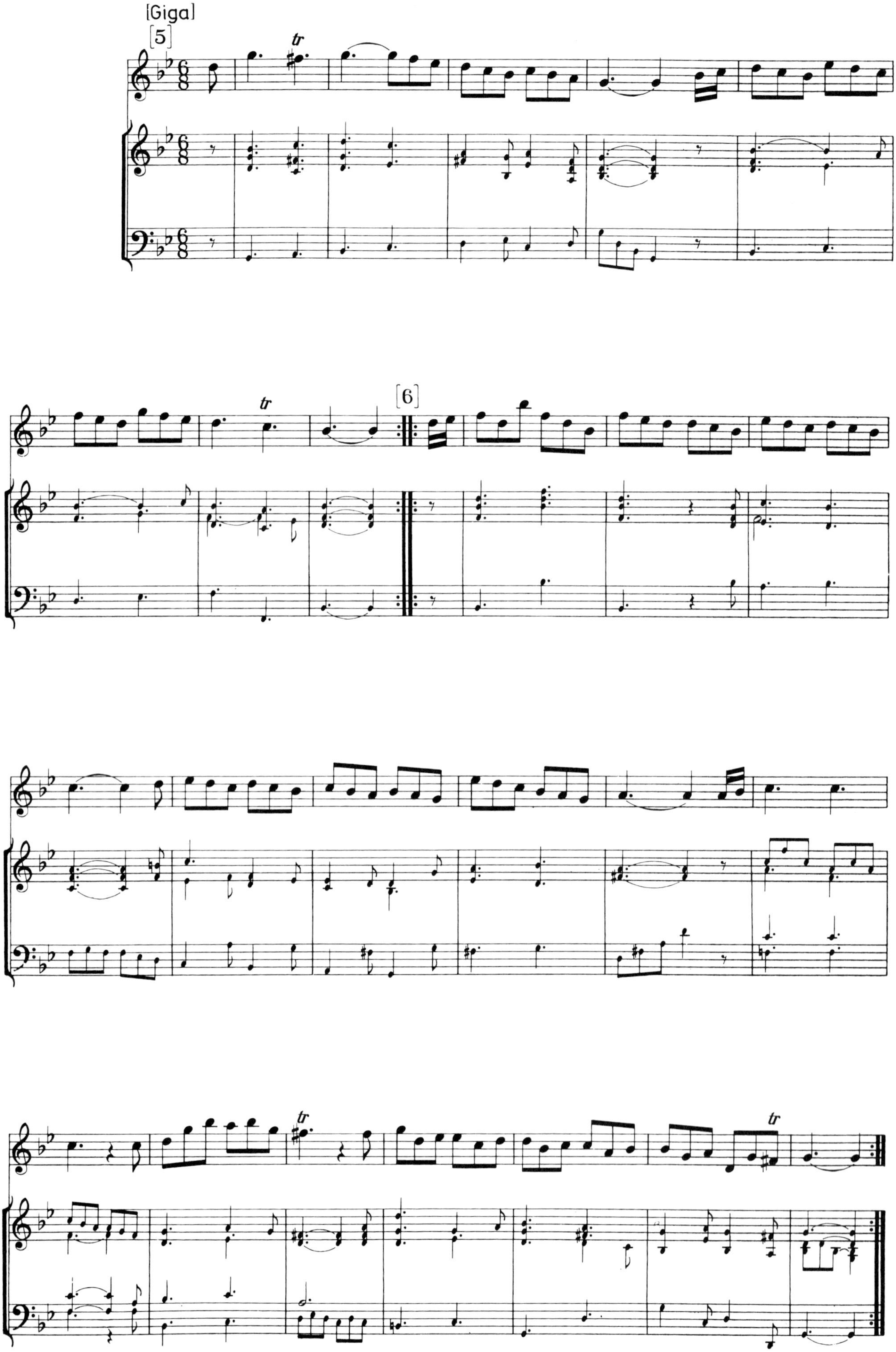
[Giga]
[5]
tr
[6]
tr
tr
tr

67. Sonata on "The lea rig"

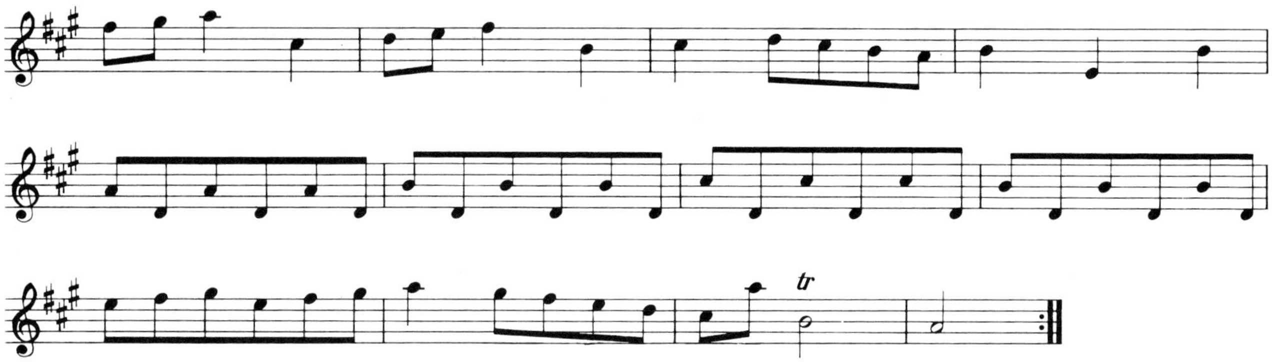

Tempo di Gavotta

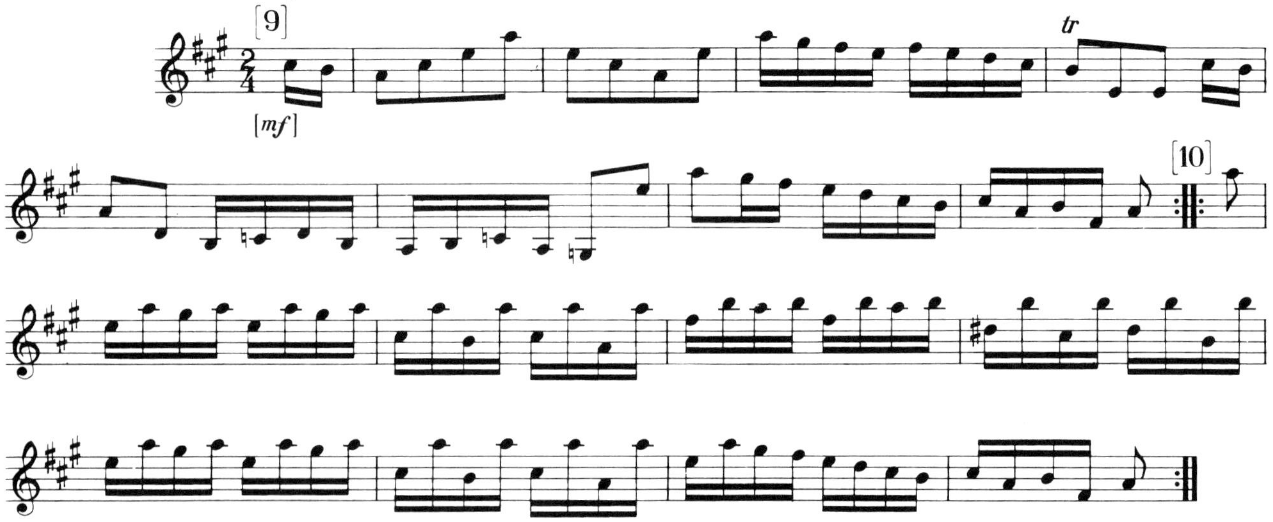

Giga. Allegro

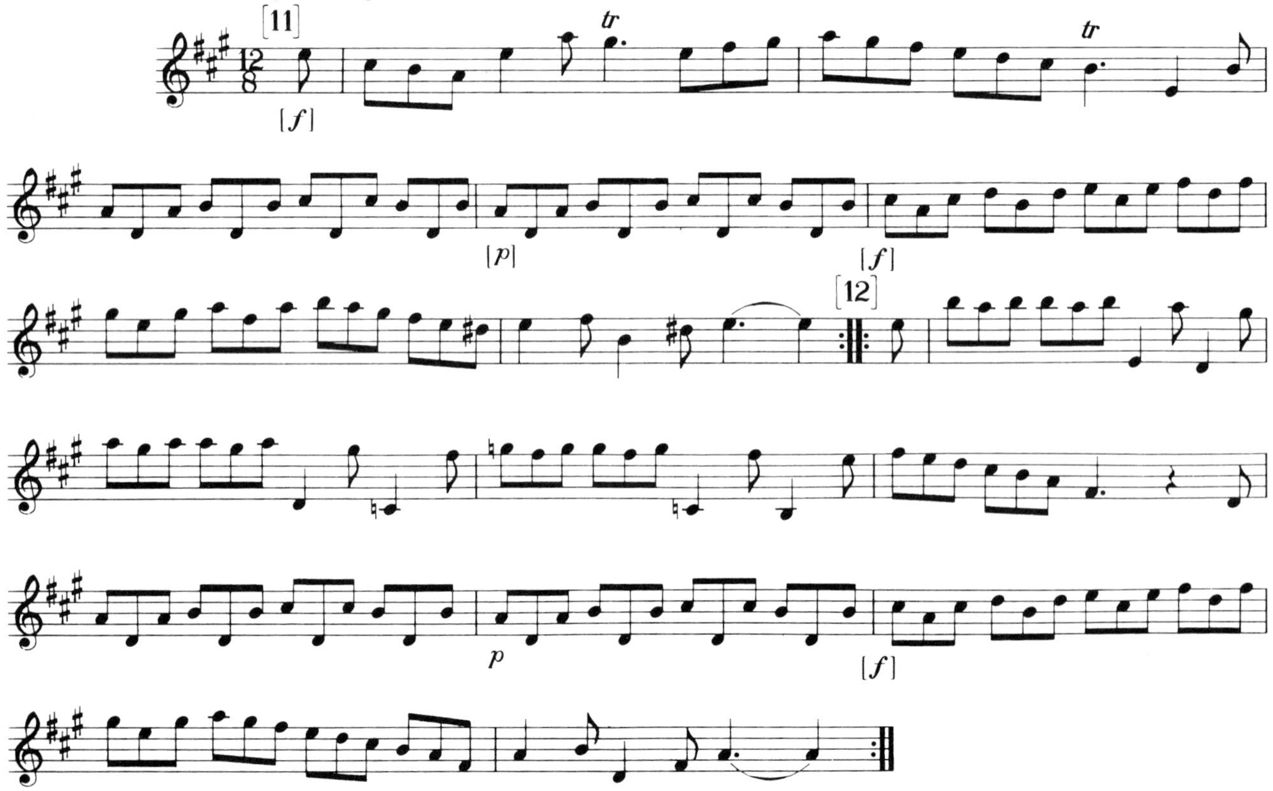

[Reel.] Presto

68. Sonata on ''Pinkie House''

ROBERT MACKINTOSH (c. 1745-1807)
and CHARLES McLEAN (fl. 1736-40)

repeat continuo for strains 3 – 4 [Andante], 5–6 [Allegro], and 7 – 8 [Tempo 1]

186

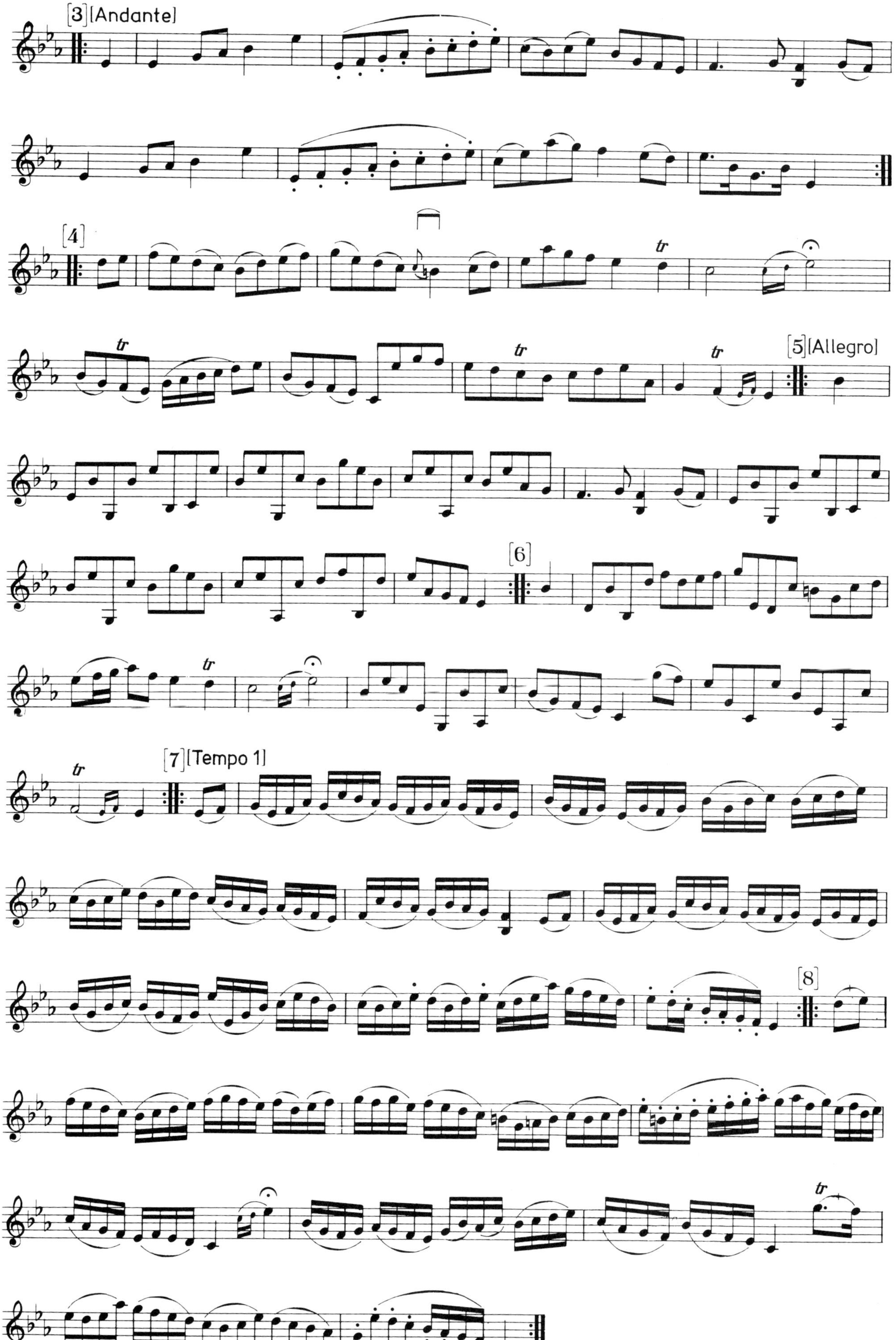
[3] [Andante]
[4]
tr
[5] [Allegro]
[6]
[7] [Tempo 1]
[8]

[9] Minuet

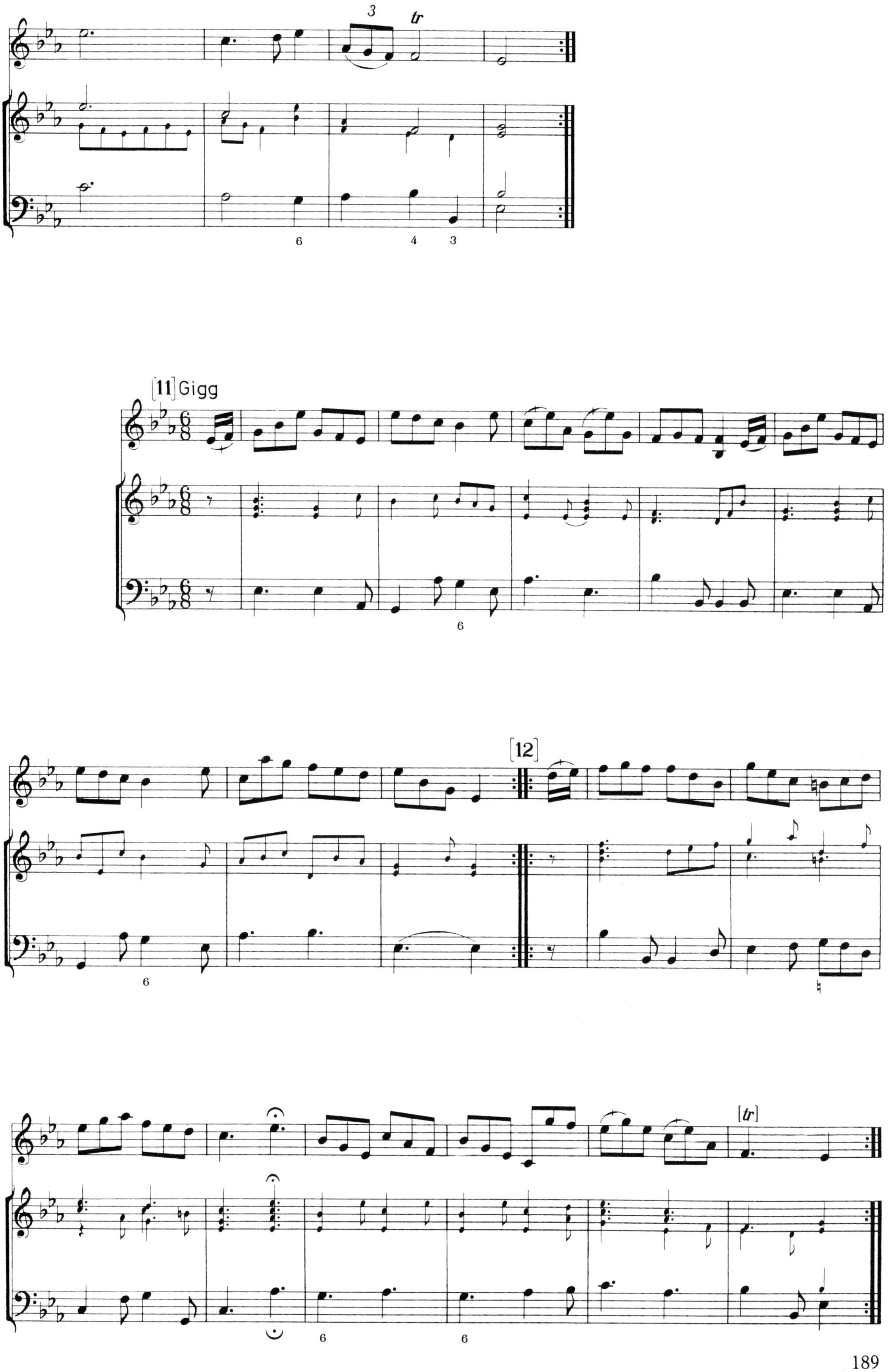

3
tr
6
4 3
[11] Gigg
6
[12]
6
[tr]
6
6

NOTES ON THE MUSIC

65 *Sonata on 'Bonny Jean of Aberdeen'*
Source: Munro's *Scots Tunes,* p.20.
This is the seventh and finest of Munro's twelve Scots-tune settings. Munro marked them for transverse flute; but they are violinistic in idiom, and contemporary MS. copies suggest that they were more often played by fiddlers than by flautists.
Revisions: several of Munro's continuo figures are clearly wrong (e.g. the $\frac{6}{4}$ figure in strain 1 bar 7). I have let the figures stand but have sometimes not followed them when realising the continuo part
   strain 2 bar 8 vln notes 2–3 orig quavers
   strain 4 bar 7 bass notes 3–4 orig crotchets
   strain 6 bars 1 and 9, vln notes 1–2 orig crotchets
   strain 6 bar 14 vln notes 3–5 rhythm editorial (cf. strain 5 bar 14); source has ♩♪♩
   strain 14 bar 4 bass note 2 orig *D*.

66 *Sonata on 'Twas within a furlong of Edinburgh town'*
Source: McFarlane MS., vol.iii no.214. Violin part only.
This sonata is based not on a genuine traditional tune, but on a mock-Scottish theatre-song by Henry Purcell, composed in London in 1694. McLean probably wrote the sonata soon after his move to Edinburgh in 1738; he took certain liberties with Purcell's song, altering its opening, compressing it from 16 bars to 12, and adding repeat-signs halfway. He must have written an accompaniment to it, but none has survived; so I have supplied an editorial accompaniment based on Purcell's original harmonisation.
   The McFarlane MS. version is the only surviving text, and is far from ideal. The McFarlane copyist, David Young, decided to transpose the piece up into A minor to make it easier to play. After writing out the Andante in transposition he then accidentally copied the Minuet at pitch in G minor. Realising his mistake, but not wishing to re-copy the page, Young hastily added a note: 'N.B. This Minuet by mistake is written out a Note too low, it must therefore be play'd a Note higher on the Violin or German Flute, and on the same Key with the first two Strains', and finished the job by transposing the Giga, once more, into A minor. This muddle at least proves that McLean wrote the sonata in G minor (also the key of Purcell's song). I have transposed the Andante and Giga back down again.
Revisions: title as first line of Purcell's song; the source has 'Edinburgh Town'
   strain 3 bar 4 note 1 orig a note lower (grace-note *b♭'*, main note *a'*)
   strain 5 bar 8 orig at pitch (not transposed up a tone as the rest of the strain).

67 *Sonata on 'The lea rig'*
Source: Riddell's *Scotch, Galwegian and Border Tunes,* p.28.
See Table VIII, above, for other texts of this sonata. For this edition the source has been checked against the texts in the McFarlane and Sharpe MSS.
Revisions: strain 3 bars 1 and 3, note 9 as McFarlane; source has *a'*
   strain 4 bar 1 note 3 as McFarlane and Sharpe; source has *e"*
   strain 4 bar 4 note 9 *tr* orig a note later
   strain 5 upbeat orig crotchets
   strain 7 bar 2 note 2 *f* deleted
   strain 10 bars 2 and 6, note 7 as McFarlane; source has *b'*

strain 10 bar 4 note 7 as McFarlane; source has $c\sharp''$
strain 10 bar 8 note 5 orig crotchet
strain 12 bar 3 note 1 $\sharp$ from McFarlane
strain 12 bar 6 *p* orig a bar earlier
strain 13 bar 3 note 7 as McFarlane; source has $g\sharp''$
strain 14 bar 4 note 3 orig $f\sharp''$.

68 *Sonata on 'Pinkie House'*
Source: *McLean* collection, p.6.
The question of how Mackintosh came to re-write this sonata of McLean's is discussed in the
Introduction (pages 11–13) and in Chapter VII above (pages 165–66).
Revisions: strains 2, 4, 6, and 12, bar 4, pause orig on note 1
  strain 6 bar 5 note 3 orig $b\flat'$
  strain 6 bar 7 note 5 orig c''
  strain 11 bar 6 bass note 2 orig $e\flat$
  strain 12 upbeat vln orig quavers
  strain 12 bar 3 bass note 4 orig $B\natural$

CHAPTER VIII

Sonatas

THIS chapter is about European art-music sonatas written by Scottish composers, which feature the violin as their main instrument.

Sonatas were, obviously, a more rarified kind of violin music than any of the pieces so far discussed in this book. They were impossible to play without an advanced technique; impossible to write without a high level of formal musical education. While composers of Scots-fiddle pieces generally limited themselves to re-arranging other people's work, or to writing tunes not more than 16 bars long, the composer of a sonata needed the training and self-confidence to create a piece of 7 to 10 minutes' duration. So it is hardly surprising that the Scottish composers who attempted sonatas were few; McGibbon, McLean, Oswald, Reid, Foulis, Kelly and Mackintosh make up almost the complete list.

Nevertheless, the violin sonatas written by Scottish composers had many points of contact with the local fiddle tradition during the period 1730–80. The sonata-composers were nearly all figures who were also active in fiddling; and it is likely that fiddlers throughout Scotland knew that these sonatas existed, and respected them as a 'top genre' of the instrument, even if they did not aspire to playing them themselves.

William McGibbon

McGibbon was the first Scottish composer to write sonatas, and in many ways the finest one. His output consisted of 24 trio-sonatas for two violins or two flutes and continuo (four sets of 6, c.1727, 1729, 1734, and c.1745), and 6 sonatas for solo violin and continuo (1740). His first set of trio-sonatas was not published and survives only in an incomplete manuscript. The second set, however, was an important piece of trail-blazing, for McGibbon published it at his own expense and seems to have had no difficulty in selling the copies. They were the first instrumental pieces in Italian-baroque style ever to be printed in Scotland. (It is interesting how closely McGibbon's 1729 sonatas followed on the heels of the first traditional music to be printed in Scotland, Adam Craig's collection of c.1727 and Alexander Stuart's of c.1728.)

No. 6 in D is the finest sonata of the 1729 set. It is scored specifically for flute, violin, and accompaniment (the other sonatas in the set have optional scorings: either two violins, or two flutes, or one of each) and uses the contrasted timbres of the instruments imaginatively. In the last movement, for instance, the flute and violin exchange parts between bars 4 and 6:

192

The second movement of the piece includes a splendid written-out cadenza for the violin, notable as the most difficult violin passage to be published in Britain up to that date. The flute is silent in this section:

The other five sonatas of the 1729 set are less adventurous, and concentrate on more basic types of instrumental writing. McGibbon's 1734 set is also fairly run-of-the-mill apart from Sonata no.5 in G, which contains two ambitious fugal movements.

The solo sonatas of 1740 mark a new period in McGibbon's work. His early sonatas are all marred by awkward corners where he has not managed to solve elementary problems of part-writing; but the 1740 set stands on a much higher technical level. It was probably competition from Barsanti, Oswald, and McLean, all of whom moved into Edinburgh between 1735 and 1738, that caused McGibbon to raise his standards. All six of the 1740 sonatas are good, the best being No.2 in D, which has a dramatic opening worthy of Handel:

Andante

Violin

Harpsichord, Cello

followed by a Corellian *giga*:

Allegro

Violin

Harpsichord, Cello

and ending with a brilliant Minuet and variations.

Title-page of McGibbon's trio-sonatas of 1734 (Rowe Library, King's College, Cambridge).

McGibbon's last set of trio-sonatas (*c.*1745) looks equally good; but unfortunately only violin 1 parts of them survive, so we can only guess at their overall quality.

McGibbon's sonatas bear no marks of local origin: they could equally well have been written in London, Rome or Amsterdam as in Edinburgh. His *La folia* variations (McFarlane MS., vol.iii no.194), however, though they are just as European in general style, do contain one noticeable Scottish finger-print. It occurs in this passage (the bass line of the extract is editorial):

Fast

The lop-sided arpeggio (bracketed) is a traditional Scots-fiddle figure which also occurs in, for instance, strain 6 of *Saw na ye my Peggie* (**7**). It is an interesting case of McGibbon letting his mask slip momentarily while writing a European piece.

Charles McLean

McLean wrote one set of 12 sonatas, published in 1737. Nos. 1–8 of the set are for violin and continuo, nos. 9–12 for flute and continuo. They were printed in Edinburgh by Richard Cooper, the engraver who had already produced Craig's and Stuart's Scots-tune collections and McGibbon's 1729 and 1734 sonatas; the book was actually published, however, from Aberdeen, where McLean was living at the time.

Nothing is known of McLean's life before 1736. But it is likely that he was born in the north-east of Scotland around 1712 and educated at the Aberdeen burgh music-school, for his sonatas have an awareness of 17th-century music which was almost certainly the product of an old-fashioned education. His Sonata no.6 in C minor, for example, ends with a movement which would not have been out of place in a viol fantasy a century earlier:

Vivace

and the main movement of Sonata no.3 in A is in the style of a 17th-century organ toccata:

Sonata no.1 in D also has sections in organ-toccata style, alternating with short fugal passages.

However, McLean was also capable of writing fluently in more up-to-date idioms. Sonata no.2 in G minor includes a fashionable 1730s minuet:

and Sonata no.9 in D opens with a movement clearly modelled on Handel:

Despite certain technical flaws, McLean's sonatas are lively and excitingly varied as a set. It is sad that he seems to have written no more sonatas after 1737.

James Oswald

Oswald composed several sonatas during the Scottish period of his life to 1741, but they are unfortunately all lost. In 1734, while still an obscure dancing-master in Dunfermline, he advertised in the press to invite subscriptions for his forthcoming *Collection of Minuets*, adding at the foot of the advert:

> The author has by him several Sonatas and Solos, one of which is to be published along with this collection: if it is well received, the rest, with some other pieces of Musick, may in time be published.
> (*Caledonian Mercury*, 12 August 1734)

The minuet collection was duly published on 16 January 1736. As has been mentioned earlier, however, no copies of it are extant, so we have no way of knowing what even the one sonata which reached print was like.

Oswald did, however, write further sonatas after his move to London. Many of these are markedly Scottish in style; they can perhaps be regarded as exile's music, self-consciously Scottish pieces written to express the composer's nostalgia for his home country.

Oswald's finest set of London sonatas is his *Airs for the four Seasons* for violin (or flute) and continuo. Published in 1755 and reprinted in 1756 with an additional part for 2nd violin (or 2nd flute), it consists of 48 self-contained pieces, each named after a different flower and arranged in four seasonal groups. Oswald seems to have got the idea for this work from James Thomson's poem *The Seasons* (1728), which contains a descriptive passage mentioning 18 types of flower:

> Fair-handed Spring unbosoms every grace;
> Throws out the *Snowdrop* and the *Crocus* first,
> The *Daisy, Primrose, Violet* darkly blue,
> And *Polyanthus* of unnumbered dyes,
> The yellow *Wallflower*, stained with iron brown,
> And lavish *Stock* that scents the garden round. . .

Out of the 18 flowers in this list, 10 appear in the Spring section of Oswald's *Airs* and 7 more in the Summer, Autumn and Winter sections, so it is probable that Oswald used this passage as a starting-point for his work.

The 'Narcissus' Sonata (Spring, no.4) is typical of the set. It is in two movements, a pastorale in Scottish pentatonic style:

Air: Pastorale Andante

followed by a jig which could well be a traditional tune:

Giga. Vivace

It makes the narcissus out to be a very Scottish sort of plant.

Elsewhere Oswald seems to have had actual traditional tunes in his mind while composing. His 'Snowdrop' Sonata (Winter, no.11), for example, begins with the same melodic figure as *My Nanny-O*, and the first phrase of its last movement is identical to the opening of *Charlie is my darling.*

Oswald was clearly pleased with his *Airs for the four Seasons,* for he wrote a second set, containing another 48 pieces, during the 1760s. The complete series of 96 sonatas is one of the most remarkable achievements of any Scottish composer.

John Reid

Reid has already appeared briefly in Chapter II. He was born at Straloch, Perthshire, in 1721, into a landowning Highland family; he read law at Edinburgh University and then went into the army, where he rose to the rank of general and eventually retured rich. Nothing is known of his musical training, but he was evidently an expert amateur flautist. (In his later years, bearing in mind that he had enjoyed studying at Edinburgh University and playing music more than anything else in his life, he left the bulk of his fortune to the University with instructions that it should found a music department. Edinburgh University built the Reid School of Music in 1860 as a result of his bequest.)

Reid wrote two sets of 6 sonatas for violin (or flute) and continuo, published in 1756 and 1762. These are like Oswald's in having a strong Scottish flavour while being basically Italian-baroque in style. The masterpiece among them is Sonata no.2 in G from the 1762 set, presented in this chapter as no. **69**.

Some doubts have been expressed from time to time as to whether Reid could really have composed his fluent and sophisticated sonatas unaided. Friedrich Niecks, the sixth Reid Professor of Music at Edinburgh University, ungratefully suggested in 1908 that Reid probably wrote 'only the germs' of his pieces, and that 'trained musicians shaped, elaborated, harmonised, and instrumented them' (Tullibardine, p.391n.). Given that this theory is correct, the person most likely to have assisted Reid with his compositions is James Oswald. Reid and Oswald knew each other well, for Reid spent a lot of time in London and Oswald was his publisher; and Reid's 1762 sonatas are in fact mysteriously re-attributed to Oswald in a later edition.

All the same, Reid's sonatas have certain features which are unlike the work of any other composer. The Sonata in G **(69)**, for example, though it resembles Oswald in general style, is constructed with a meticulousness and sense of detail which are hardly characteristic of Oswald at all. The unexpected way in which the opening violin theme (bar 1) is recapitulated in the cello part (bar 22); the subtelty with which the Moderato theme (bar 73) is reharmonised on its third appearance (bar 89); the neat manner in which the cello's rhythmic figure ♩ ♪ ♩ in the last movement (bars 98, 100, 125, etc.) is actually structural, being derived from the main violin theme (bar 93); the clever anticipation of the violin's arpeggio theme at bar 150 by the cello a bar earlier; all these are details which Oswald would greatly have enjoyed, but which he would never personally have taken the trouble to write. So it is probably fairest to assume that Reid wrote his excellent sonatas without any help from outside parties.

David Foulis

Foulis is a composer we have not met before; like Reid, he was an amateur musician. A younger son of the Foulis family of Ravelston, he was born near Edinburgh in 1710 and read medicine at Edinburgh University and at the University of Leiden in Holland. He returned to Edinburgh in the mid-1730s to become a distinguished medical practitioner and treasurer of the Royal College of Physicians (see Johnson, 'Dr. David Foulis'). For Foulis, as for Reid, composing was a spare-time hobby: apart from a few short tunes, he wrote only 6 sonatas for violin and continuo over a period of 25 years, from *c.*1748 to his death in 1773. His sonatas were printed in about 1774.

Foulis was not as well trained musically as he was medically; but his sonatas are surprisingly good, with a natural elegance and an instinctive feel for what works well on the violin. Sonata no.1 in E flat is the best of the set. It begins with a slow movement of the French-overture type:

proceeds to a fast movement with a neat canonic opening:

then to an expressive slow movement:

Adagio

and finally to an extended minuet with unusually complex rhythms:

Non troppo allegro

The Earl of Kelly

Kelly has already appeared in Chapter VI as a composer of minuets and symphonies; he also, in 1769, wrote 6 trio-sonatas for two violins and continuo. These are run-of-the-mill in some ways, and contain several ideas which Kelly re-worked from earlier compositions; but they also have many fresh, spontaneous passages. Sonata no.1 in A, for example, opens with a delightful lyrical theme:

Andante amoroso

The best sonata of the set is probably no.4 in C.

Kelly's trio-sonatas are German in style, and are symptomatic of the general move towards German expressiveness which was affecting European art music at that time. A point worth considering is that this change in European fashion caused the gap between art music and Scots fiddle music to widen. During the period 1700–60 a great deal of effort had been put into modernising Scots fiddle music to bring it into line with the upright, Italian-baroque style of Corelli and Handel. Now, however, art music began to introduce dynamic contrasts, long legato bowings, new types of rhythm, far-flung modulations and other devices which had no connection with Scottish music at all. Scots fiddle music did eventually catch up with some of these innovations, but for the moment, art music had forged ahead into new territory.

J. G. C. Schetky's 6 trios for two violins and cello, op.1, written in Edinburgh in 1773, demonstrate this point very clearly. Schetky was German and had recently arrived in Scotland, and his work was thoroughly abreast of Continental trends; his Trio no.4 in F, for instance, has this novel modulatory passage in its first movement:

Anything less like Scots fiddle music can hardly be imagined.

German traits are also apparent in Robert Barber's 6 trios for harpsichord, violin and cello, op.2, composed in Aberdeen in 1782. Barber's Trio no.2 in C opens with a Romantic, fantasia-like movement not unlike the beginning of Beethoven's 'Moonlight' Sonata; bars 7–14 are as follows:

Larghetto

It is significant that Barber was not a native Scot, but had been born and educated in Newcastle. Barber was typical of many immigrant composers who worked in Scotland in the 1780s and 1790s. Highly trained in foreign parts, almost totally ignorant of Scottish traditional music, they changed the face of art music in Scotland so rapidly that it was soon impossible for any native Scottish composer whose main reference-point was fiddle music even to contemplate making a contribution to it.

Robert Mackintosh

Mackintosh was the last Scots fiddler in the 18th century to attempt sonatas. He probably wrote several, but only one of them has come down to us; it is in G minor, for violin and continuo, and was published in his *Airs, Minuets, Gavotts and Reels* collection of 1783.

Mackintosh's G minor sonata is in many ways an excellent piece. It opens with a heroic Allegro:

leading to a Handelian slow movement:

and then to a Corelli-like *giga*:

The first movement of the sonata tries hard to achieve a contemporary idiom; nevertheless, its natural bent is clearly towards the music of 50 years earlier, the period of McGibbon and McLean. Its mixture of a modern surface and an underlying conservatism is, in fact, very similar to that already discussed in regard to Mackintosh's *Pinkie House* setting **(68)** in Chapter VII. Mackintosh's G minor sonata thus marks the end of a period in which European sonatas and Scots fiddle pieces could coexist fruitfully with each other.

69. Sonata in G

General JOHN REID (1721-1807)

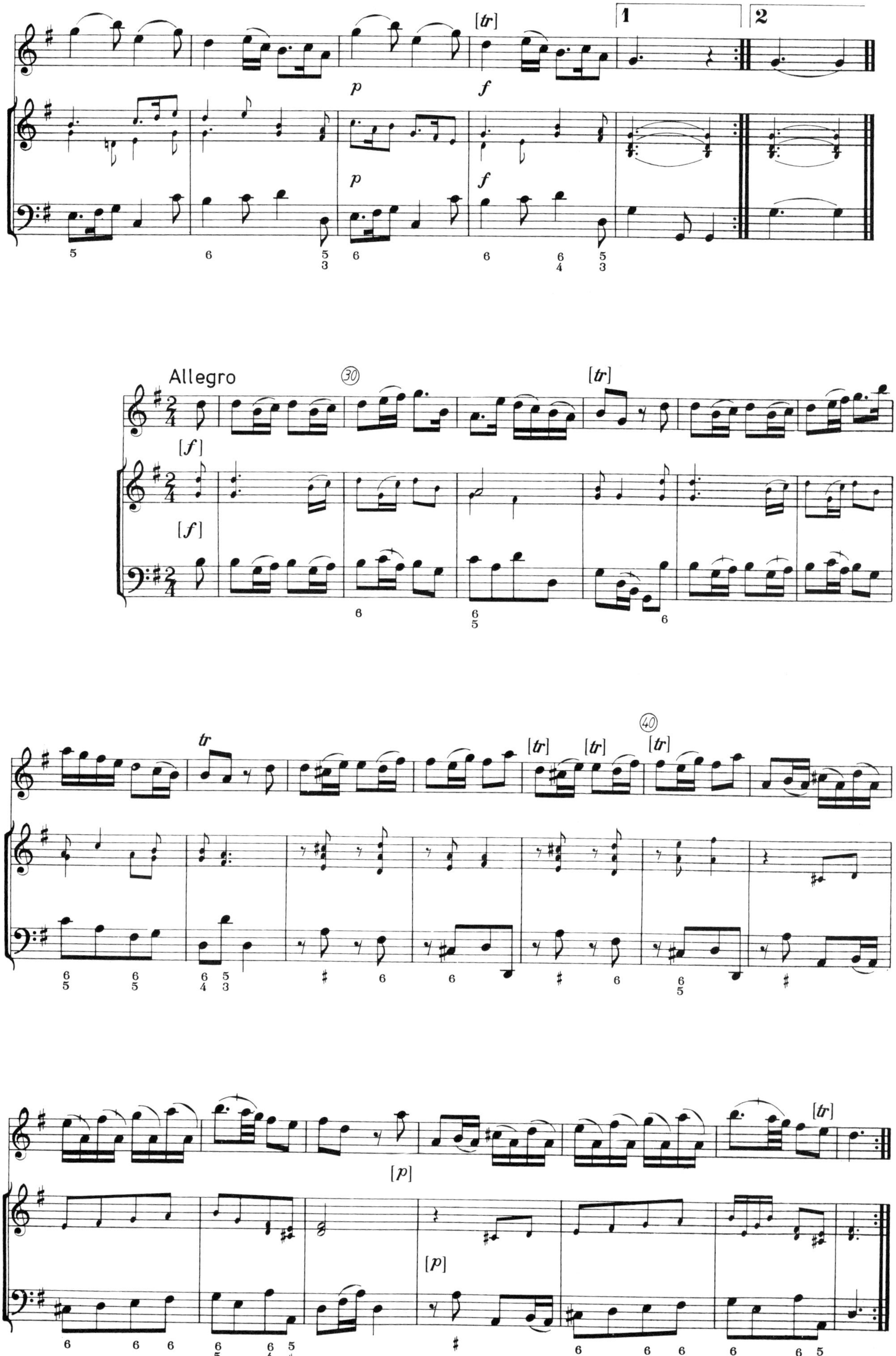
Allegro
[tr]
tr
p
f
[f]
[p]
1
2
30
40

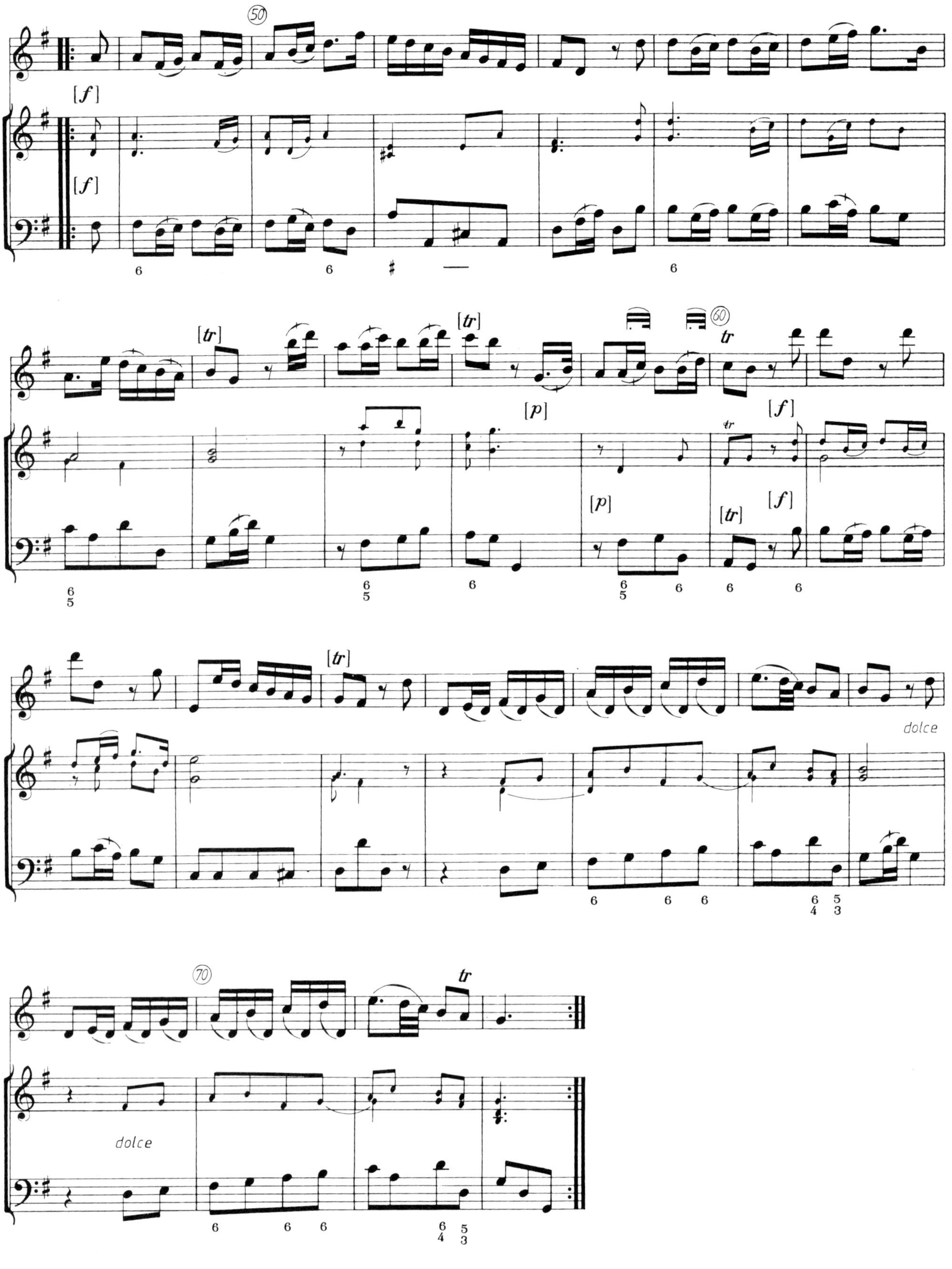
50
[f]
[f]
[tr]
[tr]
60
tr
[p]
[p]
[f]
[f]
[tr]
[tr]
dolce
70
tr
dolce

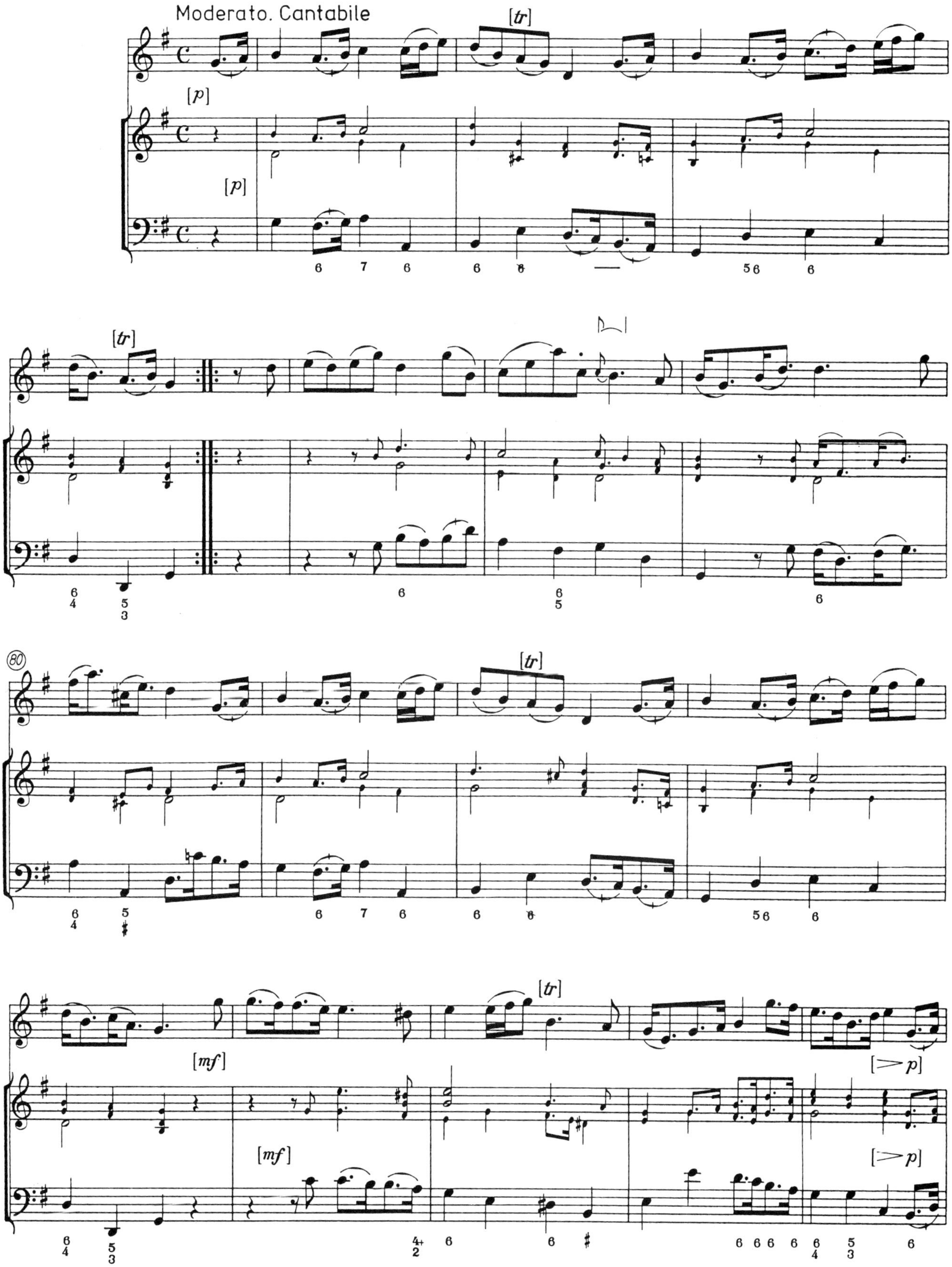
Moderato. Cantabile
[tr]
[p]
[p]
80
[mf]
[mf]
[> p]
[> p]

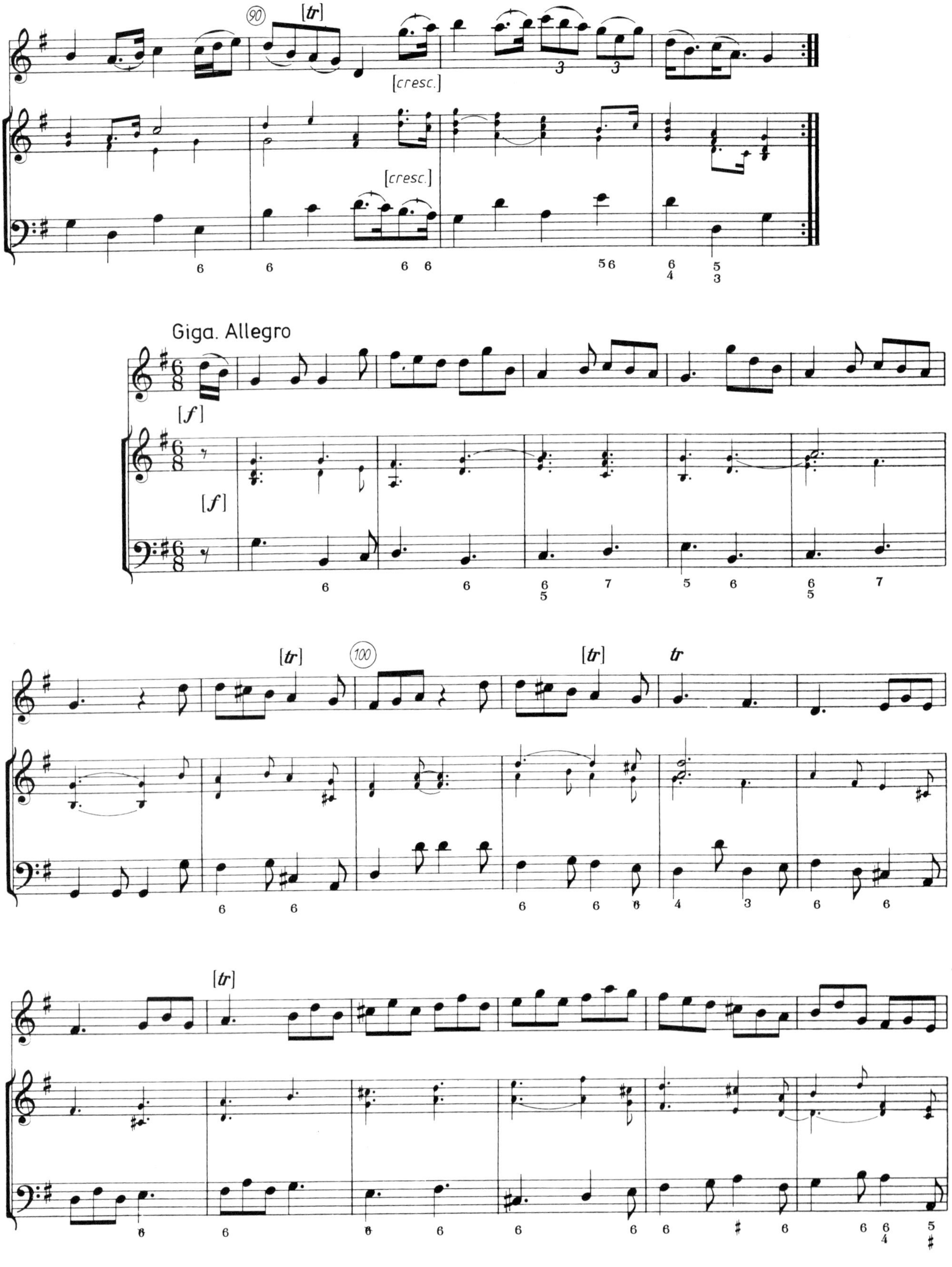
90
[tr]
[cresc.]
[cresc.]
Giga. Allegro
[f]
[f]
[tr]
100
[tr]
tr
[tr]

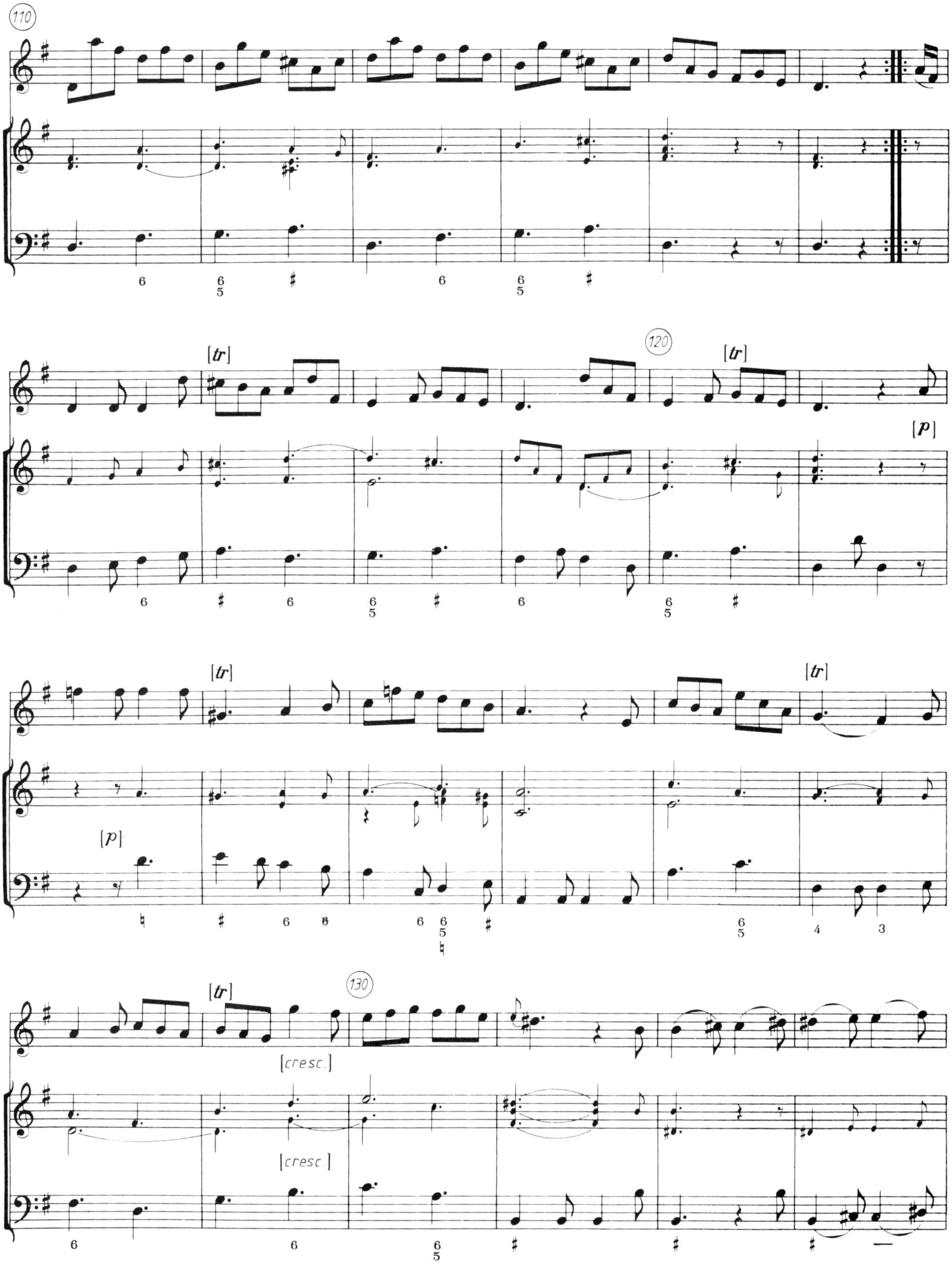
110
[tr]
120
[tr]
[p]
[tr]
[tr]
[p]
[tr]
130
[cresc.]
[cresc.]

210

NOTES ON THE MUSIC

69 *John Reid: Sonata in G*
Source: Reid's *Second Sett of Six Solos*, p.4.
Revisions: the bracketed decorations throughout the violin part are 18th-century ones, written
into the British Library copy of the source by an unknown hand
   bar 28b is editorial.

CHAPTER IX

Reels, Hornpipes, Strathspeys and Jigs from 1760

WE must now look at Scottish dance music during the last forty years of the century. Some aspects of this chapter may seem controversial to some readers; a fair proportion of this music has survived to the present day, but the ideas which today's fiddlers have about it are by no means entirely in accord with the historical facts.

Eighteen tunes are presented here. Nos. **70–75** are reels, **76–77** are hornpipes, **78–82** are strathspeys, and **83–87** are jigs. This selection gives a fairly representative picture of the period, so long as the reader realises that about 200 times as many of these tunes were current at the time.

A typical dance band in the late 18th century would have consisted of two to four fiddlers and one cellist (see Johnson, *Music and Society,* pp. 121–2). The cellist, however, could be dispensed with; nor was it absolutely necessary for a band to have more than one fiddler — except for reasons of fatigue and volume of sound — since the fiddlers would all play the tune together in any case. (They might divide into two parts for minuets; see Table IV on page 147.)

Manuscript books usually give only the fiddle parts of dance tunes; printed collections normally give cello parts as well. These printed cello parts are generally very rudimentary, consisting of long strings of repeated tonic, dominant, and flattened-7th notes buttressed by cadences at the end of each strain; it is unlikely that many cellists bothered to learn them exactly, since they could just as easily have made up their own. Cello parts to a tune tend, anyhow, to vary between one printed collection and another, showing that they were not regarded as definitive. For this reason I have not given them with every tune in this chapter but have only presented four samples, alongside one reel (no. **75**), one hornpipe **(77)**, one strathspey **(82)**, and one jig **(87)**. Interested readers can easily learn how to write them themselves in the correct style.

Cello parts are hardly ever printed with harpsichord continuo figures, and it seems that most dance bands did not have harpsichords to fill in the background harmony. This would have been desirable in theory; in practice, however, using a harpsichord would have meant transporting one to the venue every time the band played — an impracticable task by horse and cart over 18th-century roads. Bands probably used a harpsichord or spinet only when playing at country houses which already had one *in situ*.

Robert Burns' poem *Tam o' Shanter,* written in 1790, contains a passage which mentions the four current types of Scottish dance-tune:

> Tam saw an unco sight —
> Warlocks and witches in a dance;
> Nae cotillon brent new frae France,
> But hornpipes, jigs, strathspeys and reels
> Put life and mettle in their heels.

This passage gives the reader a general impression that these dance-tunes were all ancient. Reels and jigs had certainly been going in Scotland since at least the 16th century; but hornpipes had been imported from England only in the late 17th century, and strathspeys had become popular throughout Scotland as recently as the 1760s, having before then been mostly confined to the Spey valley in Inverness-shire. (From 1760 to 1800 strathspeys were often referred to as 'Strathspey reels', meaning the kind of reels that fiddlers played on Speyside. To avoid confusion, the normal type of reels were sometimes called 'Atholl reels' at this time.) Many individual tunes were even more recent, as brand new, in fact, as any cotillon one could name. Of the six reels presented here, nos. **70** and **71** were old, but **72** and **73** had been newly written in the mid-18th century, **75** written *c.*1790, and **74** composed by Nathaniel Gow only a year or two before 1800. Both hornpipes (**76** and **77**) seem to be late 17th-century ones; but of the strathspeys, only **78** was old, the others being the work of known composers writing between 1775 and 1790. Of the jigs, **83** and **84** were old, but **85** was written by Niel Gow around the 1770s, **87** by Joseph Reinagle about 1783, and **86** by an anonymous composer in 1787. In other words, Scottish dance music was being very rapidly and excitingly modernised, at the time Burns wrote his poem.

Dance music had suffered a partial eclipse during the 17th century. This was due to the Church of Scotland's repressive attitude towards dancing. When the Reformed Church came to power in 1560, it set out to gain control over all public entertainments liable to encourage high spirits and lead to promiscuity, until by the 1640s it was able to launch a violent anti-sex campaign, based somewhat shakily on New Testament theology. Dancing was one of its main targets. Music, a naturally liberating and subversive medium, was thus polarised as an enemy of the Church; for what was the good of hours of sermons on the virtues and practical advantages of chastity, if people forgot the message the moment a fiddler struck up a Scots reel? So ministers thundered not only against the rakes and fallen women in their districts, but also against anyone who played the fiddle and dared to teach it to their children.

It was mainly the middle classes and the respectable poor who were affected by the Church's propaganda. Those at the bottom of society continued to dance and play, despite public opinion and the Kirk Session's disciplinary committee. The upper classes also continued to dance; they were a law unto themselves, untouchable by the Kirk and capable of defending their behaviour on theological grounds, should the need arise. (David's harp-playing before Saul — 1 Samuel 16, 14–23 — was a useful text to throw into an argument with a minister about music.)

This situation continued until the beginning of the 18th century, when the growing enthusiasm for music all over Europe seriously weakened the Church of Scotland's position. The Church's distrust of fiddle music did not, however, simply lie down and die. It was still rampant in Ayrshire in the late 18th century, as can be seen from various angry fulminations in Burns' poems. (In *Tam o' Shanter*, for instance, Burns is clearly taking a malicious delight in showing the Devil playing reels and strathspeys — a picture dear to Kirk elders' hearts.) It resurrected itself in the Highlands and Islands in the late 19th century; there are many horrifying stories from this period of ministers ordering public bonfires of fiddles, excommunicating farmers for holding barn-dances on their premises,

Q

and so reducing the demand for fiddles that the instruments had to be sold off at auctions at nominal prices. Even today, most Scottish people experience a sudden levity, a lifting of a burden from the heart, on hearing their first reel or jig of an evening; this feeling is probably a psychological throwback to the 17th century.

It seems to have been the top of society, rather than the bottom, which regenerated Scottish dance music after the worst period of religious repression was over. The Scottish upper classes were envious of the country dances enjoyed by their counterparts in England, and determined to import the fashion and give it a Scottish cultural slant. Aristocratic dancing-clubs were opened in Edinburgh in the early years of the 18th century, despite religious opposition; and it seems to have been common in the 1730s for country-house parties to be devoted to experiments with new dances, designed to go with Scots reels and jigs. Two of David Young's manuscripts record the results of such experiments: the 'Duke of Perth's manuscript' (1734) and 'A collection of the newest countrey dances perform'd in Scotland' (1740). Both manuscripts give detailed instructions for the dance steps, and fiddle sets of the accompanying tunes.

By the mid-century the middle classes were becoming converted to dancing once more. Tentatively, at first; if the minister preached against dancing, and the laird and his guests did it every weekend, were they to follow the precept of the one or the example of the other? However, the Church lost the battle. Dancing-masters set up practices all over the country, first with a small trickle of pupils, then with a huge flood of them; and for the first time, a market appeared in Scotland for printed books of dance tunes.

Some Scottish dance music had already been printed in England. The first collections to be produced specifically for the Scottish market, however, were Neil Stewart's *Newest and best reels or country dances* (*c.*1761–5) and Robert Bremner's *Scots reels or country dances* (*c.*1765). These books had similar contents as well as similar titles. Both contained large numbers of ancient tunes appearing in print for the first time, showing that half-forgotten reels and jigs had been dug out of people's memories and written down, to meet the sharply increased demand. Many old tunes were also written down in manuscripts at this time.

The situation had a stimulating effect on composers. So many dances were going on that almost any tune would get performed somewhere, and many composers tried their hands at writing new dance music. Their efforts were generally rather old-fashioned, showing few of the modern traits of long variation sets of the same period; they wrote tunes to fit the existing repertory, and continued to use such traditional procedures as gapped scales and double-tonic sequences. Nevertheless, the new dance tunes tended to be more harmonically focussed, and to have a stronger sense of European tonality, than the earlier reels and jigs. This can be seen, for instance, by comparing *Mrs Fordyce of Ayton's strathspey* (**81**) and *Colonel Hamilton's delight* (**87**) with the earlier dance tunes in Chapter I.

Dance tunes as local celebrations

Many new dance tunes were written in the second half of the century to celebrate the districts where the composers lived. There was a series, for example, with titles in the form

'The lads of. . .' or 'The lasses of. . .' (insert place-name). The impulse behind such pieces was the same as that which led Burns, on mentioning the town of Ayr in *Tam o' Shanter*, to add:

> (Auld Ayr, wham ne'er a town surpasses
> For honest men and bonny lasses.)

Once one district had got a tune into circulation in honour of its local girls, other districts were obliged to follow suit, until the repertory was full of tunes like *Lasses of Duns, Lasses of Stewarton, Lothian Lasses, Haddington Lasses, Ayrshire Lasses, Lasses of Irvine* and *Clydeside Lasses.*

Another series were tunes celebrating bridges. Many new bridges were built in Scotland at this period, often improving the quality of life for a whole area by cutting out lengthy detours and dangerous fords on main roads. Fiddle-composers seem often to have been on hand to express the community's feelings with a new tune. One instance concerns the composer William Marshall:

> When the beautiful new bridge over the Spey [at Craigellachie] was finished [in 1815], Marshall, who had himself been a zealous promoter of the undertaking, was requested by the gentlemen interested to compose a tune to celebrate its name, and he instantly produced one of his best strathspeys, called *Craigellachie Bridge.*
>
> (Preface to Marshall's 1845 collection)

Daniel Dow's reel *The Bridge of Perth* was probably composed under similar circumstances. No anecdotes are recorded, but the tune was printed for the first time in 1773, and the bridge over the Tay at Perth was completed in 1772, so the two are almost certainly connected. Further tunes of this type, all anonymous, are *The New Bridge of Glasgow* (bridge completed 1768), *The New Bridge of Edinburgh* (1769), *The New Bridge of Rutherglen* (1776), *The South Bridge of Edinburgh* (1787), and *The New Bridge of Ballater* (1811). *The South Bridge of Edinburgh* is given here as no. **86**.

Dance tunes as tools for professional advancement

In contrast to communal-celebration pieces were dance tunes written for upper-class patrons. These had titles like 'Lord . . .'s Strathspey', 'Miss . . .'s Reel', 'The Earl of . . .'s delight' (insert patron's name) or '. . . House', 'The Highway to . . .' (insert patron's residence). Dedications to corporate bodies like dancing clubs and hunts were also common, the titles then taking the forms 'The . . . Assembly' or 'The . . . Hunt's favourite'. Nos. **72, 74, 80–82** and **85–87** are examples of such tunes.

Scottish dance music started being dedicated to patrons, in significant quantities, only around 1770. Up till then no large sums of money were to be made from playing and composing dance music, so fiddlers had no special reason to ingratiate themselves with the upper classes.

Up to 1750 or so, most fiddlers were amateurs who earned their livings from other, non-musical jobs. Band engagements were mostly unpaid, undertaken simply in return for food and drink. It was true that money tended to change hands when a band played at the 'big house' in the district, on the principle of *noblesse oblige*, but even here there was no competition for privilege between one band and another. No band travelled more than a few miles to play, so the laird had no choice over which band to hire: it had to be the local one. He got exactly the same services for his weekend house-parties as the farmer did for his harvest-home dance, or the blacksmith for his daughter's wedding reception.

After 1750 this situation changed in many parts of Scotland. Far more money was being spend on dancing, and many more band engagements were paid. Some fiddlers were able to give up their other jobs and earn their livings from teaching dancing and violin, and from playing. Bands multiplied; some were better than others; the better ones commanded higher fees; higher fees made it a viable proposition to travel 30 or more miles from home to play. It was suddenly possible for a band to win a reputation outside its immediate locality, and to make real money.

This depended, however, on personal recommendations in high places, for which it was necessary for fiddlers to attract the aristocracy's attention. How better to do this than to compose dozens of new dance tunes and dedicate them appropriately? Minuet tunes with dedications had already set a precedent for this: see Chapter VI. Among the fiddlers who became famous in the 1770s, John Riddell and Daniel Dow promoted themselves simultaneously through minuets and reels, while Robert Mackintosh wrote minuets first and reels and strathspeys afterwards. By the 1780s a large proportion of all new dance music was being written with a view to professional advancement.

Blueprint for a ducal orchestra at Blair Atholl

We should pause for a moment to consider how this development appeared from an aristocrat's point of view.

There is no doubt that the Scottish landowning classes were looking for something new to patronise in the musical line at this time. Virtuoso harp-playing was already a thing of the past. Bagpiping was still going strong in the Highlands, but it had acquired a bad odour in some circles from its association with the Jacobite rebellions of 1715 and 1745, and it seemed old-fashioned compared with recent musical developments on the Continent, which were nearly all centred round the modern Italian violin. An obvious course would have been for them to have poured energy and money into promoting European art music in Scotland.

There was a well-established tradition in German-speaking countries at the time for princes and dukes to maintain small orchestras at their stately residences. These court orchestras not only played background music for dinners and dance music for balls, but also pioneered the latest German symphonies and concertos at private concerts; they were a main cause of the ascendancy of German art music over Italian during the period 1740–80.

Several of the richest Scottish aristocrats could have afforded a court orchestra of this type, had they wanted one: for instance, the Duke of Argyll at Inveraray Castle, the Duke of Gordon at Gordon Castle, the Duke of Atholl at Blair Atholl, and the Earl of Haddington at Mellerstain House in the Borders. Founding one would have meant adding

20 musicians to the household staff, on the same wages as valets or senior gardeners, plus a *maestro di cappella* and a deputy *maestro* who would have carried the same rank as the factor and the butler. Scotland was still largely a feudal country in the mid-18th century, and there is no doubt that the tenants of these dukes would have borne the increased taxes and conspicuous spending involved at least as stoically as their German counterparts did. Presented in the right way, a local court orchestra was something they might even have come to be proud of.

How would the Duke of Atholl, say, have gone about starting a household orchestra in 1753? The first task would have been to find a suitable *maestro di cappella*: someone who combined the talents of violinist, harpsichordist, composer, teacher, concert organiser and personnel manager. Nicolo Pasquali, an energetic 35-year-old Italian who worked freelance in Edinburgh, would have been ideal for the job. For the deputy *maestro*, Francesco Barsanti (see Chapter II above) would have been a good choice: he was an excellent composer, a skilled oboist, flautist, and woodwind teacher, and though already about 62 would have come back to Scotland from London like a shot, offered such a post. The rest of the orchestra could have been recruited locally. The Atholl valley was full of fiddlers and well supplied with dance-band cellists, and a year's practice in sight-reading and ensemble would have turned a group of such players into an effective string section. The rank-and-file woodwind could similarly have been recruited from local bagpipers and players of the stock-and-horn (a type of pastoral oboe which was popular in the district: see Johnson, *Music and Society*, p.100), though in this case the musicians would have had to be re-trained on instruments slightly different from those they were accustomed to. Here, too, however, a year's practice on regular wages would have developed the skills needed.

Once the orchestra had shaped up, Pasquali and Barsanti would have composed new symphonies and concertos for it; the Earl of Kelly would come to Blair Atholl frequently as visiting composer; and Robert Mackintosh — born in the village of Tulliemet, only a few miles away — would have gravitated into the orchestra in his late teens, and would not have needed to go to Edinburgh to fulfil himself as a violinist and composer.

The reason why the Duke of Atholl, and other Scottish aristocrats, did not take such a step must have been that they felt European art music to be too foreign a form for everyday use. They had been educated to appreciate it intellectually; but for them, as for the lower classes, it was Scottish music which really spoke to the heart. Thus the aristocrats' patronage of European music went no further than taking out subscriptions for the Musical Society's concerts in Edinburgh, and occasionally playing chamber music themselves for fun.

What the Duke of Atholl did instead

Instead, the Duke of Atholl put a great deal of encouragement and goodwill behind the Gow family of Inver, near Dunkeld.

A great deal has been written about the Gows, but their history is still somewhat obscure. It is likely that they were the Atholl valley's outstanding fiddlers as far back as the 17th century; they seem to have been weavers to trade. Niel Gow (*b*.1727) was the first member of the family, as far as anyone knows, to earn his living from music, and his four sons, William (*b.c.*1755), Andrew (*b.c.*1760), John (*b.c.*1762) and Nathaniel (*b.*1763), all became famous as musicians.

The Duke of Atholl is traditionally given most of the credit for raising the Gow family from obscurity to fame. Research has not yet uncovered exactly how he did this: it is likely that the Duke discovered Niel Gow's talents, invited him to play at Blair Atholl and at his other residences, paid him well, passed the word round his friends that Gow was available for outside work, and so got him professionally launched. He probably also encouraged Gow to send his sons away to study, and pulled strings to get them engagements in Edinburgh and London; Andrew and John eventually settled in London, and William and Nathaniel in Edinburgh. The Duke's reward for his enterprise was to have his name associated with a famous family of musicians, and to have a constant supply of first-rate music on his doorstep: very similar, in fact, to the rewards he would have reaped from forming a court orchestra.

It is worth noting that Niel Gow did not take to this patronage entirely kindly. (The same could probably be said of the other outstanding fiddlers of the period, if we knew more details; they probably all saw patronage as a professional necessity, but a mixed blessing.) Niel was not temperamentally cut out to be an aristocratic lap-dog. All contemporary accounts describe him as *honest*; in Protestant terms this meant a person of integrity, one who would not be compromised by others' vested interests. Niel was not interested in moving permanently from his native village to the bright city lights, and said so. In his old age he would hardly stir from his house, so that distinguished people like Robert Burns had to go to Inver if they wanted to meet him. Moreover, though obviously fond of most of his patrons (see his jig *Dunkeld House*, no. **85**, written for John Murray, fourth Duke of Atholl, which has an unmistakable air of friendship about it), he had a habit of pulling their legs in conversation if they leaned on him too hard; as in the following anecdotes (re-worded from Murdoch, p.43):

I.

Scene: the A9 road south of Dunkeld.
    TWO POMPOUS GENTLEMEN: Are you not Niel Gow, the fiddler?
    GOW (cautious): Aye.
    TWO POMPOUS GENTLEMEN: Then you're the very man we've
        come all this way from Glasgow to see!
    GOW: Then you're the mair fules — Ah wadna gang half as far tae see you.

II.

Scene: Gow's parlour at Inver.
    DUCHESS OF GORDON: Oh Mr Gow, I've not been at all *well*
        lately — in the mornings my head swims — a sudden giddiness
        comes upon me —
    GOW: Ah ken whit ye mean, yer leddyship — when Ah've been fu' [drunk]
        the nicht before it's like a haill bike [swarm] of bees bizzing
        in ma bunnet.

Paradoxically, Gow's stay-at-home habits and quick repartee only added to his lustre: patrons saw them as endearing eccentricities rather than as responses to their own treatment of him. They added the last, perfect touch to Gow's image, and made him a legend in his lifetime.

The Duke of Gordon undertook a similar piece of patronage at this time with another first-rate fiddler, William Marshall. Marshall, like Gow, seems to have become an aristocratic protégé almost by accident; he was born at Fochabers in 1748, and entered the Duke's household in a menial capacity at the age of 12, gradually being promoted to butler and then to factor in charge of the extensive Gordon estates in Banff and Aberdeenshire. Meanwhile, in 1781, he published *A Collection of Strathspey Reels* which was acclaimed throughout Scotland. His *Miss Admiral Gordon's Strathspey* **(80)** first appeared in this collection.

Gordon was delighted to have such an excellent fiddler among his employees. But Marshall, though he dedicated a fair number of the 250-odd tunes which he composed to the Duke and his relatives, avoided a full-time musical career. He published no further collection of his tunes until his old age, in 1822, and retained his integrity by holding down the responsible factorship for quarter of a century, and by having a range of demanding intellectual hobbies like astronomy, surveying, and clock-making.

The Gow collections

The Gows became much more commercially orientated in the 1780s, when Nathaniel Gow reached maturity. Their first notable success was their *Collection of Strathspey Reels* of 1784, which was published as 'by Niel Gow at Dunkeld'; it was, however, nearly all Nathaniel's work. This collection deserves to be studied in detail.

Nathaniel had left Perthshire for Edinburgh at an early age. He was a precociously talented youth, and soon found his feet in the capital; according to Glen (*SDM*, vol.ii), he took violin lessons from Robert Mackintosh and trumpet lessons from Joseph Reinagle senior, and joined McGlashan's dance band as cellist. By the age of 19, at the end of 1782, he was also a member of the Edinburgh Musical Society's orchestra. Living in the town containing nearly all Scotland's music printers, he was highly aware of the collections of Riddell (*c.*1770), Dow (1773 and *c.*1780), McGlashan (1778 and 1781), Angus Cumming of Grantown (1780), Robert Ross (1780), Marshall (1781), Mackintosh (1783), and Isaac Cooper of Banff (*c.*1783); it was almost certainly he who decided that it was time the Gow family produced one, too.

Many years later, Nathaniel admitted that he had 'set and prepared for publication' the tunes in his father's collections (see the article on his father which he contributed to Sainsbury's *Dictionary of Musicians*, 1827). In fact, Nathaniel probably organised the entire operation, from formulating the editorial policy and harmonising the tunes to liaising with the printer and collecting money from the subscribers. It was an impressive achievement, especially considering that he was only 21 when the first volume came out.

The 1784 Gow volume differed from the collections of Riddell, Dow and Mackintosh in that it was not entirely devoted to original compositions. It included many old Highland airs (presumably as played by Niel Gow) as well as many new tunes fashionable in

Edinburgh, written by composers outwith the Gow family. What Nathaniel did, in fact, was to make a selection of about 80 pieces from his own Perthshire–Edinburgh knowledge of the repertory — mostly choosing very fine ones which had not been published before — and clap his father's name over the top of them.

Nathaniel thought out his editorial policy carefully (it also served him for the follow-up collections of 1788, 1792, and 1800). He omitted composers' names from the book except where the composers were upper-class, on the grounds that, if a tune lacked a high-class pedigree, it was better to present it as 'traditional'. Joseph Reinagle junior's authorship of *Colonel Hamilton's delight* **(87)**, for example, he quietly suppressed, though he must have known who had written it, since he was a trumpet pupil of Reinagle's father. (He did probably get Reinagle's permission before printing the piece.) He even suppressed the fact that some of the tunes were his own and his father's work, changing his mind about this later once he realised that Gow authorship was, on the whole, a credit point.

Nathaniel re-titled many of the new tunes in the book to make them more attractive to prospective customers. *The South Bridge of Edinburgh* **(86)**, for instance, became *The Haddington Assembly*, a patron's piece rather than a communal-celebration one. He also re-titled old tunes, giving them hybrid names like *Wat ye wha I met the streen or Lord Haddo's Favourite* (cf. no.**49**).

Crass and obvious though this seems today as a way of marketing a book — and it must have been pretty transparent, even in the 1780s — it worked; Nathaniel had sized up his customers accurately. Nearly 1,000 copies of the 1784 volume were subscribed for, an out-and-out record for any Scottish music book up to that time. Several aristocrats placed huge orders: the Duke of Atholl, Duke and Duchess of Gordon and Lady Charlotte Murray, for example, took 6 each, while the Duchess of Atholl and Duchess of Hamilton took 12. The 1788 volume did, if anything, even better. This collection was dedicated to the 'Noblemen and Gentlemen of the Caledonian Hunt', and had a cover illustration showing a fox on the run; its opening piece was a slow air entitled *The Caledonian Hunt's Delight*. (The tune was written by James Miller, an Edinburgh solicitor; Gow presumably thought up the title. It is nowadays known as *Ye banks and braes*, after the words which Burns wrote to it in 1792.) The subscription list tells its own tale: 'THE CALEDONIAN HUNT, 60 copies'.

The Gow collections were a milestone in Nathaniel's career. They proved to him that he had outstanding talents as a publisher; and from 1784 onwards, publishing was to be an essential part of his life. He formed several partnerships, ran a series of successful music shops in Edinburgh, and turned a blind eye to the fact that most of what he marketed was inferior to the music he composed himself in his spare time. By 1820 he was the richest musician Scotland had ever produced, with an elegant house in the Edinburgh New Town and an entrée to the leading artistic salons of the day. Finally, in 1827, he went spectacularly bankrupt in the company of Sir Walter Scott and the literary publisher Constable.

The collections were also a milestone in the history of Scots fiddling. They were, of course, only one set of fiddle-books among many published at the end of the 18th century; other worthwhile collections were issued by, for example, such fiddlers as Robert Mackintosh, John Bowie of Perth, Charles Duff of Dundee, Alex Leburn of Auchtermuchty, Archibald Duff of Montrose, Robert Petrie of Kirkmichael in Perthshire,

James Walker of Dysart, and John Morison of Peterhead, and such publishers as James Aird. But none of these collections captured the new spirit of Romanticism, which was building up powerfully in Scotland in the 1780s, as perfectly as the Gow volumes did.

Nathaniel probably did not set out deliberately to give the Gow collections a Romantic slant; it arose partly unconsciously, from the mood of the times, and partly accidentally, as a by-product of his editing methods. But it was there, on every page: an enticing, spell-binding vagueness as to what was old and what was new. Users of the Gow volumes could never be quite sure which tunes were ancient ones (fitted with new titles), which were modern (with the composers' names omitted), and which were an editorial mixture of the two. Nor did they want to find out; what they wanted was a sense of mystical participation in an age-old tradition, handed down intact and gleaming to the present day, and presided over by a figure whose Highland honesty was a legend in itself. Niel Gow's name was a crucial asset to the collections; without it, they would not have taken nearly as deep a hold on the public.

After the Gow collections, who could doubt that the hundreds of dance tunes written in response to the recent vogue for dancing were anything other than a genuine part of Scottish tradition? The figure of Niel Gow sanctioned every tune in the Gow books as 'traditional' — in spirit if not in letter — and by implication, every other reel, hornpipe, strathspey and jig composed in Scotland since 1760. The fact that very few dance tunes had been written at all during the century and a half before 1760, that the tradition had become dangerously attenuated at that time, passed from view: the Church of Scotland had laid a curse on dance music, but Niel Gow had exorcised it. Henceforth, the dance tunes of the late 18th century could be regarded as the heirs and successors to those of the 16th century.

Scots fiddling thus turned a corner into a new era. Perhaps the most portentous new idea to appear at this time was the assumption that short dance tunes were the central part of the tradition; the longer fiddle forms, pibroch, variation sonatas and long variation sets, on which so much attention had been lavished in the earlier part of the 18th century, were suddenly seen as peripheral. This will be discussed further in the Conclusion.

70. Green grows the rashes

71. The flowers of the forest

72. The Duke of Perth's reel

73. St. Bernard's Well

[Brisk]

74. The Earl of Dalhousie's reel

NATHANIEL GOW (1763-1831)

[Brisk]

75. The De'il's among the tailors

76. Dusty miller

77. Welcome home, my dearie

78. O'er the muir among the heather

79. Rose Street strathspey

ROBERT FERGUSON (*fl.c.* 1790)

80. Miss Admiral Gordon's strathspey

WILLIAM MARSHALL (1748-1833)

81. Mrs Fordyce of Ayton's strathspey

ROBERT MACKINTOSH (c. 1745-1807)

82. Sir Archibald Grant of Monymusk's strathspey

DANIEL DOW (1732-83)

83. I'll lay no more with my mother

[Brisk]

84. Greensleeves

[Brisk]

85. Dunkeld House

NIEL GOW (1727-1807)

86. The South Bridge of Edinburgh/
The Haddington Assembly

R

87. Colonel Hamilton's delight

JOSEPH REINAGLE (1762-1836)

NOTES ON THE MUSIC

70 *Green grows the rashes*
Source: Gillespie MS., p.91.
This tune was printed in Stewart's *Reels* in a similar version. It was already ancient in the
1760s; it is recorded back as far as the 1680s in fiddle manuscripts.
Revisions: key-signature orig four sharps, due to a mistaken afterthought on the copyist's part
(cf. nos. **36, 60**)
    strain 1 bar 3 notes 1–3 editorial; source has a dotted crotched *c"*
    strain 2 bar 2 note 9 orig *g"*
    strain 2 bar 3 note 4 orig *f♯"*

71 *The flowers of the forest*
Source: Gillespie MS., p.90.
This tune is best known as a song, lamenting the battle of Flodden in Northumberland in
1513; see Harper for a detailed account of its history. The reel version given here is recorded
only in the Gillespie manuscript.
Revisions: strain 3 repeat orig written out in full.

72 *The Duke of Perth's reel*
Source: Stewart's *Reels*, p.4. Bass omitted.
This is the earliest printed form of this famous piece. It is usually played today as a country
dance in 2/4 time.

73 *St Bernard's Well*
Source: Sharpe MS., p.69.
St. Bernard's Well is a mineral spring by the Water of Leith, on the outskirts of Edinburgh
New Town. The tune was printed in Stewart's *Reels* in two alternative versions, entitled
respectively *Bernard's Well* and *Shamboe Breeches*. Its first strain is based on the 16th-century
passamezzo moderno chord sequence; see page 19.
   The slurs in the opening bars are somewhat ambiguous; the tune may well have been played
both as:

and as:

Revisions: strain 1 bar 4b note 8 orig a crotchet
   strain 2 bars 2 and 4a: *f♮'s* from Stewart.

74 *The Earl of Dalhousie's reel*
Source: Nathaniel Gow's *Lady Mary Ramsay's Strathspey*. Bass omitted.
This little-known reel was composed by Nathaniel Gow around 1800, and shows his
willingness to experiment with 'difficult' flat keys in dance music.
Revisions: repeats orig written out in full.

75 *The De'il's among the tailors*
Source: Macgoun's *Five fashionable Reels*.
An early text of this famous reel, which was probably composed around 1790.
Revisions: bass orig adapted for keyboard, with most of the notes doubled in octaves.

76 *Dusty miller*
Source: Gillespie MS., p.98.
There are other versions of this hornpipe in the McFarlane MS. (vol.ii no.165) and in
Bremner's *Reels* (p.27). The tune may originally have been English, but it was well established
in Scotland by the late 18th century. It had local Scottish words, which Burns re-wrote in
about 1790.
Revisions: strain 2 repeat omitted
   strain 2 bar 1 note 3 orig dotted crotchet
   strain 2 bar 5 notes 3–5 orig g'' (dotted crotchet), $f\sharp''$ (quaver), $f\sharp''$ (crotchet).

77 *Welcome home, my dearie*
Source: Stewart's *Reels*, p.20.
This hornpipe has associated words, like no. **76**; a fragment of them is preserved in the
original title of the source: 'You've been long away. Wellcome home my Dearie'.

78 *O'er the muir among the heather*
Source: Stewart's *Reels*, p.9. Bass omitted.
This tune was current as a reel in the early 18th century; the strathspey version given here
seems to have been made about 1760.
Revisions: strain 1 bar 2 note 8 orig g'.

79 *Rose Street strathspey*
Source: Sharpe MS., p.217. Bass omitted. A second text on the same page gives the piece
transposed down into B flat.
Rose Street is a narrow lane behind Princes Street, in the New Town of Edinburgh, so it is
reasonable to suppose that the composer of the piece, Robert Ferguson, lived in Edinburgh
himself. Little is known of Ferguson, but he is probably to be identified with 'Robert
Ferguson, Edinburgh' who subscribed for vol.iii of Niel Gow's *Strathspey Reels* in 1792; and
the Sharpe MS. includes another strathspey of his with a local Edinburgh title, *Bruntsfield
Links*. He should not, however, be confused with the Edinburgh poet Robert Fergusson, who
died in 1774.
Revisions: strain 2 bar 4b note 8 orig a crotchet.

80 *Miss Admiral Gordon's strathspey*
Source: Marshall's *Strathspey Reels*, p.3. Bass omitted.
This is the first printed text of Marshall's most famous strathspey, for which Burns later wrote
the lyric 'Of a' the airts the wind can blaw'.

81 *Mrs Fordyce of Ayton's strathspey*
Source: Mackintosh's *Sixty-eight new reels*, vol.i p.6. Bass omitted.
This strathspey was published in 1792. Mrs Fordyce (née Miss Catherine Maxwell) had had
dance-music dedicated to her before, as the Earl of Kelly (see Chapter VI) wrote a minuet for
her in the 1760s. Note Mackintosh's choice of a 'difficult' flat key for the piece.
Revisions: a few rhythms normalised.

82 *Sir Archibald Grant of Monymusk's strathspey*
Source: Dow's *Thirty-seven new reells*, p.5.
This is the earliest text of Dow's celebrated strathspey. It is still popular today, and is usually known simply as *Monymusk*.
Revisions. title editorial; source has 'Sr Arch^d Grant of Monemusk's Reel'
    strain 2 repeat orig written out in full.

83 *I'll lay no more with my mother*
Source: Gillespie MS., p.97.
This jig seems not to have reached print in the 18th century. The title means 'I won't need to share a bed with my mother any longer (as I'll soon have a husband)'.
Revisions: key-signature orig two sharps
    strain 1 bar 6 notes 1–3 editorial (cf. strain 1 bar 2); source has $f\sharp$ ", *e"*, *d"*
    strain 1 bar 7 note 6 orig *c"*.

84 *Greensleeves*
Source: Gillespie MS., p.96.
This jig is a Scottish version of the famous 16th-century English tune, with some characteristic melodic changes (note the modal F naturals instead of F sharps at cadences). Another, longer, text of this setting occurs in the Sharpe MS. (p.23).
Revisions: strain 1 bar 4, quaver *d'* omitted at end of bar
    strain 2 bar 4 note 2 orig *g"*
    strain 3 bar 4 as Sharpe; source is a 5th lower
    strain 3 bar 5 as Sharpe; source has *f" c" a' f" c" a'* (quavers)
    strain 3 bar 7 notes 4–6 orig a note higher.

85 *Dunkeld House*
Source: Niel Gow's *Strathspey Reels*, vol.i p.20. Bass omitted. Ascription to Gow from the second edition of the collection.
This jig is still popular in Scotland. Dunkeld House was one of the residences of Gow's patron the Duke of Atholl.
Revisions: strain 1 bar 7 note 2, $\sharp$ from the second edition
    strain 2 repeat orig written out in full.

86 *The South Bridge of Edinburgh/The Haddington Assembly*
Source: Sharpe MS., p.223. Alternative title from Niel Gow's *Strathspey Reels*, vol.ii p.23.
This jig was almost certainly composed by an Edinburgh fiddler in the autumn of 1787, to celebrate South Bridge's opening: see page 215.
Revisions: strain 2 repeat orig written out in full
    strain 2 bar 6b note 8 orig *c"*.

87 *Colonel Hamilton's delight*
Source: Niel Gow's *Strathspey Reels*, vol.ii p.6. Ascription to Reinagle from the Sharpe MS., p.236, and from Davie's *Caledonian Repository*, ser.1 pt.iv p.32.
This jig is still popular in Scotland; it is nowadays known as *Hamilton House*, and is often played in A, with the opening chords omitted.
    Reinagle was born in Portsmouth in 1762 of an Austrian father and a (probably) Scottish mother. He moved to Edinburgh in his childhood, where in due course he became leader of the orchestra at the Theatre Royal. He left Scotland early in 1784, working in Dublin and London and then settling in Oxford as a cello-teacher. This jig must therefore have been written in 1783 or slightly earlier.

CHAPTER X
Special Effects

THE 18th-century fiddle repertory included a small number of pieces which used special violin effects. Most of these pieces can be classified under genres which we have already discussed: *The hen's march* (88), for example, as a march in Baroque-trumpet style, and *The sow's tail* (90) as a long variation set. However, the special-effect element in them is so strong that each one also has a sense of uniqueness, almost as if it were a genre in itself. So it is worth devoting this last chapter to a brief survey of these pieces.

Hit her on the bum was the only Scots-fiddle piece in the 18th century to use left-hand pizzicato — or, indeed, pizzicato of any kind. It appears in Bremner's *Scots Tunes* of 1759 as a 9-strain variation set. The pizzicato occurs in strain 7:

Bremner probably composed this strain himself, inspired by the display tricks of Italian virtuoso violinists; it had no imitators during the 18th century. Later, however, a few more fiddle tunes appeared using the same effect. Davie's *Caledonian Repository* contains two: a version of *The reel of Tulloch* (30) with pizzicato notes added, and a tune called *The cat wi' the lang tail*. Scott Skinner developed the idea further, notably in his composition *Le Messe*, published in 1904. No further Scots-fiddle pieces with pizzicato have been written since Skinner's time.

The hen's march (88), in contrast, is unique in being a sort of miniature concerto, with a middle section where two solo violins imitate hens clucking in a farmyard. The version given here was familiar to nearly every Scots fiddler in the late 18th century. Like the pizzicato section of *Hit her on the bum*, it was probably the work of Robert Bremner; it appeared for the first time in his *Airs and Marches* of *c.*1756–61.

Bremner composed (or arranged) this piece against a background of European precedents. There was a general vogue for imitating bird-calls in European instrumental music in the early 18th century, and another 'Hen's march' had appeared as part of a London pantomime about five years earlier (see Fiske, p.235, for a quotation; it is very similar to Bremner's piece). In addition, the first eight bars of the tune were very typical of the trumpet marches currently popular in London. Bremner, nevertheless, deserves the credit for putting the piece together in what Scotland regarded as its definitive form.

The hen's march tune is still popular in Scotland, and is nowadays known as 'The hen's march ower the midden'. It has been arranged for many instruments, including organ and brass band, and is usually played on the fiddle today as a solo rather than as a duet.

What makes *Marriage and money* (89) unique is the fact that the tune has no stopping places; every cadence is gently undermined as it approaches, and the next section follows without the melody being broken at any point. Each section may also be lengthened by improvisation, and can lead into any other section, giving the piece a completely fluid form.

It is likely that fiddlers who played this piece carried no fixed form for it in their heads. They would know its main themes by heart and, when the time came to play, would start at the beginning and see what the mood of the moment brought forth. Performances may well have lasted up to quarter of an hour on some occasions (see Riddell's *Scotch, Galwegian and Border Tunes*, p.ii). One text of it is entitled *The dandling o' the bairns*, suggesting that it was sometimes played with endless repetitions to help children to get to sleep.

The piece is difficult to bring off in performance, and probably only very fine players attempted it. As well as the text given here, which was written down in Edinburgh in 1740, versions are recorded from Glasgow in 1710, and from Newton Stewart in about 1705.

Finally, *The sow's tail, with variations* (90) contains a section where the fiddler is instructed to bow on the wrong side of the bridge, to give a sound like a pig squealing. The variations were mainly the work of an East Lothian landowner, William Nisbet of Dirleton; the bowing effect seems to have been a pure inspiration on his part. The piece makes a splendid conclusion to a concert: and, for that matter, to an anthology of music.

88. The hen's march

? ROBERT BREMNER (c. 1713-1789)

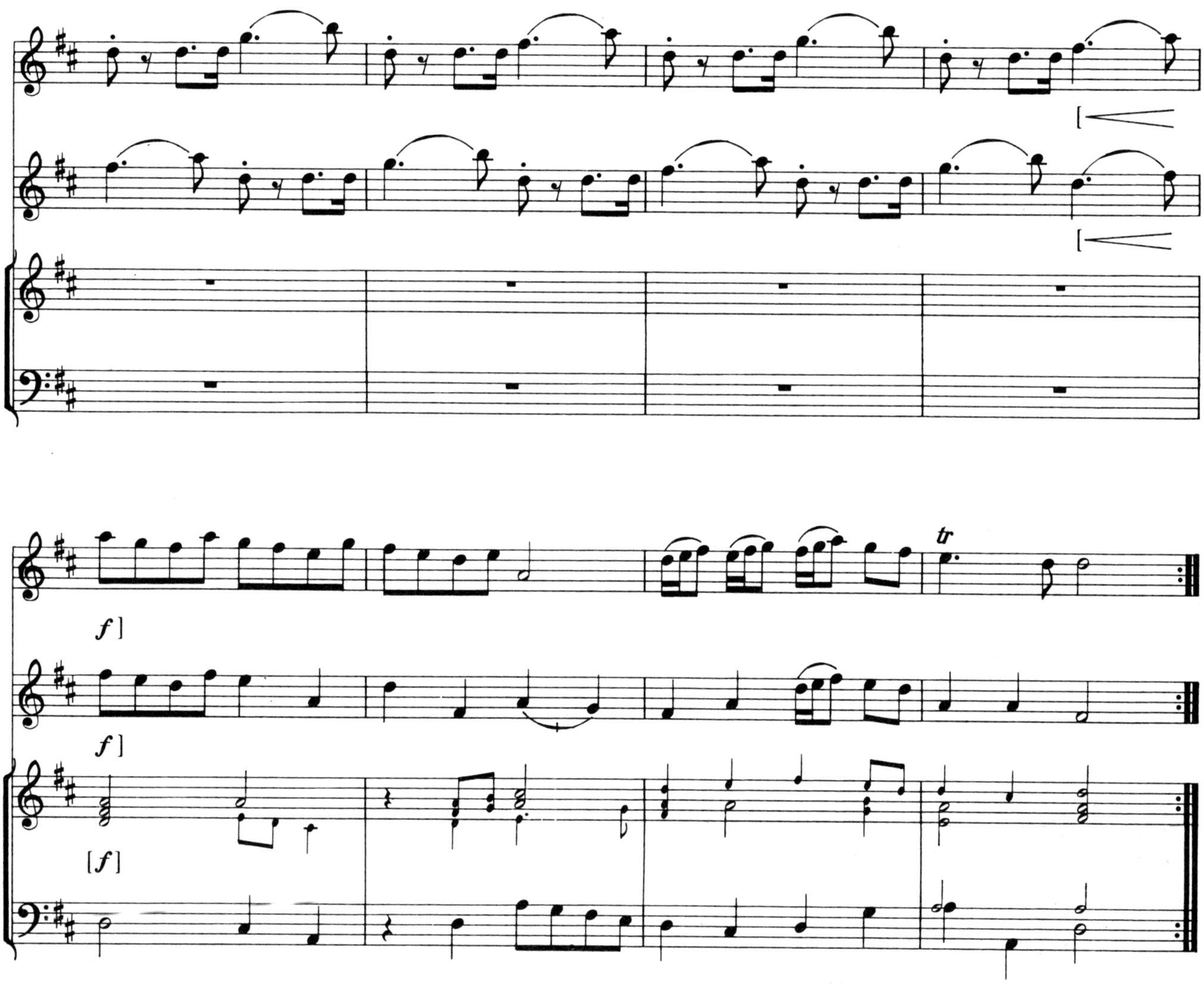
tr
f]
f]
[f]

89. Marriage and money

90. The sow's tail, with variations

set by WILLIAM NISBET of DIRLETON (c. 1710-1783)

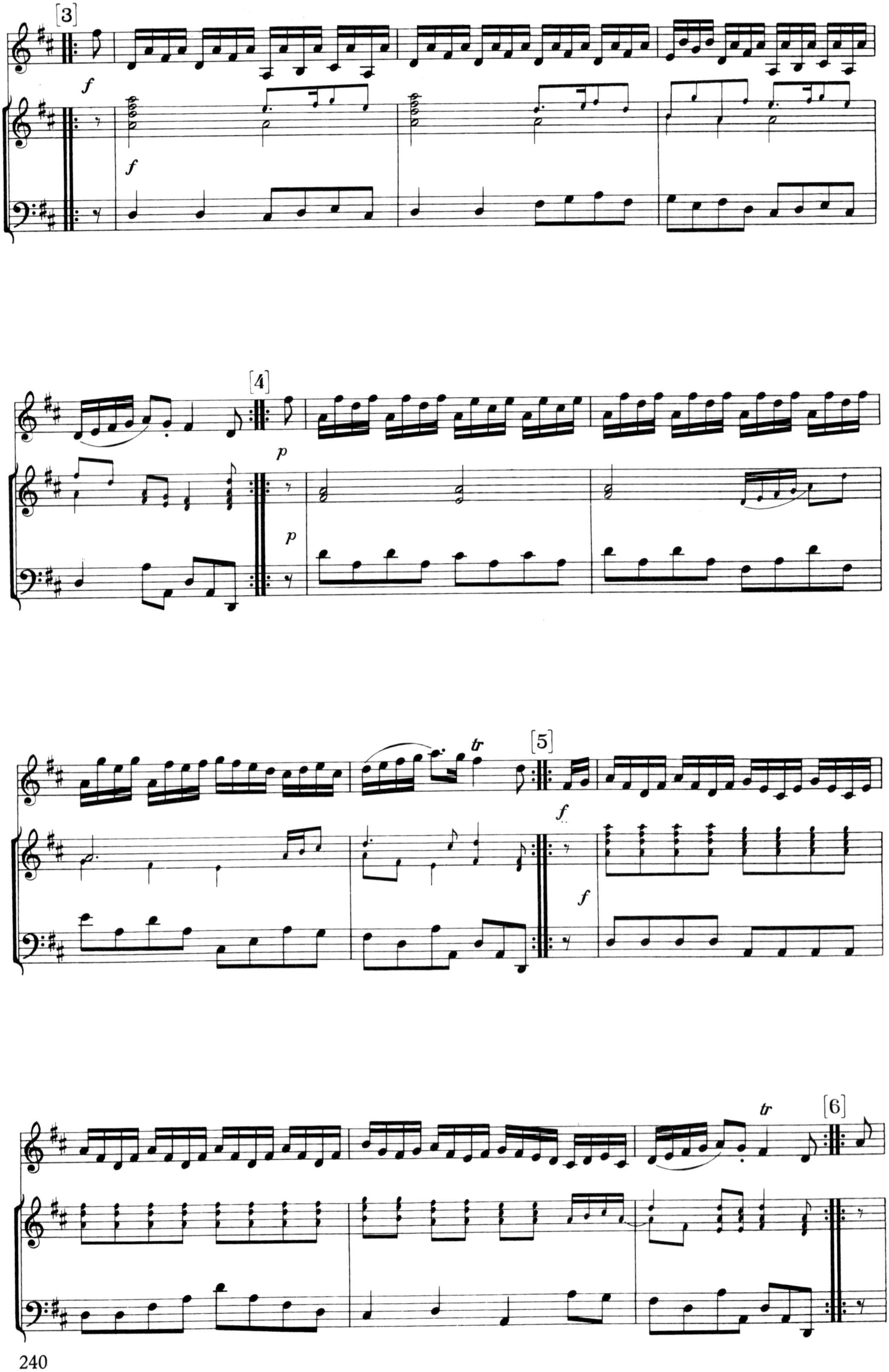
[3]
f
f
[4]
p
p
tr
[5]
f
f
tr
[6]

[lower notes, cello]

* 'The time of the Rests the Bow of the Violin to be drawn behind the Bridge in Imitation of a Sow' [note in source]

242

NOTES ON THE MUSIC

88 *The hen's march*
Source: Bremner's *Airs and marches*, p.64.
The earliest Scottish version of this famous occasional piece.
Revisions: strain 2 bars 6 and 8, 1st vln note 3 orig *g″*
   strain 2 bar 8, 2nd vln notes 3–4 orig a 3rd higher.

89 *Marriage and money*
Source: McFarlane MS., vol.iii no.68.
There are other texts of this piece in the Sinkler MS., p.16 (entitled *Dunnigall's rant)* and in
Riddell's *Scotch, Galwegian and Border Tunes*, p.8 (entitled *The dandling o' the bairns*).
Revisions: 'Andante' heading from Riddell
   scordatura prefatory stave editorial
   bars 33–40 repeat orig written in full
   bars 41–58 repeat orig shown by *segno* marks
   bar 53 notes 4–5 orig *a' b'*
   bar 81 note 5 orig *a'*
   bar 90 note 2 as bar 4 note 2; source has *b'*
   bar 91 note 6 as bar 5 note 6; source has *b'*
   bar 110 notes 5–6 orig a 3rd lower.

90 *The sow's tail, with variations*
Source: Niel Gow's *Strathspey Reels*, vol.ii p.32.
Nisbet of Dirleton was an East Lothian laird and amateur musician, who was a member of the
Edinburgh Musical Society for much of his life. The Earl of Kelly (see Chapter VI) dedicated
a minuet to his daughter.
   The *Sow's tail* tune had been popular for many years before Nisbet wrote these variations; it
had words satirising George I's love-life. Nisbet's double-stopped figure in strain 6 is derived
from Corelli's violin sonata *La folia*, op.V no.12.
   The piece is still frequently played in Scotland today. Most present-day performances,
however, consist only of the Intro plus strain 12 — oddly omitting the basic tune altogether.
Revisions: 'Intro' is editorial; the source has 'Sym' (symphony), meaning the same thing
   Intro, strains 3, 5, 11 and 12: octave doublings in the keyboard left hand omitted
   Intro bar 4 vln note 6 orig *e'*
   strain 3 bar 3 vln note 1 orig *d'*
   strain 5 bar 3 vln note 7 orig *d'*
   strain 6 upbeat: *p* deleted, vln orig *f♯″*
   strain 6 bar 4 vln note 6 orig *f♯″*
   strain 8 upbeat vln orig quaver *a'*
   strain 8 bar 3 vln note 1 orig *d'*
   strain 8 bar 4 vln editorial; orig as strain 11 bar 4
   strain 10 bar 1 bass, notes 1 and 3 as strain 10 bar 2; source has *d*s
   strain 11 upbeat vln orig *f♯″*
   strain 12 upbeat vln orig quaver *d'*, tied to the previous note.

Conclusion: Fiddle Music after 1800

BY the time the 19th century opened, fiddle music presented a quite different picture from that which it had had in 1760. Large areas of the repertory had changed dramatically. The 'Scots drawing room' pieces and the variation sonatas, which were tied to European art-music styles of the 1730s and 40s, had reached the end of their natural life-span. Minuets had disappeared. Scordatura was still being used, but scordatura pieces were no longer being written down. Scottish composers had stopped writing violin sonatas. Fiddle pibrochs were probably still being played, but no more of them were printed; the army's patronage of bagpiping and the Royal Highland Society's competitions had brought pibroch on the pipes forward to such an extent that fiddle pibroch now seemed a second-rate art form. Even the long variation sets, which had taken pride of place in fiddlers' manuscripts for most of the 18th century, had been pushed to one side. In the centre of the picture, instead, were hundreds of short dance tunes, some of them old but the vast majority new ones, composed within the previous forty years.

As we have seen in Chapter IX, there were good reasons why so many new dance tunes should have been written at the end of the 18th century, and why they were promoted so energetically: Scotland was desperately short of dance music, and many fiddlers were keen to have professional careers. Another reason, which we have not so far mentioned, was that many of the older tunes had bawdy titles or were associated with obscene lyrics. Two of the tunes in this book, for instance, have rude titles (nos. **11** and **61**), and several more had rude words (nos. **7, 15, 32, 35, 37, 50, 67, 70,** and probably also nos. **76, 78** and **90**).

The 18th century was a licentious age, when men were given to expressing themselves in no uncertain terms about the less polite functions of women. (No doubt women did about men, too; only women were not normally given to writing fiddle tunes.) At the end of the century, manners changed: people rapidly became less outspoken about sex, eventually reaching the extreme Victorian position where the entire subject was taboo in polite company. From 1800 onwards, therefore, fiddlers could not play old tunes like *The Highland lassie's lovely thing, Jockie's fu' [drunk] and Jennie's fain [eager], Whip her below the covering, The bride has a bonny thing, Wanton towdie [female genitals], Had [hold] the lass till I win at her* or *I'll hae her awa [have it off with her] in spite o' her minnie [mother]* in company without causing grievous embarrassment. (The first of these tunes is in the George Skene MS.; the next three in the McFarlane MS.; the next two in the Gillespie MS.; the last in *Flores Musicae*.) This was another reason for the repertory to be overhauled as fast as possible.

Long variation sets did not survive these upheavals very well. A few of them continued to be played: the *Reel of Tulloch* variations **(30)**, for example, lasted another hundred years and were reprinted in Skinner's *Harp and Claymore* collection in 1904, while the *East Neuk of Fife* variations **(34)** are still partly known to fiddlers today. A large number of sets, however, were lost because they were based on tunes with licentious words, and few new sets were written to replace them. Many of the new tunes in the late 18th century would actually have been extremely suitable for variation treatment. But Scotland's leading fiddlers were all busy with dance music from 1780 to 1810, and had no time for long-winded recital pieces which their clients, on the whole, did not want to hear; and by the end of that time the secret of writing long variation sets had largely been lost. As we have seen, the earlier 18th-century variations were composite works, which had been built up over several decades. It was not a genre that could be recreated overnight.

The demise of the long variation set was also due, however, to changes in Scotland's entire cultural outlook.

The influence of Romanticism on Scots fiddling has already been discussed in Chapter IX, from the point of view of old *versus* new tunes. Another aspect of it which is important for this study is the fact that the Romantics turned away from formal, learned types of art towards simpler, more spontaneous modes.

Jean-Jacques Rousseau in the 1750s had extolled the virtues of peasant culture, claiming that unlettered countrymen lived closer to basics than educated townsmen did, and that this was manifested in the way countrymen expressed themselves in words and music. Rousseau's ideas spread round Europe like wildfire; all of a sudden, cultured men grew weary of mannered elegance and began to look for deeper truths in more primitive art. James Macpherson's Ossian epics in the 1760s, which were loosely based on traditional Gaelic bardic verse, were enormously popular because they captured the 'primitive' spirit so well. Another example of the new ideology was Robert Burns' enthusiastic reception in Edinburgh in 1786 as a 'heav'n-taught ploughman', though Burns' poems were not in the least crude or uncivilised, but merely written (mainly) in Ayrshire dialect.

It was inevitable that moves would be made to identify Scots fiddling, also, as a primitive peasant culture. This was somewhat awkward at first, since everyone in Scotland knew that music was a highly technical business, and that learning the fiddle took years of practice and often involved formal lessons. The Gow collections helped; but blurring the distinction between old and new tunes they encouraged the idea that most fiddle music had been written in the distant past — or could have been — when composers were simple peasants and the instrument was played more spontaneously than at present. The idea was nonsense, but persuasive; and once it caught on, the long variation sets and other extended fiddle forms were doomed. People could easily believe that short, 16-bar reels and jigs, written in conservative styles, were the work of peasants, but the long variation sets were too intellectual, too obviously influenced by recent European art music, to pass muster. They could not be fitted into the new ideology, so they were quietly allowed to die.

The peasant myth of Scots fiddling was held in check to some extent, up to the 1830s, by the existence of the two virtuoso players Nathaniel Gow and William Marshall. Gow lived in Edinburgh, Marshall on Speyside, and both were well known to be educated, articulate middle-class men. But when Gow died in 1831 and Marshall in 1833, Scots fiddling was left without a figurehead for more than a generation; no other really outstanding player came to the fore until Scott Skinner reached maturity in the 1860s. A line of nationally-renowned fiddlers which went back to William McGibbon had been broken; with strange consequences.

James Scott Skinner (1843–1927) was a virtuoso in an age which had forgotten what Scots-fiddle virtuosi were like. Born in Banchory, he went to Manchester at an early age to join a juvenile orchestra and take violin lessons from a member of the Hallé Orchestra; he returned to Scotland as the most polished native fiddler the country had ever seen. From the 1860s until his death he gave concerts constantly and composed over 600 tunes, many of which are now firm favourites. He was indisputably the finest player of his day; no other fiddler could remotely be compared to him until Hector Macandrew arrived on the scene in the 1930s. Nevertheless, Skinner's career was out of step with his era. The peasant myth was entrenched by this time. Trained European musicians living in Scotland despised Scots fiddling, almost to a man; and the general public saw agricultural labourers (whom there was a fashion for photographing, standing with instruments outside cowsheds) and mendicant players like John Rodgers (who used to board express trains at Stirling, play to the passengers, and alight again at Dunblane: see Murdoch, p.48n.) as the most typical representatives of the tradition. Skinner, from this point of view, was an impostor and a poseur. Many of his patrons unconsciously saw him in this light even while they applauded his formidable technique. It was only other fiddlers who took him seriously as a musician.

Skinner was aware of the effect he was having on his contemporaries, and became alternately aggressive and defensive about it. This can be seen, for example, in his advice to young players — 'Procure a solid Teacher' — which he presented as a daring paradox; in the 18th century it would have been the most obvious common sense. His advice continues (*Guide to Bowing*, p.32):

> All these men [Niel Gow, Robert Mackintosh, etc.] did good work, but would have soared even higher had they received a good sound training in manual equipment.

The reference to Mackintosh here is particularly interesting. By Skinner's time, Mackintosh was remembered only as a composer of reels and strathspeys; the peasant myth had caused everyone to forget his minuets, variation sonatas, and art-music sonatas. In reality, however, Mackintosh had been very similar to Skinner in training, outlook, and personal temperament. Had Skinner known more of the true facts about Mackintosh, and about the other great 18th-century fiddlers, he might well have felt less out on a limb himself.

After Skinner's death in 1927 Scots fiddling went through a bleak period; few tunes of any lasting value were composed, and the accordion seemed all set to oust the violin from its traditional position in Scottish music.

Since the Second World War, however, fiddling has made a triumphant comeback, with a brand-new ideology attached to it. On top of the peasant myth, we now have the working-class myth: fiddling has become part of 'folk music', an expression of working-class protest against the capitalist system. Many dance tunes from the period of Marshall, the Gows and Mackintosh are still current, and they seem to work quite well with this new left-wing interpretation laid upon them, though William Marshall, who was factor to a powerful Highland landlord, wrote his most famous strathspey for the daughter of an admiral, and voted Tory all his life, would have found the idea preposterous.

One distinct advantage which the working-class myth has over the peasant myth is that there is now no objection to Scots fiddlers being educated. Where the archetypal peasant was an illiterate, the archetypal proletarian attends study-groups in order to get even with the bosses. Hence formal tuition in fiddling has blossomed in recent years, at summer schools and at master-classes attached to folk festivals. The first comprehensive instruction-book for Scots fiddlers ever written, Alastair Hardie's *Caledonian Companion*, appeared in 1981. Most of today's leading fiddlers are famous as teachers no less than they are as players; some of them even have regular jobs giving (art-music) violin lessons in schools, the state education system thus subsidising their lives and unwittingly acting as a patron of fiddle music. John Knox and the other leaders of the early Reformed Church, who drew up plans for universal education in Scotland but loathed fiddling and dancing, would turn in their graves at the thought.

Scots fiddling is remarkably resilient. Over the centuries it has been drastically and painfully re-shaped to fit the ideologies of each successive period and yet it has survived, if not exactly intact, at least alive and kicking. This is a surprising and heartening phenomenon; it shows that music is a more permanent, useful thing than the ideas about it which are in vogue at any given time. As I write these last words, on 14 February 1983, fiddling in Scotland is in a healthier state than it has been for many generations. I hope this book contributes to its success in the future.

References

a. MANUSCRIPT MUSICAL SOURCES (chronological order)
NLS = National Library of Scotland

SKENE, JOHN, of Hallyards, Midlothian. Mandora book, *c*.1620. NLS Adv.MS.5.2.15.

'Lessones for y^e violin'. Fiddle book from Newbattle Abbey, Midlothian *c*.1680. NLS MS.5778.

'Leyden lyra-viol manuscript'. Lyra-viol book, Scottish, *c*.1695. Newcastle University Library.

'Balcarres lute book'. Lute book from Balcarres House, Fife, *c*.1700. John Rylands Library, Manchester.

GAIRDYN, JAMES. Fiddle and vocal book, Scottish, 1700–*c*.1740. NLS Glen 37.

THOMSON, JAMES. Recorder and fiddle book, ?Edinburgh, 1702–*c*.1720. NLS MS.2833.

HUME, AGNES. Vocal, fiddle and keyboard book, Scottish, 1704. NLS Adv.MS.5.2.17.

BOWIE, GEORGE. Fiddle book, Edinburgh, 1705. In private ownership of Dr. Francis Collinson. NLS MS.Acc.5462.

SINKLER, MARGARET. Fiddle and keyboard book, 'written by Andrew Adam at Glasgow October the 31 day 1710'. NLS Glen 143.

BROWN, MARTHA. Keyboard and vocal book, 'boght at Inverary 1714'. North Ayrshire Museum, Saltcoats.

SKENE, GEORGE, of Skene, Aberdeenshire. Fiddle book, 1717–*c*.1740. NLS Adv.MS 5.2.21.

CUMING, PATRICK. Fiddle book, Edinburgh, 1723–4. NLS MS.1667.

McGIBBON, WILLIAM. [Six sonatas for two violins and a bass, first set]. Violin 1 and bass parts only. Edinburgh, *c*.1727. Library of Congress, Washington.

DIXON, WILLIAM. Fiddle book, Perthshire, 1733–8. Sandeman Library, Perth (Atholl Collection N27).

'Duke of Perth's manuscript'. Book of country-dance tunes and dancing instructions made by David Young for the Duke of Perth, 1734. In private ownership of the Earl of Ancaster, Drummond Castle, Crieff, Xerox copy in NLS, MS.Acc.7722.

'A collection of the newest countrey dances perform'd in Scotland'. Book of country-dance tunes and dancing instructions made by David Young, Edinburgh, 1740. Bodleian Library, Oxford, MS.Don.d.54.

'McFarlane manuscript'. Fiddle books, 3 vols., made by David Young for Walter McFarlane of that ilk, Edinburgh, 1740. NLS MSS.2084, 2085. Only vols. ii and iii survive. Vol. i was borrowed from the Society of Antiquaries of Scotland by a Dr William Farquharson in March 1806, and was never returned, though the Society wrote letters to Dr Farquharson about it until December 1819.

GILLESPIE, JAMES. Fiddle book, Perth, 1768. NLS MS.808.

NLS Adv.MS.5.2.20. Unnamed fiddle book, Scottish, *c.*1770.

NLS Adv.MS.5.2.25. Unnamed fiddle book, Scottish, *c.*1770.

NLS Ing.12. Unnamed flute book, Scottish, *c.*1770.

'Brown manuscript'. Fiddle book owned by the Brown family of Elgin, *c.*1775. NLS MS.3378.

'Little manuscript'. Fiddle book, Dumfriesshire, *c.*1775. Given to the Rev. James Little, minister of Colvend, Dumfriesshire, who passed it to Robert Riddell, who in turn presented it to the Society of Antiquaries of Scotland in 1785. NLS MS.2086.

TROTTER, WILLIAM. Fiddle book, Whitsome, Berwickshire, 1780. Edinburgh Central Library.

NLS Glen 228(3). Unnamed pages of fiddle tunes, Scottish, *c.*1780.

'Sharpe manuscript'. Fiddle book, Edinburgh, *c.*1790. Owned by Charles Kirkpatrick Sharpe during the second quarter of the 19th century. NLS Ing.153.

SHIELS, THOMAS. Fiddle book, Crieff, 1820–1. In private ownership of Mrs Anne Macaulay until 1982; now in the Reid Library, Edinburgh.

WEBSTER, JAMES. Fiddle book, New Deer, Aberdeenshire, 1839. Aberdeen University Library MS.2421.

b. PRINTED MUSICAL SOURCES (alphabetical order)

AIRD, JAMES. *A selection of Scotch, English, Irish and foreign airs.* 6 vols. Glasgow, [1782–1803].

ANDERSON, TOM and SWING, PAM. *Haand me doon da fiddle.* Stirling, 1979.

BARBER, ROBERT. *Six trios for a harpsichord, violin obligato and bass, op.2.* London, [1782].

BARSANTI, FRANCESCO. *A collection of old Scots tunes.* Edinburgh, [1742].

—— *Nove overture a quattro, op.4.* ?Edinburgh, *c.*1743.

BOWIE, JOHN. *A collection of strathspey reels and country dances.* Edinburgh, *c.*1789.

BREMNER, ROBERT. *A collection of airs and marches.*　Edinburgh, *c.*1756–61.

—— *A curious collection of Scots tunes.* Edinburgh, [1759].

—— *A collection of the best minuets.* London, *c.*1765.

—— *A collection of Scots reels or country dances.* London, *c.*1765.

—— *A collection of Scots tunes . . . by William McGibbon. With some additions by Robt Bremner.* 4 vols. London, [1768].

CAMPBELL, JOSHUA. *A collection of the newest and best reels and minuets.* Glasgow, *c.*1780.

CLARKSON, JOHN. *A complete collection of much admired tunes . . . arranged for the Piano Forte.* Edinburgh, *c.*1800.

COOPER, ISAAC. *Thirty new strathspey reels.* Banff, *c.*1783.

CRAIG, ADAM. *A collection of the choicest of the Scots tunes.* Edinburgh, *c.*1727. (2nd ed., 1730).

CUMMING, ANGUS. *A collection of strathspey, or old Highland reels.* Edinburgh, 1780.

DAVIE, JAMES. *The Caledonian Repository.* Series i, Edinburgh, 1829. Series ii, Aberdeen, *c.*1850.

DOW, DANIEL. *Twenty minuets and sixteen reels or counrty dances.* Edinburgh, [1773].

—— *A collection of ancient Scots music.* Edinburgh, [1776].

——*Thirty-seven new reells and strathspeys.* Edinburgh, *c.*1780.

DUFF, ARCHIBALD. *A collection of strathspey reels.* Edinburgh, [1794].

DUFF, CHARLES. *A collection of strathspeys, reels, jiggs, &c.* Edinburgh, *c.*1792.

Flores Musicae, or the Scots musician. Edinburgh, 1773–*c.*1775.

[FOULIS, DAVID.] *Six solos for the violin . . . composed by a gentleman.* [Edinburgh], *c.*1774.

GOW, NATHANIEL. *Lady Mary Ramsay's strathspey and the Earl of Dalhousie's reel, a new medley.* Single sheet, Edinburgh, *c.*1800.

—— *A select collection of original dances.* Edinburgh, *c.*1815.

—— See also GOW, NEIL.

GOW, NEIL. *A collection of strathspey reels.* [Edited by Nathaniel Gow.] 4 vols. Edinburgh, [1784, 1788, 1792, 1800]. (2nd ed. of vol.i, *c.*1792).

HARDIE, ALASTAIR J. *The Caledonian Companion.* London, 1981.

KELLY, EARL OF. *Six overtures in eight parts, op.1.* Edinburgh, 1761.

—— *The periodical overture in eight parts,* xvii (Symphony in E flat). London, [1767].

—— *Six sonatas for two violins and a bass.* London, [1769].

—— *The favourite minuets perform'd at the Fête Champêtre.* London, c.1775.

LEBURN, ALEXANDER. *A collection of new strathspey reels.* Edinburgh, [1793].

MACDONALD, REV. PATRICK. *A collection of Highland vocal airs.* Edinburgh, [1784].

McGIBBON, WILLIAM. *Six sonatas for two German flutes or two violins and a bass.* [Second and third sets.] Edinburgh, 1729, 1734.

—— *Six sonatas or solos for a German flute or a violin and bass.* Edinburgh, 1740.

—— *A collection of Scots tunes.* 3 vols. Edinburgh, 1742, 1746, 1755.

—— *Six sonatas for two German flutes or two violins with a thorough bass.* [Fourth set.] London, c.1745.

McGLASHAN, ALEXANDER. *A collection of strathspey reels.* Edinburgh, [1778].

—— *A collection of reels, consisting chiefly of strathspeys, Athole reels, &c.* Edinbugh, [1781].

MACGOUN, A. *Five fashionable reels or strathspeys.* Single sheet, Glasgow, c.1800.

MacKAY, ANGUS. *A collection of ancient Piobaireachd.* Edinburgh, 1838.

MACKINTOSH, ROBERT. *Airs, minuets, gavotts and reels, op.1.* Edinburgh, [1783].

—— *Sixty-eight new reels, strathspeys and quicksteps.* 4 vols. Edinburgh, [1792, 1793, 1796]; London, [1804].

—— See also McLEAN.

McLEAN, CHARLES. *Twelve solos or sonatas for a violin and violoncello, op.1.* Edinburgh, 1737.

—— *A collection of favourite Scots tunes . . . by the late M^r Ch^s McLean and other eminent masters.* [Edited by Robert Mackintosh.] Edinburgh, [1772]. With MS. ascriptions of some items on NLS copy Glen 228(1).

MARSHALL, WILLIAM. *A collection of strathspey reels.* Edinburgh, [1781].

—— *Scottish Airs.* Edinburgh, [1822].

—— *Volume 2nd of a collection of Scottish melodies.* Edinburgh, 1845.

MORISON, JOHN. *A collection of new strathspey reels.* Edinburgh, [1800].

MUNRO, A[LEXANDER]. *A collection of the best Scots tunes.* Paris, 1732.

OSWALD, JAMES. [*A collection of minuets.* Edinburgh, 1736.] No copies extant.

—— *A curious collection of Scots tunes.* Edinburgh, *c.*1739.

—— *The Caledonian Pocket Companion.* 15 vols. London, *c.*1747–69.

—— *Airs for the four Seasons.* 2 series. London [1755], *c.*1765.

—— *A collection of Scot's tunes with variations.* London, *c.*1756.

PETRIE, ROBERT. *A collection of strathspey reels, &c.* 3 vols. Edinburgh, *c.*1795–1800.

PLAYFORD HENRY. *A collection of original Scotch-tunes (full of the Highland humours) for the violin.* London, 1700. (2nd ed., 1701).

PURCELL, HENRY. *Musick's Handmaid Part II.* London, 1689.

REID, JOHN. *Six solos for a German flute or violin with a thorough bass.* London, [1756].

—— *A second sett of six solos for a German flute or violin.* London, [1762].

RIDDELL, JOHN. *A collection of Scots reels or country dances and minuets, with two particular slow tunes.* Ayr, *c.*1770.

RIDDELL, ROBERT, of Glenriddell. *A collection of Scotch, Galwegian and Border tunes.* Edinburgh, [1794].

ROSS, ROBERT. *A choice collection of Scots reels or country dances and strathspeys.* Edinburgh, [1780].

SCHETKY, J. G. C. *Six trios for two violins and a violoncello, op.1.* London, [1773].

STEWART, NEIL. *A collection of the newest and best minuets.* Edinburgh, *c.*1760–78. 64-page edition, NLS MH.s.123, inscribed 'El[izabeth] Rose, Kilravock'; 92-page edition, NLS MH.s.52(1).

—— *A collection of marches and airs.* Edinburgh, *c.*1761–5.

—— *A collection of the newest and best reels or country dances.* Edinburgh, *c.*1761–5.

SKINNER, JAMES SCOTT. *The Harp and Claymore.* London, [1904].

STUART, ALEXANDER. *Musick for Allan Ramsay's collection of Scots songs.* Edinburgh, *c.*1728.

WALKER, JAMES. *A collection of new Scots reels, strathspeys, jigs, &c.* 2 vols. Edinburgh, [1797].

YOUNG, JOHN. *A collection of original Scotch tunes for the violin.* London, *c.*1720.

c. COMMENTARIES (alphabetical order)

CAMPSIE, ALISTAIR K. *The MacCrimmon legend.* Edinburgh, 1980.

CANNON, R. D. 'The Battle of Harlaw: a lost piobaireachd?' in *Piping Times,* xxvi/12. Glasgow, September 1974.

COLLINSON, FRANCIS. *The bagpipe.* London, 1975.

ERLAM, H. D. 'Alexander Monro, primus' in *Edinburgh University Journal,* xvii. Edinburgh, 1954.

FISKE, ROGER. *English Theatre Music in the 18th Century.* London, 1973.

GLEN, JOHN. *The Glen collection of Scottish Dance Music.* 2 vols. Edinburgh, 1891–5.
—— *Early Scottish melodies.* Edinburgh, 1900.

HAWKINS, SIR JOHN. *A general history of the science and practice of music.* 5 vols. London, 1776.

GROVE, SIR GEORGE. *A dictionary of music and musicians,* 1st ed. 4 vols. London, 1879–89.

JOHNSON, DAVID. *Music and Society in Lowland Scotland in the 18th Century.* London, 1972.
—— 'The Earl of Kelly's minuets'. Unpublished Royal Musical Association paper, Glasgow, 19 March 1977.
—— 'Musical traditions in the Forbes family of Disblair, Aberdeenshire' in *Scottish Studies,* xxii. Edinburgh, 1978.
—— 'Dr David Foulis, medic and musician' in *Edinburgh Medicine,* xv. Edinburgh, July 1982.

MURDOCH, ALEXANDER G. *The Fiddle in Scotland.* Glasgow, 1888.

REESE, GUSTAVE. *Music in the Renaissance.* London, 1954.

SAINSBURY, JOHN. *Dictionary of musicians.* 2 vols. London, 1827.

SCOTT, SIR WALTER. *Redgauntlet.* Edinburgh, 1824.

SIMPSON, CLAUDE M. *The British broadside ballad and its music.* New Brunswick, 1966.

SKINNER, JAMES SCOTT. *A guide to bowing.* London, c.1905.

STENHOUSE, WILLIAM. *Illustrations of the lyric poetry and music of Scotland.* Edinburgh, 1839.

TULLIBARDINE, MARCHIONESS OF. *A military history of Perthshire, 1660-1902.* Perth, 1908.

Index

a. PEOPLE

(**Bold** type indicates a complete text of a composition by the person referred to)

Anderson, Tom 109
Arthur, Edna 3
Atholl, Duke of 216-8, 220, 233

Baillie, Peter 66-7, 69
Balcarres, Duke of 150, (MS.
    owned by) 15-6, 33
Barber, Robert 201-2
Barsanti, Francesco 2, 6, 35, 36,
    38, **41**, 63, 193, 217
Beck, Mr 15-6
Beethoven, Ludwig van 166, 201
Bocchi, Lorenzo 144
Bonnie Prince Charlie 105
Bowie, George (MS. owned by) 16,
    32, 33
Bowie, John 220
Bremner, Robert 2, 5, 6, 8, 38, 40,
    56, 64, 66, 69, 102, 103, 104,
    105, 107, 109, 118, 126, 143,
    145, 167, 214, 232, 234, **236**,
    243
Brown family (MS. owned by) 39,
    108, 109, 117, 147, 148, 159
Brown, Martha (MS. owned by) 14
Bruford, Alan 123
Burgoine, General John 159-60
Burns, Robert 3, 64, 102, 124,
    212-3, 215, 218, 220, 232, 245
Byrd, William 126

Campbell, Joshua 146, 149
Campbell, Mr, of Ardchattan 124,
    125
Campsie, Alistair 122
Carsewell, Bishop Donald 123
Clark, James 39
Clarkson, John 146
Clerk, Sir John, of Penicuik 144
Collinson, Francis 123
Constable, Archibald 220
Cooper, Isaac 7, 219
Cooper, Richard 195
Cope, General Sir John 105
Corelli, Arcangelo 3, 4, 5, 35, 37,
    38, 39, 74, 141, 162-3, 201,
    203, 243
Craig, Adam 2, 6, 35, 37, 38, 63,
    162, 192, 195
Cuming, Patrick (MS. owned by)
    15, 33, 166
Cumming, Angus 219

Davie, James 63, 233, 234
Dixon, William (MS. owned by) 70

Dow, Daniel 2, 5, 7, 8, 67, 141,
    142, 145, 146, 147, 148, 149,
    150, **154**, 159, 215, 216, 219,
    228, 233
Drummond, William, of
    Hawthornden 142
Duff, Archibald 220
Duff, Charles 7, 220

Ferguson, Robert **226**, 232
Filtz, Anton 148
Forbes, William, of Disblair 2, 8,
    11, 12, 37, 38, 63, 67, **77**, **78**,
    102, 162
Foulis, David 192, 199-200

Gairdyn, James (MS. owned by) 14,
    119
George I 243
Gillespie, James (MS. owned by) 8,
    9, 10, 14, 19, 32, 33, 67, 69,
    104, 109, 146, 150, 159, 167,
    231, 232, 233
Glen, John 11, 63, 105, 219
Gordon, Duchess of 218, 220
Gordon, Duke of 3, 216, 219, 220
Gow, Andrew 218
Gow, Nathaniel 2, 5, 7, 38, 39, **61**,
    64, 109, **115**, 118, 149, 218-21,
    224, 231, 245, 246
Gow, Niel 2, 5, 39, 64, 67, 105,
    109, 118, 124, 149, 217-21,
    229, 232, 233, 243, 245, 246
Gow, William 218
Grant, Daniel 9, 11

Handel, George Frideric 38, 39, 74,
    194, 196, 201, 293
Hardie, Alastair 107, 109, 149, 247
Hawkins, Sir John 162
Haydn, Franz Josef 38-9, 166
Hume, Agnes (MS. owned by) 33

Johnson, James 9

Kelly, Thomas Alexander Erskine,
    sixth Earl of 2, 143, 145, 146,
    147, 148, 149, 150, **154**,
    159-60, 192, 200-1, 217, 232,
    243
Knox, John 247

Leburn, Alexander 7, 220
Leyden, John (MS. owned by) 162
Little, Rev. James (MS. owned by)
    104, 141, 166

Macandrew, Hector 246
Macdonald, Rev. Patrick 5, 124,
    125, 142
McFarlane, Walter, of that ilk (MS.
    owned by) 2, 4, 9, 10-2, 37, 63,
    66, 67, 68, 102, 103, 104, 117,
    119, 124, 141, 159, 161, 162,
    164, 165, 166, 167, 190, 195,
    232, 243, 244, 249
McGibbon, William 2, 5, 6, 7, 8,
    33, 35, 37-8, 39, **42**, **44**, **46**,
    48, 63, 104, 141, 144, 148, **152**,
    159, 161, 164, 192-5, 203, 245
McGlashan, Alexander 3, 5, 7, 8,
    219
MacKay, Angus 122
Mackintosh, Robert 2, 5, 7, 9, 10,
    11-3, 37, 67, 145, 146, 147,
    149, 150, 160, 161, 165-6, 167,
    186, 191, 192, 202-3, 216, 217,
    219, 220, **227**, 232, 246
McLachlan, John 2, 15-6, **30**, 33,
    38, 63, 144
McLean, Charles 2, 5, 7, 9, 10, 11,
    12, 13, 35, 37, 38, **86**, 103,
    105, 144, 161, 164, 165, 167,
    180, **186**, 190, 191, 192, 193,
    195-6, 203
Macpherson, James 245
Marshall, William 3, 7, 121, 149,
    215, 219, **227**, 232, 245, 246
Mary, Queen of Scots 3
Miller, James 220
Monro, Alexander 162
Morison, John 221
Morison, Rory Dall 64
Mozart, Wolfgang Amadeus 143,
    149
Munro, Alexander 2, 6, 9, 10, 11,
    12, 13, 35, 36, 38, 161, 162-4,
    166, 167, **170**, 190

Nairne, Lady 33
Niecks, Friedrich 198
Nisbet, William, of Dirleton 235,
    239, 243

O Catháin, Rory Dall 64
Oswald, James 2, 6, 7, 8, 35, 36,
    37, 38, **51**, **53**, 63, 64, 67-9,
    95, 104, 107, 109, 124, 126,
    138, 142, 143, 144, 159, 161,
    162, 164, 192, 193, 197-9

Pasquali, Nicolo 217
Perth, Duke of (MS. owned by) 67,
    214

Petrie, Robert 220
Playford, Henry 6, 14, 15, 33
Purcell, Henry **84**, 103, **180**, 190

Ramsay, Allan 34-5, 63, 102, 103, 106, 118, 142
Reid, General John 2, 38, 192, 198-9, **204**, 221
Reinagle, Joseph (senior) 219, 220
Reinagle, Joseph (junior) 220, **230**, 233
Riddell, John 3, 7, 8, 145, 146, 147, 150, 216, 219
Riddell, Robert, of Glenriddell 7, 14, 39, 74, 124, 161, 167, 190, 235, 243, 249
Rodgers, John 246
Ross, Robert 105, 219
Rousseau, Jean-Jacques 245

Schetky, Johann Georg Christoph 145, 146, 147, 149, 150, **158**, 160, 201
Scott, Sir Walter 68-9, 220
Sharpe, Charles Kirkpatrick (MS. owned by) 66, 117, 118, 141, 146, 167, 190, 231, 232, 233
Sinkler, Margaret (MS. owned by) 32, 33, 104, 159, 243
Skene, George, of that ilk (MS. owned by) 14, 32, 33, 105, 118, 119, 120-1, 244
Skene, John, of Hallyards (MS. owned by) 63, 64
Skinner, James Scott 103, 109, 234, 244, 245-6
Skirving, Adam 105
Stamitz, Johann 145
Stenhouse, William 1, 105, 142
Stewart, Neil 6, 143, 145, 147,

159, 160, 214, 231, 232
Stuart, Alexander 6, 35, 36, 38, 39, 192, 195

Thomson, James 197
Thomson, James (MS. owned by) 32
Thomson, William 35
Trotter, William (MS. owned by) 39, 105, 109, 118, 146

Walker, James 221
Webster, James (MS. owned by) 103
Wigton, third Earl of 123

Young, David 2, 4, 11, 12, 32, 65, 67, 68, **79**, **81**, **82**, 102-3, 119, 124, 167, 190, 214
Young, John 6

b. TUNES

(**Bold** type indicates a complete text of the tune)

Aileen Aroon 10
Allan Water 14, 17, **23**, 31, 32, 65, 67, 69, **81**, 102
Anthony Murray's reel 109
Appin House 109
Ayrshire Lasses 215

Babbity Bowster 36
Barbara Allan 10, 12, 37
Battle of Falkirk, the 126
Battle of Harlaw, the 14, 121, 123, 124, **135**, 142
Birks of Invermay, the 9, 11, 12, 37
Black and the brown, the *see* The horseman's port
Black Jock 31, 37, 65, 66, 70-2, 73, 74, **86**, 103, 107, 244
Black Sloven 106, 108, **111**, 115
Bonny Christy 163
Bonny Jean of Aberdeen 9, 10, 11, 12, 13, 15, 36, 161, 163, 164, 166-7, **170**, 190
Braes of Ballenden, the 10, 149
Bride has a bonny thing, the 244
Bride next 14, 18, **26**, 32
Bridge of Perth, the 215
Bring her ben and bore her better 8
Bruntsfield Links 232

Caber feigh 10, 12
Cailleach odhar 10, 12, 13, 65, 67, 72, **79**, 102, 120, 121
Capillaire minuet, the 143, 148, 149
Cat wi' the lang tail, the 234
Cauld kail in Aberdeen 120-1

Charlie is my darling 198
Clydeside Lasses 215
Collier's daughter, the 14, 15, 18, 19, **27**, 33
Colonel Hamilton's delight 213, 214, 220, **230**, 233
Coming through the rye *see* The miller's wedding
Corn rigs 9, 163
Cowdenknowes 35
Craigellachie Bridge 215
Cromlet's lilt 164
Cumha Easbuig Earraghàidheal 14, 121, 123, **131**, 141
Cumha Iarla Wigton 14, 121, 123, **132**, 141

Dandling o' the bairns, the *see* Marriage and money
De'il's among the tailors, the 213, **225**, 232
Desperate battle, the *see* Battle of Harlaw
Donald McIntosh 106, 108, **113**, 117, 120, 121
Drunken wives of Carlisle 18, 19, **29**, 33, 119, 120, 121
Drunken wives of Fochabers 122
Duchess of Buccleuch's minuet, the *see* Miss Jeanie Maxwell's minuet
Duke of Argyle's strathspey, the 38, 107, 109, **115**, 118
Duke of Perth's reel, the 213, **223**, 231
Duncan Davidson 39

Duncan Gray 8, 31, 65, 67, 72, 73, **94**, 104, 244
Dunkeld House 213, 218, **229**, 233
Dunnigall's rant *see* Marriage and money
Dusty miller 213, **225**, 232, 244

Earl of Dalhousie's reel, the 149, 213, **224**, 231
East Neuk of Fife, the 40, 65, 66-7, 69, 70, 72, 73, **92**, 104, 244
Ettrick Banks 164

Flowers of the forest, the 8, 213, **223**, 231
Fox lamentation, the 106, 108, **112**, 117
Fy gar rub her o'er wi' strae 163, 164

Galway's lament *see* Miss Carmichael's minuet
General Burgoine's minuet *see* Mrs Grant of Arndilly's minuet
Gie the mawking mair o't *see* Drunken wives of Carlisle
Gilderoy 10
Gowd on your gartens, Marion **23**, 32
Green grows the rashes 213, **223**, 231, 244
Greensleeves 20, 71, 148, 213, **228**, 233
Grieg's pipes 19, 117
Gum-ga'd aiver, the 14, 119

Had awa frae me, Donald 9
Had the lass till I win at her 244
Haddington Assembly, the *see* South Bridge of Edinburgh
Haddington Lasses 215
Hare among the corn, the 65, 70, 73, 74, **100**, 105
Hen's march, the 234–5, **236**, 243
Highland battle, a 63, 64, 120, 124, 126, **138**, 142
Highland Hunt, the *see* The fox lamentation
Highland laddie 14, 15, **22**, 32
Highland lassie's lovely thing, the 244
Highlander's farewell, the 65, 73, **98**, 105, 120
Hit her on the bum 234
Horseman's port, the 14, 18, **28**, 33, 126
Humours of Glen, the 10

I'll hae her awa in spite o' her minnie 15, 244
I'll lay no more with my mother 213, **228**, 233
I love my love in secret 14, **26**, 31, 33, 164
I wish I were where Helen lies 14, 17, **22**, 32, 162

Jackie Latin 10
Jockie's fu' and Jennie's fain 244
Jockie was the blythest (bravest) lad 10, 149, 165
John come kiss me now 15, 20, 164
John Ochiltree 165
John Paterson's mare *see* The horseman's port
Johnnie Cope 10, 20, 31, 65, 66, 67, 73, **97**, 105, 148
Johnnie Faa 36, **41**, 63

Killiecrankie 14, 15, 17, **24**, 32, 125
Kilrack's reel 109

Lady Anne Lindsay's minuet 150
Lady Binnie's minuet *see* Lady Sophia Hope's minuet
Lady Cassilles' lilt *see* Johnnie Faa
Lady Jean Lindsay's minuet 8, 145, 150, **154**, 159
Lady Margaret Lindsay's minuet 150
Lady Sophia Hope's minuet 150
Laird of Cockpen, the *see* When she cam ben, she bobbit
Laird o' Drumblair, the 109
Lament for Abercairney 124
Lass of Livingston, the *see* Highland laddie
Lass of Patie's mill, the 165
Lasses gar your tails toddle 9, 14, 20, **27**, 33, 244

Lasses likes nae (drinks at) brandy 10, 12
Lasses of Duns 215
Lasses of Irvine 215
Lasses of Stewarton 215
Lea rig, the 9, 65, 67, 73, **96**, 104, 161, 165, 167–8, **183**, 190, 244
Leith Wynd 37, 39, **42**, 63
Loch Erroch-side 124
Logan Water 9
Lord Forbes' march *see* Pìobaireachd Dhomhnaill
Lord Kelly's reel 145
Lothian Lasses 215
Lumps of puddings 65, 69, 70, **95**, 104

Mackintosh's lament 119, 120, 123, 124, 125, **134**, 142
McLachlan's Scotch measure 15
Macpherson's testament 14, **23**, 32
Maggie Lauder 8
Maltman comes on Monday, the 65, 66, 73, **89**, 103, 107
Marriage and money 14, 235, **238**, 243
Mary Scott, the flower of Yarrow 146
Messe, le 234
Miller's wedding (daughter), the 107, **114**, 118, 244
Miss Admiral Gordon's strathspey 121, 219, **227**, 232
Miss Babie Gray's minuet 8, 150
Miss Carmichael's minuet 146, **153**, 159
Miss Catherine Maxwell's minuet 232
Miss Faw's minuet 146, **153**, 159, 244
Miss Grant's minuet 148
Miss Jeanie Maxwell's minuet 150
Miss Kinloch's minuet 145, 149, **158**, 160
Miss Nisbet of Dirleton's minuet 243
Miss Stewart's minuet 148
Monymusk *see* Sir Archibald Grant of Monymusk's strathspey
Mount your baggage 31, 65, 73, **99**, 105
Mrs Fordyce of Ayton's strathspey 149, 214, **227**, 232
Mrs Grant of Arndilly's minuet 145, 146, 147, 148, 149, **154**, 159
My ain kind dearie O *see* Lea rig
My dear, durst I but mow you *see* Miller's wedding
My Nanny-O 10, 12, 13, 37, 65, 67, **77**, 102, 162, 198
My wife's a wanton wee thing *see* Bride next

Nancy's to the greenwood gane 9, 10
New Bridge of Ballater, the 215
New Bridge of Edinburgh, the 215
New Bridge of Glasgow, the 215
New Bridge of Rutherglen, the 215

O dear mother (minnie) 162, 164
O'er the muir among the heather 213, **226**, 232, 244
Old Ireland rejoice 10, 12
Old Sir Symon the king 31, 65, 70, 72, **84**, 103
Old woman in the glen, the *see* Barbara Allan

Pentland Hills 36, 39, **51**, 63, 69, 126
Pinkie House 9, 11, 12, 13, 37, 161, 164, 165–6, **186**, 191, 203
Pìobaireachd Dhomhnaill 120, 121, 122, **130**, 141
Polwarth on the green 164

Reel of Tulloch, the 31, 65, 67, 73, **82**, 102, 119, 120, 121, 234, 244
Robaidh dona gòrach 38, **61**, 64
Rory Dall's port 36, 38, 39, **53**, 64
Rose Street strathspey **226**, 232

St. Bernard's Well 20, 213, **224**, 231
Saw na ye my Peggie 14, 17, 18, **24**, 31, 32, 195, 244
Shamboe breeches *see* St. Bernard's Well
She grip't at the greatest o't *see* East Neuk of Fife
She rose and let me in 164
She's sweetest when she's naked *see* Miss Faw's minuet
Sir Archibald Grant of Monymusk's strathspey **228**, 233
Sir Roger de Coverley *see* Maltman comes on Monday
Soldier's lady, the *see* Mount your baggage
Sour plums of Galashiels, the 14, 16, **25**, 31, 32, 35, 69, 163
Souters of Selkirk, the 9
South Bridge of Edinburgh, the 213, 216, 220, **229**, 233
Sow's tail, the 234, 235, **239**, 243, 244
Sweden's march, 1, 20, 65, 72, **98**, 105
Sweet pudding *see* Lumps of puddings

There's nae luck about the house 20
There's three good fellows ayont yon glen 20, 37, 38, 39, **44**, 63

Through the wood, laddie 39, **46**,
    63, 69
Tullochgorum 124
Twas within a furlong of
    Edinburgh town 37, 161, 164,
    180, 190
Tweedside 37

Up and waur them a', Willie 10, 20
Up in the morning early 20

Up tails a' 37, 65, 67, 73, **78**, 102,
    162

Wanton towdie 244
Wat ye wha I met yestreen 106,
    114, 118, 220
Weel may the keel row 10
Welcome home, my dearie 213,
    226, 232
When she cam ben, she bobbit 14,

15, 20, **30**, 31, 33, 37, 38, 39,
    48, 63, 148, 244
Whip her below the covering 244
Wife of my ain, a 65, 68, **76**, 102
Will you go to Flanders? 38, 39,
    56, 64
Willie was a wanton wag 10, 12, 39
Willie Wink's testament 19, 106,
    112, 117, 120
Winter nights are long 35